STUDIES IN

MAJOR LITERARY AUTHORS

edited by
WILLIAM CAIN
WELLESLEY COLLEGE

T0347427

A GARLAND SERIES

PHILIP ROTH CONSIDERED

THE CONCENTRATIONARY UNIVERSE OF THE AMERICAN WRITER

Steven Milowitz

Routledge
Taylor & Francis Group

LONDON AND NEW YORK

First published 2000 by Garland Publishing, Inc.

Published 2016 by Routledge
2 Park Square, Milton Park, Abingdon, Oxfordshire OX14 4RN
711 Third Avenue, New York, NY 10017

First issued in paperback 2016

Routledge is an imprint of the Taylor & Francis Group, an informa business

Copyright © 2000 by Steven Milowitz

All rights reserved. No part of this book may be reprinted or reproduced or utilised in any form or by any electronic, mechanical, or other means, now known or hereafter invented, including photocopying and recording, or in any information storage or retrieval system, without permission in writing from the publishers.

Notice:
Product or corporate names may be trademarks or registered trademarks, and are used only for identification and explanation without intent to infringe.

Credits and acknowledgments borrowed from other sources and reproduced, with permission, in this textbook appear on appropriate page within text.

ISBN13: 978-1-138-97839-3 (pbk)
ISBN13: 978-0-8153-3957-1 (hbk)

Library of Congress Cataloging-in-Publication Data

Milowitz, Steven.
    Philip Roth considered : the concentrationary universe of the American writer / Steven Milowitz.
        p. cm.—(Studies in major literary authors)
    Includes bibliographical references and index.
    ISBN 0-8153-3957-7 (alk. paper)
        1. Roth, Philip—Criticism and interpretation. I. Title. II. Series.
PS3568.O855 Z82 2000
813'.54—dc21

                                                        00-055142

Contents

Key to Abbreviations

ROTH

AL	The Anatomy Lesson
AMC	Author Meets the Critics
AP	American Pastoral
CL	The Counterlife
CRM	I Couldn'tRestrain Myself
CWPR	Conversations with Philip Roth
D	Deception
DOF	Defender of the Faith
E	Epstein
GC	Goodbye, Columbus
I-GC	Introduction to Goodbye, Columbus: German Edition
JG	Juice or Gravy? How I Met My Fate in a Cafeteria
LG	Letting Go
MIM	The Man in the Middle
MLAM	My Life as a Man
OS	Operation Shylock
P	Patrimony
PC	Portnoy's Complaint
POD	The Professor of Desire
PRC	The Philip Roth Collection
PRD	Philip Roth Sees Double. And Maybe Triple, Too
RMAO	Reading Myself and Others
SDII	Second Dialogue in Israel

TB	The Breast
TCFAG	The Contest for Aaron Gold
TF	The Facts
TPO	The Prague Orgy
WAJ-D	Draft of Writing About Jews
WSWG	When She Was Good
ZU	Zuckerman Unbound

OTHERS

AON	The Art of the Novel : Milan Kundera
BWA	By Words Alone:The Holocaust in Literature:Sidra D. Ezrahi
HBJ	Hiding Behind James : Adeline Tintner
HJGW	Henry James as Roth's Ghost Writer : Adeline Tintner
HLE	Half a Lemon, Half an Egg : Martin Green
HT	Holocaust Testimonies: the ruins of memory: Lawrence L. Langer
INTRO	Introduction: A Philip Roth Reader : Martin Green
K&T	Kiss and Tell : Hermione Lee
MAF	Marrying Anne Frank : Sanford Pinsker
NB	A Critic's Notebook : Irving Howe
OJ	Odd Jobs : John Updike
PR	Philip Roth : Hermione Lee
PRR	Philip Roth Reconsidered : Irving Howe
R	The Rapacity of One Nearly Buried Alive: Barbara K. Quart
RD	Philip Roth's Diasporism: A Symposium : Sidra D. Ezrahi
RM	Franz Kafka: Representative Man : Frederick R. Karl
RRN	Recruiting Raw Nerves : John Updike
SFD	Selections From Diaries, 1911-1923 : Franz Kafka
SOB	The Suburbs of Babylon : Irving Howe
SW	Selected Writings: 1950-1990 : Irving Howe
TCTH	The Comedy That Hoits : Sanford Pinsker
VOS	Versions of Survival : Lawrence L. Langer
W	The Treatment of Women in the Works of Three Contemporary American Writers : Barbara Quart
WOF	World of Our Fathers : Irving Howe

Preface

Victim of gross misreadings, Philip Roth's works require new close consideration. Roth has been misread not only in regard to obvious issues of autobiography, misogyny, and anti-Semitism, but, more importantly, in terms of conception. There has been, for the forty years of Roth's expansive career, an inability, or unwillingness, to acknowledge Roth's essential concerns. Roth's varied works, when studied closely, point to a central obsessional issue, the issue of the Holocaust and its impact on twentieth-century American life.

To claim Roth as a Holocaust writer might seem absurd to those readers who have witnessed Roth's rebellious outpourings, his insistence on not being read as a Jewish writer, his fascination with sex and power, his recurring discussions of the writer's lacerating effect on his personal world and on his self, his intense excavation of the continuous battle between parents and children, and his disquieting focus on the terrible internal war between desire and conscience, but it is the contention of this essay that any reading of Roth's oeuvre that ignores his primary impetus cannot truly locate Roth's place in American letters.

This book began as an attempt to account for a personal notion of continuity in Roth's books. His novels, stories, and non-fiction all seem intricately conjoined; he is one of the few current writers who is unafraid to mine the same territory over and over again, to deepen his investigations rather than just broaden them. Noticing the plethora of Holocaust allusions from Roth's early works to his most recent, I was struck by the meager mention of the Holocaust in reviews, articles, and manuscripts that attempted to elucidate Roth's individual and cumulative works.

In early reviews of Roth's celebrated and excoriated work, *Goodbye Columbus*, there is virtually no acknowledgment of the Holocaust's presence, though the book is anchored by "Eli, the Fanatic," which directly connects the experience of the contemporary American to that of the camp survivor. The first major study of Roth, *The Fiction of Philip Roth*, by John N. MacDaniel, published in 1974, concludes that Roth is a "realistic" writer, "whose central concern is with man in society" (vi). The society MacDaniel refers to is decidedly American. He expresses some agreement with the critics who view Roth as "an apostate, as one whose style and themes place him...outside understood notions of the Jewish traditions" (3). The oversight in this early study lurks in the ease with which MacDaniel understands Roth as a writer always and only pushing against tradition, never grasping to it. MacDaniel's myopia causes him to miss any Holocaust-imaginings in Roth's fictions.

Bernard Rodgers's 1978 study, *Philip Roth*, primarily looks at the "interpenetration of reality and fantasy in the lives of |Roth's| representative Americans" (9). Rodgers's view of Roth's characters as American first explains his suggestion that "as an artist Roth has placed his faith in Realism, not Judaism" (9). Though his faith may not be in the religious ethos of Judaism, Roth's writing is indepted to the Judaism of his subject matter more than to any literary method. But, for Rodgers, neither Judaism nor the Holocaust offer any interpretative fire.

Judith Paterson Jones and Guinevera A. Nance, authors of another study titled *Philip Roth*, look to the idea of self-definition as the locus for Roth's work, ignoring that self's connection to its historical place. The Holocaust's effect on individual's complex search for self-definition is not touched on in this otherwise comprehensive study.

Murray Baumgarten and Barbara Gottfried use their 1990 survey of Roth, *Understanding Philip Roth*, to "explore the moral complexities of modern experience" (7). They do mention the Holocaust, particularly in their discussions of "Eli,the Fanatic," and the Zuckerman books, and they note that Roth "was among the first American writers to bring into his fiction an awareness of how the murder of six million Jews by the Nazis has shaped the modern world" (11). This perceptive awareness, however, does not provide any pronounced discussion of how the world is shaped by the Holocaust, and how this new modern sensibility provokes Roth's harried characters.

The most recent study, *Philip Roth and the Jews*, by Alan Cooper, looks directly at Roth's need to grapple with issues particular to the Jewish experience in America, issues primarily about the internal wrestling with the felt allegiance to the Jewish past and to American modernity. He manages to find and investigate various Holocaust references but does not suggest that they cohere; for Copper the Holocaust is just one of the forces that effects characters' sense of self. Cooper claims that "most of Roth's fiction has dealt with life in |the| imperfect postwar world," but he does not give a cogent definition of what a post-Holocaust world truly is, how the fact of genocide has altered the opportunities and imaginations of Roth's protagonists.

We live in America with the dream of the pastoral, the dream of paradise, plenty, and progress. America "was to be heaven itself" for the Jew, a world in which hopefulness could transform a brutal history (AP 122). But the pastoral is a false fantasy, as Swede Levov finds out in *American Pastoral*. The Swede tries to take "his family out of human confusion" (68), out of history, into a "post-Jewish" (73) America, but finds history, "the counterpastoral," searching him out, deposing his security (86).

"The tragedy of the man not set up for tragedy – that is every man's tragedy" (AM 86). Roth's work begins and ends in the tragedy of history, in the post-pastoral universe inherited from the fact of the concentration camps. How does one adjust to the "assailability, the frailty, the enfeeblement of supposedly robust things," Roth asks (AP 423). He has been attempting to answer that impossible question for forty years.

But what if all the quiet, the comfort, the contentment were now to end in horror?

- Franz Kafka
- *The Metamorphosis*

Now vee may perhaps to begin. Yes?

> When you admire a writer you
> become curious. You look for his
> secret. The clues to his puzzle.
>
> -Philip Roth
> -The Ghost Writer

Powerlessness haunts post-Holocaust man. The knowledge that, ultimately, one has no power over one's life, that one can, in a moment, be labeled, numbered, and shipped off towards death creates a startling ever-present vulnerability. To know, intuitively, that all that one has and all that one is is contingent upon an undeclared power not intervening, not changing the rules of life—rules that were once assumed to be incontestable and unchallengeable—keeps one forever suspicious, forever unsure, embattled, entrapped. The truth of Joyce's declaration, "You could die just the same on a sunny day," becomes only one truth that inhabits and inhibits man. Precariousness is now not only a component of bodily well-being but of freedom, of the self's ability to create its own destiny. For those ever-aware of the nightmare of the Holocaust nothing can be assumed stable or sure. The freedom one feels today is only a reminder of that freedom's possible revocation.

The testimonies and poems of survivors and victims, the histories written and recorded, and the essays fashioned from those works, remark time and time again on the helplessness of man when he is deemed the inhuman enemy of a state's ideology. How to continue in light of that knowledge, how to find meaning, how to reinvigorate will, and how to reestablish choice, become essential questions. Fear replaces hope in the concentrationary universe, the universe not only of the Holocaust-proper but of the new world created from its ashes.

David Rousset was the first to use the phrase, "I' Univers concentrationaire," as Sidra Ezrahi reports (10). For him, as for Ezrahi, the phrase describes the "self-contained world" of the concentration camp and "all aspects of the Nazi operation which were part of the master plan of annihilation and therefore common to most of the ghettos and camps" (Ezrahi 10). I have expanded the phrase to represent not only the place and period of the incarceration and extermination but the altered universe that is born as a result of unprecedented evil. It is as though, after the camps, the universe itself is impaired: hopes die, beliefs are more difficult to hold fast to, a pale hangs over the world.

In *The Professor of Desire*, Philip Roth's ninth novel, David Kepesh, a man whose tumult has reached a point of diminution, a man whose life has suddenly been brightened by new hope, expresses a profound, nagging fear of an unknown and unknowable oppressor. Having spent the evening listening to a Holocaust survivor tell his tragic tale Kepesh sits with his "innocent-beloved" girlfriend, Claire, and tells her the outline of "a simple Chekhov story" which describes his life: (261).

> Two old men come to the country to visit a healthy, handsome, young couple, brimming over with contentment. The young man is in his middle thirties, having recovered finally from the mistakes of his twenties. The young woman is in her twenties, the survivor of a painful youth and adolescence. They have every reason to believe they have come through. It looks and feels to both of them as though they have been saved, and inlarge part by one another. They are in love. But after dinner by candlelight,one of the old men tells of his life, about the utter ruination of a world, and about the blows that keep on coming. And that's it. The story ends just like this: her pretty head on his shoulder; his hand stroking her hair; their owlhooting; their constellations all in order - their medallions all in order; their guests in their freshly made beds; and their summer cottage, so cozy and inviting, just down the hill from where they sit together wondering about what they have to fear. Music is playing in the house. The most lovely music there is. 'And both of them knew that the most complicated and difficult part was only beginning' (259-260)

An ominous force, awakened by the survivor's oration, surrounds them. "Are you really frightened of something?" Claire asks Kepesh, after listening to his brooding summary (260). "I seem to be saying I am, don't I," he responds (260). As to what he's afraid of he tells her, "I don't know, really" (260). It is an unintelligible and uninterpretable fear rooted in history, ambiguous and menacing. It is the fear that Sydney, one of Roth's earliest protagonists, speaks of in Roth's first published story, "The Day it Snowed," the fear excited by the naive observation which begins the tale: "Suddenly people began to disappear" (34). Roth's first published sentence resonates backward in time, resurrecting images still so vivid in 1959, images still undigested, still impossible to acclimate. Sydney's world is the world of the unexperienced and innocent child baffled by death's power. His vision articulates that of a young America shocked into awareness of systematic murder and dehumanization. Just as Sydney's first world is forever altered, turned "inside out," so too any post-Holocaust man's view of life is altered irretrievably (35).

"The Day it Snowed" is a story of the birth of the knowledge which presages death, as Sydney is, in a heavy-handed conclusion, "crushed" by a "big black hearse," a reminder not only of death's whale-like strength but of its allegiance with mechanization (44). The hearse announces the death of childhood and of the pastoral. Roth's first fictional landscape is a post-Holocaust, post-lapsarian, post-pastoral landscape, a landscape at once terrifying and empty. The world in Roth's work is one of surprises, one in which people disappear inexplicably, as simply as snow can fall, seemingly out of nowhere.

The world is, in Roth's words, "crooked and unreal;" it is a place wherein "one feels less and less power" over one's life (RMAO 187). It is a place for which "the inevitable end is destruction, if not of all life, then of much that is valuable and civilized in life" (RMAO 187). This is the world that Roth thrusts his young protagonist into, only to have him quickly devoured by it.

In "Goodbye, Columbus" Neil Klugman recounts a dream about himself and a little black boy he has met at the library. The two outsiders are placed onto a boat that, under its own power, takes them off shore: "And though we did not want to go, the little boy and I," Neil explains, "the boat was moving and there was nothing we could do about it" (74). Like unwilling passengers on a destinationless boat, Roth's characters search for a way to regain control of their lives. But each character is struck with the "terrifying inkling," which Willard Carroll describes early in When She Was Good," "that there were in the universe forces...immune to his charm...remote from his desires...estranged from human need and feeling" (5).

One feels oneself a potential victim of a numinous extrinsic power, a Kafkaesque fiend which threatens at every turn. Like Kafka, the young Peter Tarnopol, in My Life as a Man, wonders if his life will be one of "Eviction? Confusion? Disorder?" (244). For Peter, as Kafka expresses in his Diary, misery "happens whether you like or no," and whether you expect it or no (268). Returning to the home he had a day earlier moved away from, having momentarily forgotten that he now lives somewhere else, he is impaled with terror "to find the door...wide open and to hear men talking loudly inside" (244). His world, he feels, has suddenly been taken from him. This terror comes not simply because of a childish error of memory but more importantly it is born from a world view that recognizes the barbarity of life, the tenuousness of safety. "One minute it's sunlight and the next dark," explains Leo Patimkin (GC 113). "All of a sudden, pfft!' exclaims Epstein, "and things are changed" (218). The momentary nature of one's happiness and of one's comfort is a constant source of anxiety for the characters inhabiting Roth's texts.

Some give into dismay, becoming misanthropic shells, appearing "round-shouldered, burdened," as though in flight from "a captured city" (GC 118), and some "reach out" and "grab" whatever they can get their hands on, whatever momentarily salves their pain (E 221). Some latch onto an ideology and some embrace nihilism. Some mortify their flesh and some become all-consuming carnivores. And then some few manage to neither fall into despond nor to become salacious sybarites. Some manage to negotiate a tense balance between their opposing desires and drives, finding a way to live in the unsure and devalued universe.

In that universe not only are things changed in an instant but they are changed, ostensibly, without reason or meaning. "The power to alter the course of the age, of my life and your life, is actually vested nowhere," Roth quotes Benjamin Demott approvingly (RMAO 177). There seems, in many cases, no one to assign blame to for one's personal pain. The confusion Sydney feels in "The Day it Snowed" is exemplary of the confusion of many of Roth's subsequent protagonists. Sydney asks, "What did I do? Why does everybody have to disappear on me?" (42). The question foreshadows to Novotny's query, in "Novotny's Pain," Roth's 1962 story of a soldier with a recurring backache, as to why, "Good as he had been - industrious, devoted, resolute, self-sacrificing - he would never have the pleasure of being a husband...or a comfort to his mother in her old age?" (266). He wonders, "What had he done in his life to deserve this?" (270).

And Kepesh - the same Kepesh whose fears rest not even on the quietest, most peaceful, evening of the year - must ask himself, when miraculously, horribly, he is turned into a breast, "WHAT DOES IT MEAN? HOW COULD IT HAVE HAPPENED? IN THE ENTIRE HISTORY OF THE HUMAN RACE, WHY PROFESSOR KEPESH?" (27). Characters are thrown into situations that defy understanding, that defy logic, that defy words, that defy explanation. It is as if Hardy's malevolent 'immanant-will' rules the lives of these twentieth-century men. Though the doctors tell Kepesh he has experienced "a massive hormonal influx or an endocrinopathic catastrophe, and/or a hermaphroditic explosion of chromosomes," no one knows with any degree of certainty what has caused his disfigurement (13). "Evidently," Kepesh realizes," nothing that has happened can be blamed on anyone, not even on me" (53). As Roth states, "Not all the ingenuity of all the English teachers in all the English departments in America can put David Kepesh together again" (RMAO 69). Nathan Zuckerman's back pain, in *The Anatomy Lesson* is, like Novotny's pain and like Kepesh's transformation, unclassifiable and incurable, its source impossible to uncover. In 'Courting Disaster' Zuckerman admits, "I tended, like a student of high literature or a savage who paints his body blue, to see the migraines as standing for something, a disclosure or 'epiphany'" (MLAM 55). But, as Zuckerman learns, quite often pain stands for nothing, has no retrievable cause, no substantive meaning. Things, simply, fall apart.

Epstein's rash is thought to be "prickly heat," a "sand rash" (212), or even "The syph" (216). Like the others before him Epstein insists "He was innocent," as if this declared innocence would cause the rash to disappear (217). 'Philip Roth,' in *Operation Shylock*, borrows the Jungian formulation, "the uncontrollability of real things," to express this unexplainable uninterpretability of life (237). Smilesburger calls it "Pipikism," "the antitragic force that inconsequentializes everything" (289). Giving it a name, though, does not contain or control it; nor does it soothe the fearful heart of those for whom it is a potential victimizer.

Connected to and working in tandem with all that oppresses invisibly and for no ostensible purpose are those discernible and recognizable powers that consciously and knowingly constrict man. They are what Roth refers to as "The Powers that Be," and range from the restrictive state to the restrictive religion, from the restrictive parent to the restrictive self (RMAO 3). When Epstein cries out in desperation, "When they start taking things away from you, you reach out, you grab," the "they" he attaches blame to are all those powers which conspire against the individual (221). "You Must Change Your Life," Rilke writes, and in Roth it is interpreted as a command. You, the powerless, the small, must change, a decree, not a suggestion.

In *Letting Go* Gabe Wallach comes in contact with Harry Bigoness, a representative figure for all the forces that stand above the individual, unswayed. Bigoness, Roth points out, "can't be moved by |Gabe's| intelligence, by his money, by his persuasiveness, by his moral code" (CWPR 9). The Big Ones - the ones who are in control, whose strength appears limitless, whose impersonal authority and dispassion resonate in all lives, whose decrees are meted out, whose words are acted upon, whose language is corrupt and corrupting - are ubiquitous. Of Gabe's encounter with Bigoness, Roth states, "I wanted him to come up against, at the end of the book, something that was indeed larger than him, but something that had nothing to do with being more intelligent or even more charitable than he was" (CWPR 9).

Bigoness is a concrete illustration of that force that Willard comments upon, and that Sydney, Novotny, Kepesh, and Epstein feel haunting them in every shadow. Incarnations of Bigoness are revealed in the McCarthyite actions of Mr. Wendell, in "You Can't Tell a Man by the Song he Sings," who documents both teachers' and students' behaviors and opinions on "a big card" which, he assures everyone, "would follow |them| through life," and which portends disaster for the left-leaning Russo (246), in the residents of Woodenton, who force the quiescent Holocaust-survivor, "the greenie" (281), to give up his clothes, to whom he appears to ask, "The face is all right, I can keep it? (283), in what Alexander Portnoy refers to as "this Holy

Protestant Empire" (43), in the officials and agents in Prague who follow both Kepesh and Zuckerman throughout their short visits, in the equally intrusive Israeli agents who tail 'Philip Roth' in Israel, in the Major League Baseball Association, the "Holy Baseball Empire," in *The Great American Novel*, which denies Smitty's entreaties, denies even Smitty's memories, and most hilariously in the figure of Tricky Dixon, in *Our Gang*, the personification of the tyrannical and the false, a parody of all political potentates, all dictators (16).

Dixon is the embodiment of what Norman Manea, in *On Clowns: The Dictator and the Artist*, calls "the white clown," the stark, cold, autocrat, exemplified for Manea in the figure of Nicolae Ceausescu (41). Manea contrasts the White Clown with Auguste the Fool, the subdued artist who "simply refuses" to let the White Clown dictate his life (49). But, Auguste is no dissident leading the charge against tyranny; he is, instead, the fearful, schlemiel-like man who, when forced into submission, must resist, who admits proudly, "I couldn't restrain myself" (8). It is this aspect of Manea's study that Roth finds most fascinating: "The battle not of the heroic but of the vulnerable, the weak and the unheroic to hang on and, stubbornly, against all odds, to resist their degradation" (CRM 3). For Roth, "no moral endeavor is more astonishing" (3).

This same fascination with the weak, the ordinary, the decidedly human, coming in contact and doing battle with various forms of coercion informs Roth's own fiction. It is not so much the Dixons and the Bigoness that intrigue Roth as much as those who manage to see through their hypocrisy and their lies, who manage to live in truth, in Vaclav Havel's phrase.[1] To give in to the powers that be, to submit one's self to the preset patterns of society is no remarkable feat; It is, in fact, the norm. Roth's prose focuses on how and why certain individuals, however unexceptional, are able to, to some degree or other, retain individuality in the midst of what Manea calls "the derailment of humanity itself;" how they do battle with the lie and with those who present the lie as truth (CRM 3).

This essential concern of Roth's explains his interest in oppressed European writers from Kafka to Klima, writers who investigate the individual in extreme situations, in conflict with powerful dehumanizing and corrupt political systems. His own works bridge the gap between Europe and America, focusing on the less overt ways in which man is stripped of individuality.[2] In contrast to the obvious manipulation of an authoritarian state the American reality is more obtuse and complex. There is no clear White Clown, no single Dixon to place blame upon. Roth's work speaks of the more subtle ways in which man loses his self: conformity, banality, blind patriotism, cliche, stereotype, trivialization, mechanization, a laundry list of methods and enactors of, what Noam Chomsky calls "manufactured consent," the unquestioning and obedient trust in one's world (Said 302). What Chomsky sees as "the effects of a generation of indoctrination" Roth writes in response to, pitting his frightened, groping, protagonists against various automatizing agents (Said 302). From Sydney's mother, whose attempt to stifle his growth through euphemism and lie, to the Mossad, which asks 'Philip Roth' to censor himself, these agents act, often effectively, to keep the individual in line, under control, essentially imprisoned.

Again and again characters attempt to "cut loose from what binds and inhibits" them, most often doing battle with the twin imposing threats of "the oppressiveness of family feeling" and the "binding ideas" of religion, threats which stretch across the spectrum of body and mind, the heart and the head, and which are employed synecdochically for all that represses man (RMAO 9).

Both forms of pressure are present in Roth's early, celebrated story, "The Conversion of the Jews," a story used often to explain Roth's initial impetus to create, a story usually viewed as a "moral-fantasy" (Jones & Nance 28), or, as Roth puts it, a "day dream," wherein oppressors are "magically" (CWPR 85) humbled by the young Ozzie Freedman, the personification of "the urge for individualistic freedom" (Jones & Nance 29).

Ozzie rebels against the obfuscations of his mother and of Rabbi Marvin Binder, dissenting from the illogical dogma that the students who surround him accept without disquiet. Ozzie, unlike his fearful peers, is disinclined towards "closed-mouthedness," questioning Binder on Binder's easeful rejection of the Immaculate Conception: "Jesus is historical" (139). Ozzie, refusing to digest, unconsidered, the words of authority, asks Binder, "If |God| could create the heaven and earth in six days, and make all the animals and the fish and the light in six days....and He could pick the six days right out of nowhere, why couldn't He let a woman have a baby without having intercourse?" (140-141). Ozzie is a literalist, confused when lessons learned do not correspond with new lessons or with behavior. He has wondered "how Rabbi Binder could call the Jews 'The Chosen People' if the Declaration of Independence claimed all men to be created equal" (141), and why during "free-discussion time" he feels so unfree to express what is on his mind (144).

The suggestion, most critics make, is that Binder, Mrs. Freedman, and Yakov Blotnik - "the seventy-one-year old custodian" who mumbles incoherent prayers to himself and whose thought are "fractionated...simply: things were either good- for- the-Jews or no-good-for-the-Jews" (150) - "come to represent the narrow and sterile religiosity from which Ozzie wishes to escape" (McDaniel 85), and that Ozzie is a "spiritual activist" (McDaniel 82) who moves from a constricting spiritless world to "one of spiritual freedom" (Meeter 20). Bernard Rodgers is the primary proponent of the Ozzie/Roth parallel. He calls Ozzie's action a "revolt against...xenophobia and closed-mindedness" and likens it emphatically with "Roth's own artistic revolt" (22).

These readings, defensible though they are, miss the substance of both Ozzie's 'revolt' and Roth's artistic program. For these readers the story lacks any irony: Ozzie is heroic individualism and the three elders repressive society and religion. There is no doubt that Roth uses this story, on one level, to exact criticism on those platitudinous and doctrinaire religious and secular authorities who refuse to answer or consider questions, who expect acquiescence, and who mouth the words of God without understanding what they are saying. And yet these villains are less villainous than at first imagined.

"Rabbi Binder," we are reminded, "only looked dictatorial" (149). In fact he is an unimposing and easily humbled figure, who, against the group chant of "Jump," maintains his plea, "Don't Jump! Please, Don't Jump" (153). Mrs. Freedman, a widow, is presented as a gentle and sad figure who "didn't look like a chosen person," and who, though she strikes Ozzie does so "for the first time," and without vigor (143). And Yakov Blotnik is clearly no danger to anyone, saddled with an "old mind" which "hobbled slowly, as if on crutches" (150). Though they are, indeed, single-minded and cliche-ridden they are not formidable threats; rather, they are combatants easily vanquished.

Ozzie, in many ways, is the aggressor, not merely questioning his teacher's words but insisting that the answers he receives are not sufficient, constantly claiming, "What I wanted to know was different" (141).Their conflict is essentially generational, the elder secure and dogmatic, the youth quizzical and unsatisfied with anything but faultless logic. But, where Binder attempts to answer Ozzie again and again, albeit with banalities, Ozzie rejects his answers outright, firing the accusation, "You don't know! You don't know anything about God!" (146).

It is Ozzie, not Binder, who is described as feeling both "Peace" and "Power" (149). It is Ozzie who becomes a Christ figure dancing on the rooftop to the chant of his earnest disciples, "Be a Martin. Be a Martin" (155). It is Ozzie who forces all into the "Gentile posture of prayer" (157), and compels them to "say they all believed in Jesus Christ" (158). Ozzie renounces Binder's binding dogma in favor of Christianity's, replacing Binder's cliches with his own: "You should never hit anyone about God" (158) He becomes so sure, so finally certain, that he leaps from the rooftop without fear, a believer. Ozzie, who only wanted definitive answers finds his answers in the "catechizing" of the Jews, in the language of another religion (158). His rebellion is less than "a fragile one," as Sanford Pinsker asserts; it is a fundamentally empty rebellion, a rebellion not towards freedom but towards more restrictiveness (TCTH 14). Ozzie, who initially seems to be "protesting his individuality," loses his individuality not to Binder, Blotnik, or to his mother, but to his reliance on the language of established Christianity, the language of dogma, to his assertion of power and surety (Deer 357). The story turns in upon itself, ironizing the simplicity with which Ozzie seems to find freedom.

To claim Ozzie Freedman as the personification of the activist's revolt against constrictions is to apply a facile and superficial reading to a story that demands a more complex explication. The outward simplicity of the language that Roth employs seems to invite uncomplicated interpretations. Saul Bellow chastises "The Conversion of the Jews" for being "absolutely clear" (42), and Joseph Landis states, "The point is... altogether too clear (166). And Roth, in a 1966 interview, suggests that his reading of the story is no more sophisticated than many readers when he asserts that he is no longer "at one with the ideas and feelings that had caused it to be written" (CWPR 8). Roth's statement applies to a story that is only about the absolute rejection of authority, a story which enacts a revolt. If the more complex reading is applied the story is seen as questioning both authority and the individual, both the rebel as well as the object of the rebellion.

In any reading, though, Ozzie's revolt is not commensurate with Roth's artistic program, as Rodgers claims it to be. To argue that Binder, Blotnik, and Mrs. Freedman "personify all that Roth was determined to reject in the attitudes of the Jewish environment which had surrounded him for the first eighteen years of his life" Rodgers paints a picture of Roth's work as overtly polemical, as didactic, as the work of a rebel rather than of an aesthete (22). Rodgers's claim is based on Roth's own argument that "an author's work can and should have a social impact" (61). He adds: "To Roth that impact would appear to be a subversive one" (61). Such a view of Roth places him side by side with Ozzie, a child attempting to overturn his world with an act of conversion. Roth is not such a simple subject. Rather than encouraging rebellion he investigates it in all its forms. Rather than derogating authority he questions and scrutinizes it. "I wouldn't write a book to win a fight," Roth contends, making clear his refusal to see art as a vehicle of rebellion (CWPR 193). "If you ask if I want my fiction to change anything in culture," Roth states, "the answer is still no," further subverting Rodgers's argument (CWPR 186). Roth, unlike Ozzie, embraces no position to overturn another. His fiction resonates with his "distrust of positions" of all kinds (RMAO 71). To see Roth's burgeoning writing as equivalent to Ozzie Freedman's escapade on the temple roof is to begin to study Roth from a mistaken angle.

Roth's first critics, those rabbis and readers who vehemently decried "The Conversion of the Jews," "Epstein," and "Defender of the Faith," offered Roth a much more virulent disapprobation than Binder's for Ozzie, and Roth's response has been more considered and sophisticated, more tinged with irony and doubt, than Ozzie's intuitive response. Roth's early stories were called "dangerous, dishonest, and irresponsible" (RMAO 205). He was called an "anti-Semite" and "self-hating" (RMAO 25), and was accused of "informing" on Jews by representing the lecherous Grossbart, the lusting Epstein (RMAO 217). "You have earned the gratitude," wrote a rabbi, "of all who sustain their anti-Semitism on such conceptions of Jews as ultimately lead to the murder of six million in our time" (RMAO 218). "I hated you personally every sentence of your story," another reader wrote (PRC).[3] "Medieval Jews would have known what to do with him," a "rabbi and educator in New York City" voiced (RMAO 216). A literary discussion group wrote to *The New Yorker*, after studying "Defender of the Faith," "We have discussed this story from every possible angle and we cannot escape the conclusion that it will do irreparable damage to the Jewish people" (RMAO 216). Requesting an answer to their complaints the group concluded, "Cliches like 'this being art' will not be acceptable" (RMAO 216).

Roth responded not with cliches but with unremitting earnestness, writing not only his 1963 essay, "Writing About Jews," (which summarizes and addresses those complaints) but with detailed individual letters written to rabbis and other readers. He decried their narrowness of vision, their inability to see his stories as investigations of various types of Jewish men and woman, both righteous and limited, both driven and conscience-laden, both deceitful and forthright. His book was not simply a categorizing of the evils and weaknesses of Jews, not "rassenschande," but an attempt to "redeem the stereotype," to understand and uncover both the truths and falsities embedded in the stereotype, to explore Jews as human beings, fallible and real (SDII 75). "The hope of the fiction writer is to tell the truth about experience and phenomena," Roth argues, in a draft to "Writing About Jews," not hiding ugly truth and celebrating laudatory truth (11). To adhere to his critic's suggestions, to succumb to their fear of fomenting "fuel" for anti-Semite's fire (RMAO 206), to create art while constantly asking, "What will the goyim think?" is to allow one's freedom to be taken away, to allow a restriction to be placed upon the imagination, to turn one's work into agit-prop (RMAO 212).

Likening his critics to McCarthyites and to the Russian government in its persecution of Boris Pasternak, he views their exercise as an attempt at "denying me my freedom and making me obedient to their will" (WAJ-D 11), arguing that "the only response there is to any restriction of liberties is 'No, I refuse'" (RMAO 221). Roth places the responsibility on the I, the individual, to hold fast to his sense of self by not adhering to the censoring powers, by 'writing in truth,' as Havel might term it.

Ozzie does not retain his self-hood in "The Conversion of the Jews." His recurring question, "Is it me? is it me?" reveals his loss of self (148). The language describing his actions on the roof indicate a boy out of control: "The question came to him," "he discovered himself no longer kneeling," "his arms flying every which way as though not his own," "he hadn't really headed for the roof as much as he'd been chased there" (151). He is a boy without volition, jumping because the crowd calls for it, using a language not his own. The individuality he asserts at the start of the story has disappeared. His revolt has failed. Roth's revolt is, by contrast, not only against the narrowness of his Jewish detractors but against narrowness in general. Roth resists all "untenable notions of right and wrong" (RMAO 206), using his fiction to locate "all that is beyond moral categorizing" (RMAO 207).

At the center of that resistance is an exploration of the self, the way in which a man holds back and falls victim to entrapment, the way in which a man entraps and liberates himself. "You Must Change Your Life" is not only a potential threat but, as Martin Green points out, a reminder of "the process of self-indictment" (PRR XXII). The struggle inside is as perilous as the struggle outside, the powers that inhabit a man more trying than the powers that be.

For the writer the "imaginations' systems of constraints and habits of expression," and not the critics' disdain, offer the most profound problems (RMAO 13). It is the self's limits that need to be traversed if writing is to succeed. The writing self is stymied by guilt, by fear, by history, by experience, and by indissoluble literary paradigms. Roth claims that he writes and reads fiction "to be freed from my own suffocatingly narrow perspective on life" (RMAO 120). Elsewhere he states that successful literature "allows us for awhile to be free" (WAJ-D 6). Roth's work springs from this conception of literature as potentially liberating and transforming. Like his characters the urge, the necessity, to maintain individuality, whether in style or content, is Roth's most difficult and imperative task. "What is it to be what I am?" his characters ask themselves again and again, determined to discover themselves without recourse to a preconstructed formula(I-GC 1). The discovery of the self and the retention of individuality and freedom amidst a debasing and deindividualizing world and a tortured and confused body and mind are concerns central to Roth's artistic drive, concerns which spring forth from Roth's overriding interest in the Holocaust and its lingering effects on twentieth-century man.

In an interview about the Zuckerman trilogy with *The London Sunday Times*, in 1973, Roth says of the Holocaust, "If you take away that word - and with it the fact - none of these Zuckerman books would exist" (RMAO 136). In fact to take away that word would be to erase Roth's canon. For Roth the Holocaust is the contemporary equivalent of what Harold Bloom terms Kafka's "Judaism of the Negative" (12). What in Kafka is the understood as the darkness "of the future," becomes in Roth the darkness of the past (Bloom 12). What Kafka feared and imagined became real for Philip Roth's generation; the penal colony became the death camps.

Instead of recognizing Roth's essential concern with the Holocaust and with its power to hold sway over the next generation, critics tended to use the Holocaust as a linchpin for their criticisms of his work, insisting that Roth degraded the memory of the victims by his critical and all too human portrait of Jews. In those early expressions of outrage the Holocaust is consistently invoked. Marie Syrkin's words are representative of the barbs lodged at Roth. She calls *Portnoy's Complaint* a work "straight out of the Goebbels-Streicher script" (RMAO 300). As Roth sardonically points out, "Had she not been constrained by limits of space Syrkin might eventually have had me in the dock with the entire roster of Nuremberg defendants" (RMAO 300).

Critics like Syrkin contended that not enough time had passed to write so openly about Jews. Jews, they asserted, should be exempt from criticism, their recent history made them unique, separate from other men, needing to be insulated, written and spoken about referentially, only as passive victims and heroic sufferers. For Roth the fact of the Holocaust makes it essential not to stoop to propagandizing for the Jews, not to cower in fear of the repetition of history; to present Jews as men and women, not categories, as individuals, not indistinguishable members of a group. After all, what is the fundamental difference between the Nazi picture of Jews as "wicked," and wicked only, and the fearful Jewish claim that Jews are "perfect," and perfect only? (WAJ-D 14).

Roth recognizes the validity of the fears expressed, just as he recognizes the anti-Semitic threat as real. "The difference between us," Roth writes of his critics, "is in how we choose to respond to the threat" (WAJ-D 13). While his critics espouse silence, prettified pictures, and timidity, Roth suggests vociferousness, honest, if sometimes ugly, pictures, and boldness as ways of exploring Jewish and American life after the Holocaust. It would be "an insult to the dead" six million to use their memory to stifle the artist's spirit (RMAO 221). For Roth, "The suggestion that we act willingly now the way certain Jews, in horror, grief, and shock, were forced to act then, provokes in me an outrage equaled only by my disbelief" (WAJ-D 15). To act as a victim when the victimization has ended is to hand the enemy a final victory. Roth's work is so centrally concerned with the I because it is the I that the Holocaust-architects tried to strip away. "Hitler killed nerve" (WAJ-D 18), argues Roth, and to allow nerve's death to infect the survivors is to "continue to be Hitler's victims" (WAJ-D 15). Roth's first responsibility, then, is to resist the impulse to censor himself in deference to the memory of the camps. The first I to liberate is the I of the writer.

As Sanford Pinsker points out, "If an older generation of American-Jewish writers had insisted, in Bernard Malamud's phrase, that 'All men are Jews!' Roth's vision was the converse -All Jews were also men" (TCTH 4). Roth individualizes men rather than grouping and universalizing them. Each Jew, in Roth, is differentiated from previous or future protagonists, each faces his own barriers, his own hurdles, and each responds according to his own strengths and limitations.

Many critics, including Irving Howe, find Roth's individualizing of Jews unconvincing, suggesting that Roth's Jews are de-judaized, their ties to Jewish tradition and history non-existent. Howe sees Roth as a writer submerging Jewish identity into assimilationist America, flaying the Jew from his roots, making him disappear into the mass, like Ellison's black paint disappears into a great American whiteness. Dorothy Seidman Bilik points to Roth's comments in a 1961 *Commentary* Symposium, to prove her point. In that debate Roth asked of Jews, "How are you connected to me as another man is not?" (351). However, rather than deciphered as a statement of disconnection from the Jews it is more accurately read as a declaration of connection to all men, not limited to Jews only. Jews are men, each attractive or repulsive on his own. This manner of viewing one's connection to Jews allows one a vaster perspective, allows one to deny that Jews are all one

thing, all the same. "And that is a good thing," Roth states in the same symposium, "for it enables a man to choose to be a Jew," to embrace his Judaism
and his history by choice rather than by being "turned into one, without his
free accession" (351).

His embrace of Judaism is a complex embrace, not simply the throwing
of arms blindly around all Jews and all the patriarchal Jewish beliefs and
codes but a more considered embrace, an embrace tinged with questions
and with thought. Roth does not renounce his Judaism, nor does he turn
away from its discomforting realities. On the contrary, Roth's emphasis on
the Jew as man, on the Jew as willful and complex, springs forth from a
painful need to remember and delve into the Jewish past.

What the Nazis attempted to take from Jews, and indeed from everyone,
Roth attempts to reinsert in his fiction, using the Holocaust as a lodestar to
point to the hurdles man must overcome. The most seductive hurdle the
Holocaust exposes is the hurdle of ideology, the belief in a fundamental,
absolute, indubious truth, a truth one must ascribe to unquestionably. In its
denial of self and in its elimination of choice the enactors of the Holocaust
relied on a strict ideology to enforce their will. Ideology presents itself as
the most malevolent force behind all that worked to devastate and dehumanize man in Nazi Germany. The Nazi ideology insisted that the Jews were
less than human, that they were cancers that needed to be excised.

In Roth's work, characters move across the spectrum of ideology and
nihilism. No single stance is satisfactory because each embodies an aspect
of the Nazi philosophy. The Nazi doctrine was not only a call to ideology
but, as David Hirsch points out, "a call for a return to a primordial past...a
regression to chthonic Dionysian drunkenness" (265-6). It relied not only on
the "systematic" and the "ordered" (Ezrahi 255) in man but on the "unshackled" in him as well (Hirsch 265). The Nazis tried to harness neither side of
man, allowing uncapped Dionysus to alternate with automatized and pro-
gramed Apollo. No balance, no interplay, was reached between these contradictory sides of man. The Nazi, in this illustration, is half a man (though
he feels himself to be whole, complete) turning one side of his self off while
the other performs its horrendous duties. Roth's successful men and
women find fullness in the tension between the two diverse sides of self, a
tension lessened and engorged minute by minute but never subdued, never
fully quieted. Unlike the Nazi, Roth's protagonist maintains a balance,
unable and unwilling to allow either Dionysus or Apollo full control over
him. He feels "painful points of friction," as Roth writes of the quintessential Rothian man, his father, a friction, he continues, "which yield[s], at its
best, vitality, a dense and lively matrix of feeling and response" (MIM A-32).
The maintenance of this friction, this balance, creates countless dilemmas,
neuroses, terrors, hurts, and fears, but its maintenance is the only way to
exist in a concentrationary universe.

The balance extends to Roth's style as well as to his content. Roth rejects
the temptation "to imitate" narrative techniques "verified by authority"

(RMAO 8). He rejects "literary dogma" in favor of a more individual style, one which mixes genres, which mixes the past and the present, which mixes the vernacular and the literary, which uses models and breaks free from models, which forms new paradigms only to undermine and reconsider them. Speaking of *The Counterlife*, but useful for all his works, Roth notes, "The narratives are all awry but they have a unity" (CWPR 253). In that remark he locates the pull between form and formlessness, the need for both if a work is to have validity in the changed world. His works take literary techniques and genres - naturalism, realism, anti-realism, parody, satire, thriller, confession, love-story, biography, autobiography - and turn them in upon themselves, altering the reader's perspective by diverging from the established form, by undermining expectations. Roth's style, a cacophony, a hybrid, a bringing together and a stripping apart, can best be defined as impressionism, a style inextricably bound up with the individual, the I groping for vision, a style which both is aware of the ambiguity and unsurety of the world at the same time as it retains some solidity, some structure which holds back the urge for a deconstructionist denial of all form, all truth, all meaning.

The battle is between, what will be termed, Lonoffism and Pipikism, the ordered, ideological, strict, impotent, lifeless automaton and the "protean" (OS 185), the nihilistic, "the senseless," the driven, the lustful, the uncontrolled, the unbound animal (OS 389). To keep the tension between the two and to be aware of the split is to remain viable and vibrant, functioning and potent. To shut down one side and to give the other sovereignty is to fall into the cauldron of the concentrationary universe.

"The novelist," Roth says in an interview with Asher Z Milbauer and Donald G. Watson, "suffers from serious ignorance of his obsessional theme" (10). Whether Roth suffers from that ignorance is difficult to deduce, but it is clear that when a comprehensive survey of Roth's work is undertaken the Holocaust in all its manifestations, as history, as lesson, as harbinger, as memory, as coercer, as warning, is Roth's obsessional theme.

Unlike other American writers Roth was not hesitant to investigate imaginatively the stark facts of the Holocaust period. Sidra Ezrahi describes the "slow process by which the remote event eventually entered |American| literature (179). She notes that in America "few...writers possessed the resources from which an immediate response could be shaped" (176-177). The war literature of the forties, Ezrahi argues, "established the camps somewhere on the outer boundaries of human geography" (179). American literature of the late forties and fifties investigated "the fascist threat...but not the historical events of the Holocaust" (179). The fifties, she states, were taken up with "growing documentation by survivors and historians," but little substantive fiction was created (179). Ezrahi points to the trial of Adolph Eichmann in 1961 as "a watershed in the American perception of the Holocaust," the bell that awoke the slumbering or weary writers (180). And yet between 1958 and 1959 Philip Roth was already writing and re-writing a play, titled "A Coffin in Egypt," which confronts the Holocaust directly, exploring boldly the experience of a Jewish ghetto between 1941 and 1943.[4]

The play tells its story in three relatively short acts. Act One sets the scene in Vilna, Lithuania, October 1941. Solomon Kessler, a former clerk, a simple man, "a man who has been deprived all his life" (26), a "mediocre failure," has just been made Mayor of the Jews of Vilna, by the Nazi Colonel Holtz (60). He meets with the Jewish council to explain that he is now "in charge of the Jews" (6) Rabbi David Meyer, the Chancellor of the Yesivah, refuses to acknowledge Kessler, refuses to compromise, as he will through-out the play. Rabbi Joachim Smolenskin, a wise elderly man, recognizes the need for compromise, the need to retain some Jewish authority in the midst of what he admits is an incomprehensible situation. Leo Rosenfeld, a com-munist, refuses, like Meyer, to respect Kessler's rule, promising him a revo-lution of workers. Kessler is told by Holtz that he will be able to make Vilna a prospering, culturally alive village again as long as each month he sends a thousand Jews to the extermination camps. Holtz explains that in sending a sacrifice each month Kessler will save countless Jewish lives. Kessler resigns himself to Holtz's terms believing that "Fighting them is impossible" (17). The first act ends with the first "Action" (10). An old man , the last of the thousand, asks, "What did I do? Why?" as he stops midway to the train (20). He asks Smolenskin, "Rabbi, who can be buried in a strange place?" and the rabbi tells him of Joseph's burial in Egypt, far away from the prom-ised homeland (21). The man is taken away and hit by a Nazi guard. Kessler smacks the guard, telling him, "Never lay one finger" (23). The train pulls away and the citizens of Vilna begin the mourner's prayer as Kessler screams, "Stop it! Stop mourning! I forbid mourning!" (23).

Act Two takes place in December 1942, in an ostensibly revitalized Vilna. The coffee shop is filled with Jews; music is playing. The theater, the schools, the restaurants, have been reopened, and, as Smolenskin says, It is all "Kessler's doing" (26). The two rabbis and Rosenfeld argue their various positions, Meyer and Rosenfeld secure in their rightness, Smolenskin con-sumed by doubt. Kessler enters the shop like a monarch, an air of confi-dence about him, magisterial, in control. He tells those assembled of his plan to save ten thousand Jewish lives. Five thousand workers are to be shipped to Kovno, which will become a "Jewish worker's city," and five thou-sand of Vilna's vagrants will then take their places at work (28). Kessler appoints Rosenfeld the leader of the workers in Kovno. Rosenfeld, accusing Kessler and the Nazis of "breaking the back of the resistance" by sending "the young" and "the strong" away from Vilna, declines the appointment (38). For his non-acquiescence Rosenfeld is arrested. The train for Kovno is loaded with healthy, optimistic men and women. Kessler and Meyer watch the train begin its trip, Kessler fiercely proud of his accomplishment, Meyer bitter, enraged at the decimation of his beloved Vilna. The train, suddenly, comes to a halt and the young Jews are led from the train and are massa-cred in a maze of machine-gun fire. Kessler, horrified, despondent, screams,

"I didn't do it! I didn't do it!" (42). The act ends, once again, with the mourner's kaddish, chanted this time by Kessler himself.

Act Three takes place in August 1943. The Nazis are concerned about the approaching Russian army. Vilna, it seems, will soon be overrun. Holtz presents Kessler with a scheme whereby Kessler will assume guilt for all the evils perpetrated upon Vilna's Jews in return for an assisted escape to Sweden. Kessler, while thinking over Holtz's proposal, visits the ailing Smolenskin, who despairing, wants only to die. Kessler defends his actions, claiming that everything he did he did only to save Jews. He tells Smolenskin, "Everything was black and some of us stood in front of the blackness, and we made some gestures" (58). Kessler leaves the dying rabbi to supervise what might be the last Action. He is told that they are one Jew short of their quota. Kessler moves to a microphone and addresses the crowd. "The Russians are coming," he tells them. "Go home. All of you, go home" (59). Powerless to have his words acted upon he joins the doomed Jews. The crowd begins to chant the mourner's prayer as Kessler disappears into the train.

"A Coffin in Egypt," written virtually simultaneously with the stories of *Goodbye, Columbus*, recreates the Holocaust universe while pointing towards the post-Holocaust universe that Roth's next works will take as their setting. The play begins with an overwhelming assertion of power: the imposition of a puppet government to both subjugate and palliate the frightened Jews of Vilna. Kessler's appointment is not put to a democratic vote; the Jewish council is dissolved in a moment. The power thrusts itself upon Kessler and the villagers, taking control of their lives. But that power is invisible, always at a distance, always removed. Kessler answers to Holtz, Holtz to an unseen Berlin. "I resent," Holtz tells Kessler, "that you are making this seem my idea" (13). "Kovno," he says later, "was Berlin" (48). But Berlin remains in the shadows. The power seems to emanate from nowhere.

It is not only invisible but uninterpretable. It seems to act counter-intuitively. "I don't even begin to understand," Smolenskin says. "Cossacks I've seen, pogroms I've seen. But this, giving people yellow cards, counting them off, putting them on trains, some still carrying their fiddles, their china" (17). There is no model, no precedent, to compare to the Nazi assault. All designations, all forms of knowledge and of language are undone. "What did I do?" cries the old man (20) In this new world innocence is no defense against punishment It is a world, as Primo Levi reports, in *Survival in Auschwitz*, without "Why" (7).[5]

It is a world where the strong are murdered and the mediocre are rewarded. It is a world where the definitions of good and evil are overturned. Are Kessler's actions good because they save lives or are they evil because they advance the Nazi campaign? Are Meyer and Rosenfeld good because they admonish Kessler or are they evil because they would rather submit everyone to a collective death. rather than compromise with an outside power and give up their own authority? The attack upon Vilna's citizens is more than an attack upon their bodies; it is an attack upon all that they have believed in, all that they have spoken, all that they know. It is an attack upon their sense of themselves, on their humanity. A mammoth power has arrived not only to conquer but to control, to strip its victims of their very status as human beings.

Each character reacts to this assault in a different manner, depending on his/her former life, preconceptions, and ardent beliefs. Rosenfeld uses communism as the redemptive ideology to challenge the Nazi ideology. To him Kessler is a "Fascist" (56). A true believer in the workers, in the coming of a world revolution, in Stalin as god-head, Rosenfeld promises Kessler, "There will be a new era" (56). Rosenfeld derives his strength from this belief, a belief which gives him the will to refuse Kessler at every turn, to mock and threaten him. But Rosenfeld's ideology is as limited as the Nazi ideology that he rebels against. He mimics Stalin and Lenin as Hitlerites mimic Hitler. He considers nothing, doubts nothing, sees the world in black and white. His revolt, then, is an empty one. Like Ozzie, he merely substitutes one ideology for another. He never aspires to individuality; his ideology keeps him strong but costs him his identity.

David Meyer's refusal is, like Rosenfeld's, initiated from ideological ground, his ideology being that of Orthodox Judaism. Meyer is forever quoting the bible, suggesting that martyrdom is the only solution for Vilna's Jews. For Meyer compromise is out of the question, those who do, whether they save lives or not, are collaborators, traitors to their religion. Smolenskin responds to Meyer's simplistic assertion of superiority, asking him, "How can you be so holy? How can the rest of us be so wicked?" (27). Meyer, like the Nazis, attempts to brand each man holy or unholy, hero or murderer, human or beast, "messiah" or "butcher" (36). There are no gradations. Ideology provides him with a sense of rightness, but it takes away his ability to consider, to think and rethink, making him robotized, inhuman, making him the epitome of the undone, victimized Jew.

Smolenskin resists the urge to condemn or criticize too quickly in favor of a more balanced and thoughtful approach to the unendurable situation. He is an appeaser, a realist, offering sympathy for the victims while maintaining his connection to those in charge. He tells Meyer, "A dead Jew helps nobody. We take from the Germans what life we can" (27). Smolenskin is a man of decency and of wisdom, his philosophy antagonistic to ideology.

But with his faith pulled out from under him, his town denuded, his fellow Jews at war with one another, he gives in to despair, banishing himself to his bedroom, hoping for death. When Kessler encourages him to recover the rabbi responds, "I don't have the ambition" (53). He has given up, surrendered himself to the degradation that has been foisted upon him. He appropriates the posture of a dying man though his health is fine. Nihilistically, he lies down and closes his eyes, becoming a martyr to hopelessness. Meyer and Rosenfeld find sanctuary in ideology while Smolenskin finds his sanctuary in emptiness. All eviscerate their selves.

Solomon Kessler moves within both frames, only to escape from the binds of each to unfettered self-hood. Initially he is an empty vessel, a man whose heart is "a plug of iron," a man cut in half (15). "For thirty-seven years I went through life I didn't feel a thing," he remarks (39). He is an automaton, moving through each day by rote. Thrust into a position of power Kessler finds his missing half, he finds purpose. "I...believe in what I'm doing," he says with passion (39). He finds an alternative lifestyle to his previous structureless life. He develops faith in his power, believing it to be legitimate. When he announces his plan for Kovno he says triumphantly, "They have made a concession to me. To me!" (34). He tells the Nazi guards, "I'm in charge here" (23).

But Kessler's language betrays him. He tells a crowd, "The basis for existence in the ghetto is work," echoing the Nazi cliche, "Work makes man free," exposing the extent of his indoctrination into the Nazi lexicon and dogma. In the throes of power he displays his inherent impotence. He is a puppet, mouthing the oppressor's words, no more human than he was when a non-feeling clerk. Kessler tells Smolenskin, "I suddenly was given a life, not of a bug" (55). He believes he has experienced a reverse metamorphosis, that he has finally become a man. But even in his expression of this found freedom he displays his debt to a controlling power. He is 'given' a life; he does not create or choose a life. As long as he acts as the Nazi representative he is never free.

It is when doubt enters his consciousness that he begins to extricate his self from its confinement. When Holtz asks him, towards the end of the play, "What have you been in this for in the first place?" he responds, "I don't know" (51). His belief in his role has evaporated and he is liberated. When he disobeys Holtz and tells the Jews to detrain he knows his life is in jeopardy, he knows his action will be ineffective, he knows that he has given up all roads to escape. His act of refusal is a potent act, an act born not from ideology nor from despair but from will. In the midst of the dehumanization of all that surrounds him he exercises choice thereby denying Holtz and Berlin their victory. Kessler finds, in the convergence of the twin sides of self, a freedom that no other character is able to uncover.

The battle Kessler undergoes augurs the battle Rothian man suffers time and time again, attempting to keep each side vibrant without relying on ideology or grabbing hold of nihilism. Ambiguity is the stance Rothian man finds most satisfactory, a questioning back not a rejection, a searching but not a discovery, a way of living with the "blackness" without allowing it to devour. The play itself ends ambiguously, a mourner's prayer spoken but for whom it is unclear. For Kessler? For the thousand on the train? For the mourners themselves? Or, perhaps, for the changed world, for the future, for the next generation whose duty it will be to recover meaning, to recover hope, to recover language, to recover faith, to recover the covenant, all without forgetting and without demeaning the memory.

In the end, the play asserts, it is the individual who is responsible for his own redemption. Roth's characters must risk appearing as fanatics to the world if they are to maintain their individual integrity. Two types of fanatics are illustrated and explored throughout Roth's work: The fanatic who follows blindly an ideology and the fanatic who rebels against conformity. To resist fanaticism of the first order Roth's characters must often embrace fanaticism of the second order, appearing insane to those indoctrinated many. Kessler's final action may appear as the gesture of a fanatic, the futile gesture of a man outside society, but it his his one authentic gesture, his one true assertion of self.

"A Coffin in Egypt" introduces the historical period that shapes the attitudes and visions of the characters and that shapes the very language of the texts themselves, the world that informs, impels, encourages, and entraps the next world. The situation in Vilna is not only the epitome of the situation of twentieth century man but is also the base memory that intrudes upon the more staid post-1945 world. When not involved in their own battles against disintegration Roth's characters are reflecting upon their separation from the world Vilna represents, and their connection to that world.

Never again will Roth make the Holocaust world his setting, never again will he so nakedly immerse himself in its horrors, but never will it cease to be the central subject of his work. It remains on the periphery, awakening, enervating, and informing. Its relative silence makes its force altogether more powerful.

The mix of silence and of speech is essential to Roth. His work is structured on dichotomy, on tension and balance. To write only and always about the Holocaust in its stark reality would serve to trivialize its weight, but to leave it out is impossible. Roth's work is assimilationist; it relies on a "two-way engagement," as Roth says of true assimilation: Silence and verbosity, head and heart, past and present, desire and conscience, ideology and nihilism, literature and life, all interact creating an explosion of lively tension, a burst of energy (MIM A32). It is the energy of conversation, of commingling. The conversation reinvestigates history, reimagines time, reinterprets literature, spurns cliche and stereotype, dehumanization and vulnerability, to salvage a taste of truth.

The concentrationary universe removes certainty. It creates an abyss and warns against a descent into that abyss. It demands memory and demands that memory not inhibit truth. It makes authority suspect and the invisibility of authority portentous. The man in the concentrationary universe is anxious and uneasy, fundamentally powerless. How to overcome that powerlessness and write is Roth's first concern. With language so debased how is a writer to explore the multi-faceted altered world? It is this question which Sydney asks throughout "The Day it Snowed:" How to find words to comprehend what is incomprehensible. Language resists the attempt but the attempt must be made.

"Suddenly people began to disappear." We begin with that fact, stark and plain, and from that our investigation is set afloat. How? Why? History demands investigation, demands memory. The mourner's kaddish which ends Roth's early Holocaust play is a psalm of memory and it acts as an impetus for Roth's efforts. "You must not forget anything," Roth quotes his father, echoing Elie Wiesel's plaintive cry for remembrance (P 238). To remember means not merely to record the facts but to retain the lessons.

This complex call for memory infects the whole of Roth's canon, from the young boy longing for truth to the writer questioning his motives and his debts. The Holocaust moves across Roth's work like an anomorphic design in a painting, hidden at first, but with the turn of the head and the focusing of the eyes it is readily apparent, huge, overwhelming.

Notes

1.   Vaclav Havel, in his essay, "The power of the powerless," posits, "Living within the truth, as humanity's revolt against an enforced position, is ... an attempt to regain control over one's own sense of responsibility" (62). Havel uses the dichotomy of "living within the truth" (55) and living "within the lie," the lie being the oppressive system which demands conformity (50). To live within the lie is not only to join willingly in the repressive government but to live obediently, anonymously, cowardly, unquestioningly, under that government. Havel recognizes the desire to "merge with the anonymous crowd and flow comfortably along with it down the river of psuedo-life" (55), the desire to turn one's head away from the truth of one's own enslavement, one's collaboration, but implores man to resist in any small way he can, to break "the rules of the game" and to therefore disrupt "the game as such" (56).

2.   Since 1974 Roth has been General Editor of "Writer's from the Other Europe," a series of books written by Eastern European writers whose voices were, in many cases, virtually unheard in America. The series includes: Jerzy Andrezejewski's *Ashes and Diamonds*, Tadeusz Borowski's *This Way for the Gas, Ladies and Gentlemen*, Geza Csath's *Opium and Other Stories*, Bohumil Hrabal's *Closely Watched Trains*, Danilo Kis's *A Tomb for Boris Davidovich*, Tadeusz Koniwicki's *A Dreambook for Our Time*, Milan Kundera's *The Book of Laughter and Forgetting*, *The Farewell Party*, and *Laughable Loves*, Bruno Schulz's

Sanatorium Under the Sign of the Hourglass, and *The Street of Crocodiles,* and Ludvick Vaculik's *The Guinea Pigs.*

3.   The Philip Roth Collection, in the Manuscript Division of the Library of Congress includes many unpublished letters to and from Roth, from which this has been extracted. It also includes unpublished manuscripts and drafts of stories and novels.

4.   "A Coffin in Egypt" is included in The Philip Roth Collection. I have quoted from the third draft, written October 1959. Roth describes it as a "play" but its parenthetical directions suggest that he was also considering it as a film.

5.   Levi attributes that comment to a Nazi guard, and so for many writers on the Holocaust the expression loses its validity; they do not want the terror defined by the persecutors but by the victims. Levi is a writer Roth has expressed great affection for. His poem 'Shema,' a stern call for memory, can be read as an epigraph to Roth's fiction. In *Patrimony* Roth writes of a 1986 interview with Levi: "Over the course of the four days together we had become mysteriously close friends - so close that when my time came to leave, Primo said, "'I don't know which of us is the younger brother and which is the older brother,' and we embraced emotionally as though we might never meet again. It turned out that we never did" (211).

CHAPTER ONE

The Ghost Writer

A man said to the universe:
"Sir, I exist!"
"However," replied the universe,
"That fact has not created in me
A sense of obligation."

- Stephen Crane
- Poem XXI, From *War is Kind*

The landscape is barren, cold, wintry white; daylight is fading. It seems a place for endings, for descent, escape. The "clapboard farmhouse" which sits "at the end of an unpaved road twelve hundred feet up in the Berkshires" is part of a time lost long ago, part of a pastoral America now all but vanquished (9). It is a place "where America began and long ago had ended," as the elder Nathan Zuckerman knows (11). Rather than a setting for renewal it is a setting for renunciation and departure. The two-hundred year old house is devoid of life. The words used to describe its interior are words of sterility: "plain," "pale," "bare," "colorless" (11). The trees and hills that surround the house act as a "barrier" to the outside world (38). Nature protects the house, guards it from civilization; "a thick green growth of rhododendron" and a "wide-stone wall" act like sentinels (38).

Ironically, it is into this emptiness that Zuckerman comes to find approval, acceptance, encouragement, and inspiration. From its opening *The Ghost Writer* revels in contradictions of this sort: The Jew living in "the *goyish* wilderness" (10), the writer who lives "away from all the Jews" and who writes only about Jews (67), the writer whose talent "made his every paragraph a little novel in itself" looking, in person, to be "out to lunch" (75).

Nathan's education, his growth from ephebe to artist, teaches him to accept the disparities inherent in life, and to grasp hold of ambiguity and duality as essential elements of twentieth-century art.

The Ghost Writer introduces Philip Roth's world to the neophyte and to the familiar reader; the novel acts paradigmatically, illuminating Roth's major concerns, his style, and his obsessions. To explicate Roth's eleventh novel is to open the door to his world, to shine light upon his methods, and to discover the continuity that holds together such a seemingly disparate, vastly differentiated, range of works. Zuckerman's education begins ours.[1]

The text is replete with contradictions which Zuckerman announces but dismisses quickly: E.I. Lonoff moves "with a notable lightness for such a large, heavyset man" (12). Amy Bellette confuses Zuckerman because "she could act so wise and dress up so young" (37). Lonoff is a married man whose work contains not "a single hero who was not a bachelor, a widower...or a reluctant fiance" (91). Zuckerman looks at Lonoff's typewriter and thinks, "Why a portable for a man who went nowhere?" (96). In his fiction of Amy Bellette, Zuckerman thinks of Amy/Anne "succumbing to having not succumbed" (184), and Lonoff is envisaged feeling of Amy "that she meant every word and that not a word was true" (186). The lines turn in upon themselves, sabotaging Zuckerman's early sense of simplicity.

Oxymorons proliferate: Zuckerman lives in the apartment of an "unchaste monk" (13). He describes himself as "a truthful perfidious brute" (50). He admits to "a son's girlish love" for Lonoff (74). Astonished at Lonoff's scrupulosity in both his life and in his art, Zuckerman thinks, "What a terrible triumph" (94). "Tenderness, boldness, love, and contempt," is the oxymoronic description of "Chopin's Scherzo No. 2" (97). Even the quoted Jimmy Durante number - "Did you ever have the feeling you wanted to go, still have the feeling you wanted to stay?" - relies on contradiction and antithesis (72).

Lonoff's home is not quite what Zuckerman had imagined when he envisioned the artist's life, wherein "all one's concentration and flamboyance and originality" are spent on one's creations, where everything is sprinkled with the holy water of art, where everything makes sense and is complete, simple and meaningful (11).The strangeness of his journey is accentuated when he reads Lonoff's typed quotation from James's "The Middle Years:" "We work in the dark - We do what we can - We give what we have. Our doubt is our passion and our passion is our task. The rest is the madness of art" (98). Zuckerman confusedly thinks, "I would have thought the madness of everything but art" (98). For him art has been a sanctuary for pure, uncontradictory effort, a sacred realm, separated from all the world, as the house he spends the night in is separated from civilization. "The art," he tells himself, "was what was sane, no?" (98). Zuckerman's definitions begin to fail him in the home of the master. Confusion settles over the anxious artist. He looks at James's words and wonders, "Was I missing something?" and in this initial admittance of doubt Zuckerman's Bildungsroman has in fact begun (98).

But doubt is what he had hoped to leave behind at Emanuel Isidore Lonoff's hermitage of "magical protection" and "love," the doubt he has been inundated with recently by the reaction his story, "Higher Education," has elicited from his formerly quiescent, "amiable" father (17). In its abruptness, its variation from the norm, the objection his father makes sends Zuckerman into a tailspin, leaving him unprepared to make a cogent argument for artistic sovereignty. Instead he tells his father, "Dad, go home, please," and jumps onto a bus, in effect running away from his father's words, words which claim that Zuckerman has written a story about one thing and one thing only: "Kikes and their love of money," words which arise from, and reveal, a father's particular memory and sensibility (118).

Those words are not easily left behind. But, as he sits in the awe-inspiring study of his literary hero Zuckerman recognizes his father's displeasure as a potential source of inspiration. Zuckerman is only now beginning to learn that resistance to fatherhood and resistance to coercion and to authority are the keys to his writing life. The Holocaust's existence makes the father afraid of his son's prose, and its existence makes the son even more afraid of giving into the father's authority. The fiction Zuckerman creates of Anne Frank's unknown life is a fiction that could only have been created in response to his own break with his father, for the story is one which investigates the need for fathers and the need for independence. Its evolution begins the moment Zuckerman hears the resonant slam of the bus door weeks earlier.

In Zuckerman's fiction, Amy Bellette/Anne Frank is traumatized by the Broadway "dramatization of Anne Frank's diary" (153).Watching the women in the audience cry she realizes that in order for her story to retain its power she will "have to be dead to everyone," even, most importantly, to her father (154). She believes that in order to exact revenge on her oppressors and to keep the dead alive "she would have to vanish...fatherless and all on her own" (183). Her "belief in the power of her less than three hundred pages" strengthens her "resolve to keep from her father, sixty, the secret of her survival" (183). Her desperate and painful sacrifice of her father is the sacrifice that Zuckerman feels he must make. He must give up the father, like Anne, to be faithful to his conception of the horror. He must give up his childish image of his father if his work is to have any vitality. He realizes as much when he sees that there is no scar on Amy's arm, that she is not Anne Frank at all: "No," he thinks, "the loving father who must be relinquished for the sake of his child's art was not hers: he was mine" (207).

Beyond recognizing his need for a father's resistance, Zuckerman must finally acknowledge that he has created this fiction for truly one purpose, to reconcile himself with his father. For, to give the father up would also be a betrayal of their common past. The morning after the tumultuous creative night Zuckerman admits that his father "was never out of my thoughts"

(194). The fantasy he has created allows him to imagine himself married to Anne Frank, to imagine himself introducing her to his family: "This is my Aunt Tessie, this is Frieda and Dave....This is my wife, everyone.... Remember the shadowed eyes....Remember the dark hair...? Well, this is she" (196). In his fantasy he envisions his father's response: "Anne," he says, "the Anne? Oh, how I have misunderstood my son" (196). As outraged and angered as Nathan is at his father's behavior, at his misreading of "Higher Education," and of his narrow view of art, Nathan wants his love and his approval even as he turns away. As much as he has learned how his father's active antagonism can spur his own birth of a freer, more intellectually honest creative spirit, he still fears that antagonism. As much as he longs for autonomy, he still wants a Dad-da to pat him on the *keppe*. "Oh, marry me, Anne Frank," he thinks, "exonerate me before my outraged elders" (210). "Zuckerman," argues Scott O'Donnell, "wishes...to orphan himself ..., to be his own father" (371). That wish, though, is only one part of Nathan. Like most Rothian characters, Nathan is divided, multitudinous, diverse. He is not one man but two, not just the aspiring artist but also the needful son. "It was," Zuckerman remembers, recounting the bright morning in the Berkshires, "as though not one but two suns had risen that morning" (218). Indeed, in the course of his short journey Nathan has come to understand his own duality, the dichotomy which lives within him and which makes him the artist he will become.

The son is oppressed by his father's derision and is similarly oppressed by his mother's love. The mother's power over the son is comparable in many ways to the father's, but is always more subtle, more hidden and more quiet. She is essentially a figure of warmth, but as Roth comments, "The fire that warms can also burn and asphyxiate" (RMAO 198-199). The mother's affection fosters shame as the father's rancor fosters anger.

When Nathan does not call his father for three weeks after their road-side argument his mother calls him and begins to cry. "I know its wrong to bother you," she begins, "but I can't take it anymore" (131). Mrs. Zuckerman plays peacemaker; she shows no revelatory vituperation to her son but manages to make the same complaints to him in a more covert manner. "Nathan," she tells him, echoing her husband's rational for censoring the story, "Violence is nothing new to the Jews, you know that," calling back to an inbibed memory, a memory sucked into his veins with the pure white milk (133). Attributing the comment to someone else, she asks him, "Nathan, is this true? - that...it looks like you don't really like Jews very much" (135). She adds, using apophasis, "Are you really anti-Semitic...? Me? I never heard of such a thing. But Teddy..." (136). In this backhanded way she is able to defend her husband, accuse her son, and never put herself in a position of judgment. "Please," she tells Nathan, "if you will not do anything else I ask, at least phone your father," using verbal acumen to exact guilt upon her beloved, intransigent offspring (136). That she never accuses him directly only makes his severing with her more painful. She asks him, frantically,

"What about your father's love?" (136). Her love, a mother's love, cannot be put in doubt.

Nathan hears his mother's words, words of love and sacrifice, sounding through his head as he sits down to compose his fiction. Her voice never deserts him, explaining his need to quote Anne's declaration, "I have now reached the stage that I can live entirely on my own, without Mommy's support" (173-174), a line which reverberates with his own final words to his mother on the phone, "I am on my own" (136). This assertion of freedom is easier to announce than to enact. To be free of the mother who poisoned his youth with a terrifying history is to be free of the mother who protected him from that history. To be free of mother's entrapment is also to be free of the consolation she can provide.

Feeling alienated from both mother and father, Nathan's need for impersonal authority becomes more and more pronounced. But what authority offers is only restrictions and rules. Authority becomes menacing for the young Zuckerman, who searches for its sanction so earnestly. Authority becomes authoritarian, evaluating in silence, ominously. Zuckerman, hoping for a nod from Felix Abravanel, the gargantuan figure who inspires "boundless adoration," sits and, like the prisoner before the court, expects the thumb. But Abravanel, in his vestments of authority, prefers "to look down at |Zuckerman| from along way off, like a llama or a camel" (84). He offers nothing, promises nothing; if he deigns to take notice it is with the air of a king placating his vassals. His only words are "Good luck," mechanical, social words which mean virtually nothing to the twenty-three year old writer (84). Though Abravanel seems to embody the same aura of sureness and potency that Lonoff appears to possess, he exists in a different relationship to Nathan. He is less a man than a representation, less a father than a judge. He is someone who would "not be in the market for a twenty-three-year old son" (85), someone about whom Zuckerman could never think, as he does of Lonoff, "I loved him" (72).

Abravanel resembles, in many ways, Judge Leopold Wapter, another figure of distant authority who seems to hover above and beyond ordinary men. Wapter occupies, Zuckerman reports, "a position of prestige and authority" (122). He, like Abravanel, is treated with "reverence" (123), and is explicitly compared to "President Roosevelt" (122) and "Abraham Lincoln" (124). Zuckerman's first experience with Wapter is an experience of supplication, the young boy dressing up and petitioning the pillar of the community in his imposing "chambers" (123). His indoctrination into the world of power is one fraught with fear and awe, one in which he is "instructed" on how to behave, on what to say, and on what to wear (123). Already preparing for college he is forced into the behavior of a child in order to secure a recommendation from the judge. The judge is generous and approving to the young man, benign, but that benignity only hides a felt malevolence ever-ready to show itself if the young adjurer wavers from his current straight path, as Zuckerman finds out when he receives a letter from Wapter and his wife commenting on "Higher Education."

The letter is didactic and pompous. Wapter writes of his meeting with Mr. Zuckerman, telling Nathan, "I informed him that classically, down through the ages and in all countries, the artist has always been considered himself beyond the mores of the community in which he lived" (127).

Wapter attempts to deindividualize Nathan's efforts as an artist by linking him to "the artist" in "all" countries. For if artists have "always" acted against the strictures of the community then they offer little real rebellion, as they are only performing their own timeless function in that community. Nathan's threat is minimal if he is viewed as following a classical formula rather than acting on his own volition.

Appended to the letter is a list of ten questions. By framing his complaint in the form of questions Wapter makes Zuckerman indict himself. Authority's ways are often deceptive, entrapping by trickery. In the form of questions Wapter manages to accuse Zuckerman of valuing "the cheap" and "the slimy" over "the noble and the sublime," and to admonish him for exposing Jews for the purpose of personal "financial gain" (130). The heartbroken tone of Nathan's father is substituted by Wapter's calm, assured voice, a voice without furor in its tone but loaded with virulent rebuke and disgust. Wapter never expresses an opinion; he hides within the labyrinthian lawerly language, relying on loaded questions to make his point. Wapter is never a human presence; like Abravanel, he lives in a sphere distant from others, delivering opinions upon men.

Wapter and Abravanel attempt to sap strength from Zuckerman, Abravanel in his refusal to take notice, and Wapter in his sly, disarming, disapproving letter. And yet both attempts only breed a more rebellious spirit in the formerly un-rebellious Zuckerman. Rather than constraining Zuckerman, they enable him to find strength in disobedience. In Lonoff's home Zuckerman thinks, "Wapter, that knownothing windbag! That dopey pillar" (139). Zuckerman transforms Wapter's censure into a Muse. He is enabled to give up the need for support of the impersonal authority figure, to use it as a force to resist, and to let the tension it creates release his gift.

Fathers, mothers, and impersonal authority figures all work to subvert the will of the artist. All entrap in their own way, but each is equally dangerous to the writer's fostering spirit. The break with all three forms of authority and power is an impossible one. To give up all ties to authority is not only to give up certainty and structure, but to give up all that formed one.

Parents are not only practitioners of coercion but are also sources of love and of history. Speaking of his own conflicts with family, Roth states, "The question of whether I can ever free myself from these forms of power assumes that I experience family...as power and nothing else. It is much more complicated than that" (RMAO 9). Rebellion is not as simple as jumping on a bus and turning away from the past forever. Nor is it as simple as stating defiantly, "I am on my own" (136). Nor is it as simple as substituting one father for another. The conflict with fathers and mothers is fraught with complex, often contradictory desires: the desire to leave and the desire to stay, the desire to rebel and the desire to fit in, to conform, the desire to assert independence and the desire to find comfort in the stability of tradition. Though less complex the conflict with impersonal authority is not a simple matter either. The artist both needs and rejects authority in its various incarnations; he longs for its praise and the comfort only it can give while inviting its hostility.

Authority is not only present in men or institutions but also in an individual's beliefs and preconceptions. Zuckerman has preconceptions about everything, about Lonoff, about art, about family, about Jewishness, about sex, about fame, and about love, and those preconceptions rule his thinking. His one night in the country manages to undo most of those simple conceptions, conceptions that the elder retrospective Zuckerman remembers ironically, amused by his younger self.

For the young Zuckerman there are two distinct models for the aspiring artist that he must choose between, either the Lonoffian model or the Abravanelian (Pipikian) model. The choice, as Hermione Lee explains, using Kafka's images, is between "the hunger artist and the hungry panther - half a lemon or a sausage" (PR 19). Lonoff ascribes to the same banal conceptions of man as Zuckerman. His life is all art, all hunger artist, all half a lemon. Lonoff believes a writer must conform to one of two patterns; either he must be the solitary aesthete for whom his own dictum, "Ordinary pleasures be damned," applies, or he must be the kind of writer who nourishes his craft through a constant interaction with the world (53). Zuckerman, according to Lonoff, fits into this second, Pipikian, category, the category that Abravanel epitomizes. Lonoff tells his wife and Nathan at the dinner table that "an unruly personal life will probably better serve a writer like Nathan than walking in the woods and startling the deer. His work has turbulence - that should be nourished, and not in the woods" (45). Contrasting Lonoff, Roth claims, "The best way to get the job done is to block the turbulence out so you can make your own turbulence" (CWPR 168).

Lonoff's vision of the artist is formulaic, like his daily rituals of writing. He exists in a suffocating world and is nourished from the lack of air, producing works about those who suffer the same lack. Lonoff's art is born of negation. If Judge Wapter's ten questions tell his correspondent that he "must subsume art to life," as Jeffrey Rubin-Dorsky claims, then Lonoff's actions and words tell Zuckerman that he must subsume life to art, that he must choose a lifestyle for its effects upon his craft (175). Neither Wapter nor Lonoff propose a model wherein life and art can meet and interact with one another, where a writer can both live and write and where the relationship between the two may not be correspondent, but complementary.

Zuckerman is drawn to both Lonoffian quiet and Abravanelian verbosity. The inner dispute that Lonoff has so easily resolved is unresolvable for

Nathan. It aches at him throughout the long night. It entraps him as much as his father's never forgotten face. Zuckerman suffers the Portnovian dilemma of need vs. purpose or, as Roth titles it, "The measured self vs. the insatiable self. The accommodating self vs. the ravenous self" (RMAO 70). Resolving the conflict "between the ethical and social yearning and the implacable, singular lusts for the flesh and its pleasures" is paramount in Zuckerman's mind because his conceptions of being an artist are wedded to the suppression of his own desires (RMAO 70). Though Zuckerman, in an inspired moment, adds to Isaac Babel's description of the Jewish writer "as a man with autumn in his heart and spectacles on his nose," "and blood in his penis," it is pronounced more as a "challenge" to himself then a statement of conviction (65). For everything in Zuckerman's demeanor suggests a wish for a Lonoffian life, the life that controls desire and blood. Zuckerman talks wistfully of his month at Quahsay, telling the Lonoffs of "the serenity and beauty of the place" (41). Nathan tells them, in his "innocent" voice, about "the joy of awakening each morning knowing that there were all those empty hours ahead to be filled only with work" (41). It was a time, he suggests, when he felt "pure" (42). "I could live like that forever," he tells them proudly, suggesting that the fleshy life could be renounced with ease, telling them because, as he says, "I wanted to believe it myself" (42).

Forever lasts but a short time for Zuckerman. In the midst of Nathan's unexpected, long hoped for, meeting with Lonoff, in the midst of the "house of forbearance," a house, Nathan thinks, where he "was better at suppressing...amorous impulses" than he had been in Manhattan, Nathan's flesh takes control of him (95). Seeing the as yet unidentified Amy Bellette sitting on the floor sifting through manuscripts and eating cookies Zuckerman's "irrepressible preoccupation" is awakened, making him think "of the triumph it would be to kiss that face, and the excitement of her kissing me back" (35). He admits, "For I had not stayed awake simply because I couldn't forget my father's disapproval...I had also no intention of being unconscious when the enchanting and mysterious houseguest got back to change into her nightdress on the floor above me" (140). Her allure infects Zuckerman even as he contemplates the master's bookshelf. While listening to Amy undress in the room directly above him, Nathan is taken over by his ungovernable flesh; he masturbates "on the daybed" and is left with "a sense of utter shabbiness," a sense of "shame" (151).[2]

It is that very shame that pushes him to create his fictionalized life of Anne Frank. As Joseph Voelker notes, Zuckerman's late-night experiences furnishes "in him a mood of complex misery that generates the vision contained in the novel's third chapter, 'Femme Fatale'" (90). It is within that fiction that Zuckerman shows an awareness of desire's (and shame's) animating and progenitive powers. In transforming his dilemmas onto his creation, Amy Bellette/Anne Frank, he manages to grasp hold of some fundamental truths that he has yet avoided in life.

Anne Frank, in Zuckerman's story, "couldn't sleep, sure that the Gestapo was going to come in the dark to take them away" (172). Her thoughts turn to death and incarceration: "She would see herself in a dungeon, without Mummy and Daddy - and worse" (172). She feels empty, alone. But she is revived, revitalized, her prose is given new life. "And what did it, Professor Lonoff?" Zuckerman writes. "The miracle," he answers himself, "desire" (172). Desire fills her with "a craze for life," a craze for independence, freedom (173). Even in the crowded attic, surrounded by the noises of death, she finds peace; she ignites a separate identity created from desire.

And yet desire moves in two ways: After her burgeoning desire compels her to write her father a letter suggesting that he is not needed any longer she is reprimanded by her father and begins "to cry with shame for having been too low for words" (174). Desire has made her too bold, her spirit too unbridled. Need unharnessed by conscience makes her irresponsible, false, cruel.

Desire, formless and intuitive, proves to be both painful and emboldening, as does the strict and formal conscience. Each allowed full reign over an artist creates stagnant, morally vacuous art, while conflict between the two breaths life into an artist's work. Anne seeks and finds a balance between desire and responsibility, between need and purpose, spending half her time "exclusively with Peter" (173), and half her time "off studying by herself," writing her diary (174). As Zuckerman has uncovered, desire is tempered by conscience and conscience is freed by desire.

Martin Green concludes from Lonoff's failed existence that "in *The Ghost Writer* we are told it is not our high purposes but our humble needs and cravings that make us moving creatures....the whole story tells [Zuckerman] to be carnal and acquisitive" (HLE 74). *The Ghost Writer* tells us no such thing. Carnality can make one a slave to its yearnings. The personification of the carnal, acquisitive writer, Abravanel, is pictured as equally as limited as Lonoff. They are opposite portraits of a similar ailment. Lonoff says, "the disease of his life makes Abravanel fly" (69). Though the symptoms are different, the diagnosis of the Berkshires writer is the same. These two artists are fashioned by their respective diseases, each able to create only from one limited vantage point, Lonoff from austerity and Abravanel from chaos. Zuckerman, attracted to both writers, uncovers their limitations while still a novice writer, while still unformed, un-indoctrinated. He shows himself to be, as Jonathan Brent puts it, "a centaur-like creature - Babel from the shoulders up, but Sade and Rabelais down below" (186). Zuckerman comes to define the writer not as a self-abnegating aesthete or as the self-ennobling carnivore but as the man who wrestles with the angel and the devil within himself.[3]

As writers, Anne Frank, Amy Bellette, and Nathan Zuckerman are therefore to be placed in the grouping "redface," a group Roth coined in his 1973 self-interview (RMAO 83). Roth introduces Philip Rahv's 1939 distinction between the "paleface" writer and the "redskin" writer to make clear his own position. Rahv designates two categories for American writers; the paleface (James, T.S. Eliot) is, "in every sense, refined," he "moves in an exquisite moral atmosphere," while the redskin (Whitman, Twain) is drawn to "the aggressive, the crude, and the obscene," and his "reactions are primarily emotional, spontaneous, and lacking in personal culture" (RMAO 82). Roth pictures himself, and others, as having "reconciled" what Rahv described as this "disunity of the American creative mind," by accepting the sense "of being fundamentally ill at ease in, and at odds with, both worlds," by accepting membership in neither group (RMAO 83). The "redface" finds his strength in disharmony, discord, antithesis.

In *The Ghost Writer* Zuckerman aligns himself with the redface writers, surrendering his early conceptions of what an artist should and should not be, what the artist can and cannot do. If at the start of the novel Zuckerman is attempting to find "a way to live as a writer," as Roth asserts, then by the close of the novel he has learned to reject at least two possible models, and, quite possibly, all models (CWPR 110). He has joined Roth's group.

To some critics and readers this similarity, and a few others, between author and creation implies that Zuckerman and Roth are one.[4] The assumption, so easily made, exposes a typical misreading of the text. That Zuckerman and Roth share some common traits is evident, that one is therefore a representation or equivalent of the other is not. To suggest such a correspondence is to put oneself in the camp of Lonoff, the camp of the absolutist. Roth finds the critic's impulse to locate his novels as thinly veiled autobiography repugnant. He tells Alan Finkielkraut, "You should read my books as fiction, demanding the pleasures that fiction can yield" (CWPR 121). Time and time again Roth has tried to argue against the biographical-fallacy critics employ when reading his works. He views it as a constriction of his works, an effort to latch onto some solid ground that otherwise is not present in them. In his sea of ambiguity, irony, and indecipherability they keep above water, secure on the lifeboat of autobiography. Roth asks his readers to discard their vests and their rafts and float free.

Roth's protests have been vociferous and unequivocal. He has consistently decried the attempt to read his fiction as confession (until the strange case of *Operation Shylock*). *The Ghost Writer*, he claims, is no one's autobiography except Zuckerman's. "My autobiography," Roth explains, "would consist almost entirely of chapters about me sitting alone in a room looking at a typewriter. The uneventfulness of my autobiography would make Beckett's *The Unnameable* read like Dickens" (CWPR 121). Roth insists that he has "nothing to confess," that his fiction is his attempt to "invent" "selves," not to expose his own self (CWPR 122). Roth privileges imagination and invention, and suggests that critics and readers emancipate themselves from limiting concepts of reading. "To label books like mine 'autobiographical' or 'confessional,' Roth tells Alan Finkielkraut, "is not only to falsify their suppositional nature but, if I may say so, to slight whatever artfulness leads some readers to think that they must be autobiographical" (CWPR 122).

Nathan's father's reading is an exemplar of just this kind of misreading. Mr. Zuckerman complains that Nathan "didn't leave anything out," suggesting that the story be read as a piece of family biography and not as fiction (106). By arguing that Nathan misrepresents Sidney and the rest of the family, Mr. Zuckerman assumes that Nathan intended to represent the family accurately rather than to use them as models to begin his story from.

A story springs forth from facts, but then the imagination is left to its own designs. It seems an elementary lesson but it is one that, like his father, Nathan has trouble understanding. In the course of his disagreement with his father Nathan never makes Roth's argument about the division between fiction and autobiography; he never refutes his father's contention that the protagonists are portrayals of the Zuckerman clan. He doesn't tell his father that nothing could be left in or left out because it is fiction. His response is, "Things had to be left out - it's only fifty pages" (109). When his father complains about Nathan's heroic portrait of Sidney, Nathan counters by stating that Sidney "actually existed Dad - and no better than I depict him" (117). He calls his work a depiction, making clear that he views he story in the same terms as his father. Nathan assumes that there is a continuity between a writer's private history and a writer's work, that a writer's job is to portray moments from the past in story form.

The silent house, the master's study, the sexual excitement of Amy Bellette's footsteps, the guilt of masturbating, the voices that echo in his mind, the overheard conversation, the thrill of Lonoff's praise, the tension of Hope's outburst, the books of German philosophy which line the wall and which awake historical memory, the volume of Henry James he holds on his lap, and his own confused, tormented head and heart, act as catalysts to the birth of a new artist, an artist willing to go beyond his life experiences. In the darkened study Nathan creates a fiction that, in the words that Nathan gives to Lonoff, leaves Lonoff's "poor art far behind;" a fiction which arises from observation and experience but which alters and deepens those experiences (155).

Besides using Amy as a way to investigate "his own suppressed longings and struggles for identity," and a way to come to terms with his father's disapproval, Zuckerman uses "Femme Fatale" to incorporate and expand words, ideas, and images he has come in contact with during the previous few hours (Brent 181). From the knowledge that Nathan acquires of Amy being a "Displaced" person, a "Refugee," he begins to construct an imaginary life for her (54). He keys upon Lonoff's words to Amy - "You're a great survivor" - as the nascent facts to evolve his fiction (148). He uses Lonoff's confession that he would like to live with a woman "in a villa outside Florence" (88), and turns the words over to Amy, who tells Lonoff, "This summer I saw a small stone home for rent, a stone villa on a hillside. It was outside Florence" (190). Lonoff's dreams of visits "to the Uffizi" (189) are transformed into Amy's "afternoons in the museums" (191). Lonoff's fantasy of a young woman wearing "long feminine nightgowns under her pretty robe"

(89) becomes Amy's promise to wear "lovely nightgowns to bed" (191). Amy calls Lonoff "Dad-da" in Nathan's fiction just as she does in the guest room above Lonoff's study. Echoing Lonoff's slogan, "There is no life without patience" (36) Amy reverses the words saying, "Without patience there is no life" (166). The Broadway production introduced by Wapter in his letter to Zuckerman is remade as the inspiration for Amy's letter to Lonoff. The facts become a point of departure.

For the first time Nathan's "imagination is freed from the gross weight of daily experience," as Brent argues (181). Formerly awed by the "excitement of what actually goes on," Nathan has unburdened himself from the need to report life (151). Concerned for the "thinness" of his own imagination, Nathan is compelled to construct a more fantastic fiction than ever before (151). Challenged by reality, Nathan's imagination is enlivened. Zuckerman takes his observations and metamorphoses them into something entirely new. The characters in Nathan's fiction are not Lonoff, Amy, Hope, and Anne Frank but entirely new characters developed in Zuckerman's mind and to be judged only in context with Zuckerman's creation, for, as Jeffrey Rubin-Dorsky suggests, "once experience is placed into a fictional framework it assumes an entirely different ontological status" (168). Zuckerman need no longer be bound by facts, nor need he argue for the accuracy of his depictions with his father or with anyone. Nearing the end of his visit Nathan asks himself, "But what can I know, other than what I can imagine" (221). Zuckerman now puts his trust in the anarchic, suppositional, unpredictable, un-indictable imagination. To read Nathan's story, or Roth's novel, as autobiography or confession is to fail to notice the imagination's awesome reshaping power, a power both celebrate.

Roth admits, though, that he has "drawn heavily from my general experience to feed my imagination," and, in fact, more than most authors Roth uses his own experiences liberally, making his work feel at times like confession (CWPR 121). Roth's indignant outrage at being read autobiographically, then, seems overdone, if not insincere, for far from discouraging these kinds of investigations Roth, time and time again encourages them, writing about Jews from Newark, writers, professors of literature, using his disastrous marriage as a model for the marriage of Peter Tarnopol and Maureen Johnson, in My *Life as a Man*, and in *Deception* and *Operation Shylock* writing about a character with the same name and history as Philip Roth. In *The Ghost Writer* Roth even echoes his own statements, putting them now in Zuckerman's mouth. Arguing with his father, Zuckerman tells him, "I was administering a bear hug, to tell you the truth" (119), which is reminiscent of Roth's criticism of a rabbi critical of his early works, of whom he writes, "As I see it, one of the rabbi's limitations is that he cannot recognize a bear hug when one is being administered right in front of his eyes" (RMAO 210). Zuckerman's realization of the "thinness" of his imagination in contrast to reality is an echo of an early Roth essay, "Writing American Fiction," wherein he decried the "meager imagination" in contrast to "much of American reality" (RMAO 176).

In these moments Zuckerman and Roth seem to be one, and Roth seems to be making the case for this interpretation. And yet to turn back to Zuckerman's fiction is to recall that the use of facts does not make a story true, that echoes of heard or spoken dialogue or experienced or viewed events in a story does not necessitate an autobiographical reading. Roth makes it easy to read his works as confessions; he tempts the reader with this simple solution and then condemns those who fall into his trap. That so much evidence points towards one reading, that clues are sprinkled like bread crumbs marking a path one way, does not make that direction or that reading accurate or essential.[5]

That Roth resembles Lonoff, Zuckerman, and, even, Abravanel tells readers that he is not simply any one of them. "Am I Lonoff? Am I Zuckerman?" Roth asks himself. "I could be, I suppose. I may be yet. But as of now I am nothing like so sharply delineated as a character in a book. I am still amorphous Roth" (130).

Critics have not only occluded their own visions ascribing definitive sources for characters but have displayed a similar myopia in their interpretations by assuming one literary source for the text itself. Beyond the ostensible use of writer-models there is the more apparent use, by Roth, of literary sources that interact with, and, at times, disrupt the text. As in the case of models there is no one source that clearly dictates a reading of the novel, though critics continue to assign one or the other writer or work to define Roth's work. James Joyce, Isaac Babel, Anton Chekhov, Henry James, Bernard Malamud, and Franz Kafka are all mentioned as possible ghost writers for the text. It is clear that each of these writer's work is alluded to in the novel, but it is also clear that no one text, no one author comes forth as the guide to or explicator of the jigsaw puzzle that is the novel. Rather the various texts offer instead additional pieces to investigate and compare, pieces that quietly push the reader toward a more complex reading of the book.

Far from being a "brilliant analogue for Nathan's own naive desires to fly the nets of his religion and family," *A Portrait of the Artist as a Young Man* is better read as an inversion of Nathan's growth (Fowler 173).[6] "Portrait" has been traditionally read as a story of the artist's journey towards independence of mind. Yet the story it more plainly tells is of the systematic closing down of that mind, the effects of a coercive society's victimization of its own son. *The Ghost Writer* tells precisely the opposite story. As Nathan comes to mistrust certainties Stephen learns only to reject one certainty, one truth, one ideology, for an equivalent replacement. Stephen ends his story believing in "integritas," in "wholeness," in a certain philosophy (212). Stephen ends not as an artist but as a naive, doctrinaire critic. Nathan, contrarily, learns to accept ambiguity, to accept the rising of two disparate suns. For all Stephen's concrete verbosity, it is Nathan who gains independence, for

independence is not merely a throwing away, a substitution of one philosophical truth for another, but a selection, an awareness of what to hold
onto and what to let go of.

Both novels follow the path of the aspiring artist attempting to resist the
grasp of a repressive society. Roth's novel uses Joyce's to enact a more
quixotic and confused conclusion, less definitive, more obtuse. In Joyce's
world the son still calls pleadingly to the "Old father," a victim still; in Roth's
the artist is left "making feverish notes," left to make use of the coercive
forces surrounding him both in daily life and in history (222).

In "Awakening" Isaac Babel, too, writes of the effects of the coercive powers of family and society on an aspiring artist's growth. Beyond merely aping
Babel's story, Roth draws attention to Babel to announce a more important
theme. According to Milton Ehre, in his book on Babel, "Awakening" tells
more than the story of the liberation of a young man's mind. It also tells of
"how creative expressiveness can be disciplined" (100). The tale teaches the
student and the reader that "Imagination...is cheap if not anchored in the
disciplines of craftsmanship" (100). It seems a Lonoffian lesson until it is
fully understood. Ehre goes on to explain that for Babel "craft is not a
mechanical exercise; it is an expression of love" (100). Here, then, are the
alternatives Nathan has originally been asked to choose between. Babel's
story makes clear the duality of the artist, the disharmony and rebelliousness that makes an artist's work soar.

Another central duality is discussed in a second Babel story, a parable,
"The Sin of Jesus," a story Nathan mentions (63). The conflict between mind
and body links this story with *The Ghost Writer*. Like Nathan, Arina cannot
control her desires. Though given an abstemious angel for a husband by
Jesus, Arina longs for a animalistic man who "snored and snorted" (249). In
Babel's story desire is a natural and undeniable force. "Water flows," he
writes, "stars shine, a man lusts" (55). Lust is linked to and is a part of
nature. To deny lust is to deny one's humanness. Authority commands
"purity", commands one to mortify the flesh (Babel 246). Jesus, like Lonoff,
demands unnatural discipline while Arina makes it clear that lust cannot be
contained indefinitely and should not be, that the body was created to be
put to use. Babel's two stories act and react against and with Roth's novel,
asserting the need to come to terms with both sides of the self and to disclaim or close down neither.

In Chekhov's "The Seagull" it is the writers' refusal to move beyond their
own single-mindedness that dooms them. "The Seagull," like "Portrait," is
alluded to for its representation of the failed artist, a representation which
suggests other routes Nathan might have taken. Unlike Stephen, Trigorin
and Trepliov fail not by latching onto an absolutist philosophy, but by giving into their own weaknesses.

Chekhov's voice can be heard throughout *The Ghost Writer*. Voelker claims
that "The novel begins and ends in a duet with Chekhov" (90). But Chekhov's
presence is felt most forcefully not in the novel's tonal allusions but in the

more specific echo of Trigorin's speech on his existence as a writer. As Jack Beatty points out, it is that speech "that lies behind" Lonoff's explanation of his own solitary and gloomy life (36). Lonoff tells Nathan, "If I knock off from this routine for as long as a day, I'm frantic with boredom and a sense of waste" (27). No joy is expressed, no exhilaration. Trigorin's speech expresses these same sentiments. He tells Nina, "I'm obsessed day and night by one thought: I must write, I just must....What is there radiant or beautiful in that, I ask you? Oh, it's a fatuous life...! And it's like that always, always...and I can't get any rest away from myself. I feel as though I'm devouring my own life....What a torment!" (149-151). Trigorin and Lonoff are not doubles of one another but they do share the same despondency toward their work. Both are writers who descend into an inextricable pattern, living inhuman lives.

The other writer in "The Seagull," Trepliov, parallels Nathan in his youthful desire for passion and for artistic freedom, freedom from, in this case, "the hackneyed devices of Realism" (Troyat 188). Yet, while Nathan is able to find his inspiration the forlorn Trepliov admits, "I don't know what my vocation is" (181). Trepliov and Trigorin offer two alternatives to Nathan's course: the dispirited, staid, vacuous life or the mordant and ultimately fatal melancholic life.

While Chekhov, Babel, and Joyce impinge upon the text offering the reader a variety of similar tales to inform upon and alter one's reading, no author permeates The Ghost Writer as thoroughly as Henry James. Among James's texts commented upon by critics are "The Middle Years," "The Lesson of the Master," and "The Death of the Lion."[7] As will become clear, a text that critics have ignored, "The Private Life," offers a profound insight into Roth's narrative.

Adeline Tintner reports that "Many readers of The Ghost Writer are aware of the overt prominence in it of James's short story, 'The Middle Years'" (HJGW 49). The parallels between the stories are obvious and Beverly Edwards lists most of them without suggesting any explanation for these parallels.[8] Marilyn Fowler, too, notes the similarities and concludes that both works teach the same lesson, that "art and artist are one, and their power is the power to affect" (183). However, to understand the split between the two authors is to realize that Roth's tale negates James's rather than imitates it.

Roth's narrative tells the story of an older disconnected writer, a slave to mechanized writing, one whose vision of literature is unchangeable, who will not gain any pleasure or knowledge from the young admirer's affections, while James's narrative tells of Dencombe, a master who comes to see literature in a new light, from a new angle. Doctor's Hugh's devotion "transfigured his despair" (257). Dencombe learns that art has value in its convergence with a reader's mind. "The thing is," Dencombe says on his death-bed, "to have made somebody care" (258). James's "The Middle Years" tells of a writer who even in his last breaths is capable of a great change, while Roth's story tells of a stagnant and decrepit writer victimized by his self-imposed limits.

"The Lesson of the Master" tells of the effect of the self imposition of a dictum of determinism on two writer's lives. St. George has arrived at a deterministic portrait of the artist after years of unsatisfactory effort. To him one must be true to his nature if one is to achieve "perfection" (154). He insists upon the singularity of the artist much as Lonoff does. When Paul asks St. George, "The artist - the artist! Isn't he a man all the same?" the master answers him, "I mostly think not" (172). Like Lonoff, St. George offers his student a false lesson, a lesson Overt, like Nathan, learns to reject.

Tintner argues that Roth not only appropriates James's stories and themes but also his literary technique of "pointing to a hidden form" (HBJ 50). The technique is explained as suggesting overtly a story by an author while covertly using themes and ideas from another story of that author's, an "undeclared" story (49). She points to "The Author of Beltraffio" as the undeclared story but it seems that the more hidden, ghostly story, is James's "The Private Life," a story which, when studied, clarifies a reading of *The Ghost Writer.*

"The Private Life" is a tale of the birth of the knowledge that a man and his art are two separate entities coexisting simultaneously, that one can live a sexual, social life and be an artist at the same time. Clare Vawdrey is exposed as two entirely separate beings. Early in the story the narrator declares that "Clare Vawdrey's talk suggested the reporter contrasted with the bard" (212). Later, he comes to realize, with Mrs. Adney, that "There are two of them;" two Vawdreys (212): "One goes out, the other stays at home. One's the genius, the other's the bourgeois" (212). The discovery of "his other self" (217) is to them "delightful" (212).

They have unearthed the same information Zuckerman unearths. While Lonoff and his literary precursors have been unwilling to admit this possibility into their own lives, they manage, unwittingly, to bestow this knowledge upon their respective proteges. As Zuckerman is readying himself to leave Lonoff's house Lonoff turns to him and says, "You're not so nice and polite in your fiction" (221). He adds, "You're a different person" (221). It is too late for Lonoff to put that knowledge to use, but for Zuckerman those words are liberating.

The person who is sexual and whose blood is in turmoil is different from yet joined to the meticulous and methodical craftsman. The two are distinct entities within the same body, and rather than shutting one down the artist is taught to let each flow into the other. To limit one's biformity, one's contradictory sides, is to limits one's possibility as artist and as man. The failed artists in James, in Joyce, in Chekhov, and in Roth are those who turn from this doubleness, who hide within their fortresses of certainty and of rote, or of disbelief, who in fear of the ambiguity of life and of their own divided selves bury a side of themselves in darkness.

"The Death of the Lion" elaborates upon this lesson. Neil Paraday is made the victim of a public's unwillingness to recognize two disparate sides of man. Their insistence on having Paraday read his works and appear for interviews and lectures leads not only to his untimely death but to the loss of his last manuscript. He dies, as Chapman points out, "of cold and exposure, both literal and figurative" (64). He is destroyed by lionization, by a world which demands its artists to emulate their works, to be their creations.

James's stories point to the doubleness of man, a concept central to any reading of *The Ghost Writer*. James's texts help to unravel what initially seems an unexplainable disproportion of metaphors of contradiction and negation in Roth's text. The text is seen, in the light of the Master's texts, to celebrate the essential split within a person; a split which promise not unmitigated chaos but creativity and invention.

Dubin, in Bernard Malamud's *Dubin's Lives*, finds the same dualism essential to his life.[9] Dubin develops by coming to understand that there is no one unequivocal correct portrait of any of his subjects. He accepts incompletion in his work and in his life. What he comes to realize, moreover, is the enormous distance between himself and his subjects, a distance so great that he can never surmount it. Between Lawrence and Dubin, Thoreau and Dubin, or Lincoln and Dubin is an historical period that makes an understanding of these earlier figures impossible. Dubin can never feel Thoreau's transcendent joy in nature, Lawrence's certainty and guiltless desire, Lincoln's stolidity. The world that separates them is a world torn from its mooring by an historical epoch more disastrous than any prior to it, most significantly by the Holocaust, a world where notions of transcendence, of absolute faith, of certainty must be tinged with doubt.

The two periods of history are distinct and separate, and yet they interact with one another, like Dubin interacting with his subjects but never entering their world. And it is this same distance that Roth is drawing forth when he introduces allusions to James, Babel, Chekhov, and Joyce. As Brent argues, Roth's "inheritance from Babel is adulterated....Babel was related to a world of values, [and] intentions" (185). After the Holocaust it would be more difficult to feel a kinship with the Cossacks, or to suggest the easeful balance of "Awakenings," or to portray a figure of power, like Jesus in "The Sin of Jesus," as so easily humbled. Authority has shown itself to be unrelenting and murderous. The character of Jesus takes on an ominous aura for the modern reader. So, too, Chekhov's symbolism is made more equivocal, Trigorin more inhuman, Trepliov more cowardly, after 1945. Joyce's "momentous epiphanies," Voelker argues, "prove hard to come by later in the century" (92). The powers that Stephen succumbs to show themselves as precursors to the more terrible powers. James's elegance, his sure-hand felt behind each word, is an impossibility for the modern writer. His masters are read, with belated knowledge, as the forerunners of the empty, bureaucratic, collaborators of repression.

Roth's use of these writers makes readers aware of not only his connection to them but, more importantly, his disconnection from them, his difference, a difference required by history. Not only do their texts compel us to re-read and re-interpret Roth's, but Roth makes clear that they, too, are to be re-interpreted in the light of history. Once again doubleness is asserted, separation and connection, a dialogic give and take from text to text, age to age, each forging a new understanding of the other.

Roth's extensive allusions point not only to his sense of belatedness towards those great authors but "towards the Jews of Europe" (Voelker 94). Writing after the Holocaust alters one's possibilities, one's choices. The world the European masters' write for and about has been unalterably changed. A chasm has crept in between, causing a separation between two generations, distinct like the two sides of man.

The writer who bridges that chasm, who links the old world and the new, is Franz Kafka, Roth's primary literary predecessor, his literary father. Kafka's world spans both sides of the divide. His fiction describes a world before the Holocaust at the same time as it virtually predicts the Holocaust. Kafka's world serves as a stepping stone between Roth and his literary ancestors.

Roth's novel is suffused with Kafkan puzzles and predicaments. Zuckerman, like Kafka's man, is entrapped by his father, his society, his history. He is torn in two, desiring sexuality and the aesthetic life of renunciation. Kafka's work insists on "bifurcations" and "divisions," according to Frederick Karl, just as *The Ghost Writer* depends on an understanding of doubles, of man's duality, a duality never unified completely, a duality which debilitates and gives life (RM 3). Kafka, like Zuckerman, is a "split person (RM 9), divided, as are his characters, into "two halves....the observer and the participant," or as it is transformed in *The Ghost Writer*, the artist and the man (RM 7). Division, for Kafka, is natural. And, like Zuckerman, Kafka uses his divided self to create his little masterpieces. "More than any other creative person of this century," argues Karl, "Kafka depended on the maintenance of an imbalance" (RM 7). Definitiveness, surety, and absolutes were all anathema for Kafka. His art is born of the uncertainties and contradictions of the world.

Though Kafka's fiction tells time and time again of the entrapped man there is an admittance of that man's debt to his entrapment. "Kafka," Karl maintains, "repeatedly presents characters who sympathize with their captors, whose lives would be empty without the potentiality of the tormenter" (RM 5). Karl presents two examples: "The animal in 'The Burrow,'" he points out, "gains its entire identity from its need to protect itself from whatever or whoever is moving toward it, possibly to destroy it" (RM 5). In "The Metamorphosis," Karl claims, Gregor Samsa "has little of his own...until he is transformed into a bug - he then gains...identity" (RM 5). Other examples include "The Trial," wherein K. has little to distinguish himself except his arrest and trail, and "The Penal Colony," wherein one is defined by one's crime and punishment.

In *The Ghost Writer* Zuckerman becomes aware of his own indebtedness to entrapment. The entrapment of his father, his mother, Wapter, Lonoff, his own aesthetic philosophy, and his own desperate desires, all work not only to inhibit him but also to coax him to thought and to work. In his battle against entrapment he finds his voice, his self, selves. In his fiction of Anne Frank he asks of Anne, "Truly, without the terror and claustrophobia of the achterhuis...would she ever have written sentences so deft and so eloquent and so witty? (170). His voice screams out through the mask of Anne when she thinks, "Maybe if I were locked up again in a room somewhere and fed on rotten potatoes and clothed in rags and terrified out of my wits, maybe then I could write a decent story for Mr. Lonoff" (171). Like Kafka's protagonists, Anne's life is negligible until it becomes tragic. And like Anne, Zuckerman too needs trauma to push him towards independence and individuality. K. (and Kafka's other tormented souls) Anne, and Nathan are joined together, three characters aware of a split within themselves, aware of the powers that seek to enslave them, and finally aware that that split and those powers are not simply entrapping and debilitating but give substance and can enliven.

The link between Anne Frank and Kafka is made explicit in *The Ghost Writer*. Zuckerman explains to Amy Bellette:

> "I was thinking...she's like some impassioned little sister of Kafka's, his lost little daughter - a kinship is even in the face, I think. Kafka's garrets and closets, the hidden attics where they hand down indictments, the camouflaged doors - everything he dreamed in Prague was, to her, real Amsterdam life. What he invented she suffered. Do you remember the first sentence of The Trial...? It could be the epigraph for her book. 'Someone must have falsely traduced Anne F. because one morning without having done anything wrong, she was placed under arrest'" (210).

That link is made more apparent when one considers Roth's 1973 story/essay "I Always Wanted You to Admire My Fasting; or Looking at Kafka," where Roth uses the same premise with Kafka that Nathan uses with Anne Frank, imagining him to have survived to become his hebrew-school teacher. Both fictions focus upon the unexpected results of survival. In "Looking at Kafka" Kafka survives but he "leaves no books: no Trial, no Castle, no Diaries. The dead man's papers are claimed by no one, and disappear..." (326). For Anne, survival makes her book merely "a young teenager's diary of her trying years in Holland, something boys and girls could read in bed at night along with the adventures of the Swiss Family Robinson" (181).

Survival brings its own costs, just as terror brings its own rewards. In "Looking at Kafka" it is Kafka's knowledge of his own forthcoming death that allows him to find love and to consider marriage. In "Femme Fatale" Anne's imprisonment allows her to recognize her "many buried qualities," and to view her horrid experience as "a great adventure" (173).

Both works describe powers that attempt to restrict the individual. Anne is obviously the victim of a most awesome dehumanizing power and Kafka is surrounded by father figures who compel acquiescence to their decrees. "No," writes Roth, "Thou shalt not have, say the fathers, and Kafka agrees that he shall not" (309). Both works tell of lives lived in the shadow of death, of lives constantly under attack by incomprehensible forces. And both works tell of artists who from the depth of their despair transform that despair into art. Both are essentially tales about survival. Roth makes their physical survival contingent on their artistic demise. They survive, ultimately, by dying, another contradiction.

Joseph Epstein notes the similarity between the two short works, asking sardonically, "What will be next: Martin Bormann as a counselor at a boy's summer camp in the Poconos?" (100). Epstein derides Roth for "cuteness," neglecting to recognize the distinct linkage between the two figures of Anne and Kafka (100). Roth is not simply playing the game "What if?" Kafka and Anne Frank are unique figures, unique in a way that Bormann could never be. Beyond their linkage as victims, as writers, and as sufferers, beyond the predictive element from Kafka to Frank, they are linked by their inescapable categorization as Jews. Though both Anne and Kafka exhibit little or no affinity for their religion, though neither practices Judaism, both are labeled "Jews" and therefore sanctioned for death. Anne is described as "only dimly Jewish" (178), and Kafka is quoted, by Roth, from his diary, asking, "What have I in common with the Jews?" (311). Anne and Kafka are reduced to a label. They become defined by one aspect of themselves. All individuality is shunted aside. The Nazi ideology insists upon limited and limiting definitions. It insists upon a one to one correspondence between religion and man. Kafka and Anne become interchangeable, equivalent. They are proscribed for the ovens, for the camps, as Zuckerman writes, "just for being Jews' (179).

Further, Kafka and Anne are linked by their assertions of individuality amidst a world that sees them as victims only. Had they succumbed to the invidious philosophy of singularity they would have vanished voiceless and without a trace into history. Had they accepted a Lonoffian viewpoint, accepted their oppressor's definition of them, their voices would not have echoed beyond their deaths. Kafka and Anne are presented as survivors, by Roth, because in some way they did survive; they managed to survive an attempted dehumanization. Roth resurrects their voices because theirs are voices of victory over the Holocaust, voices which were able to endure.

Kafka's work prefigures the Holocaust, Anne's recounts it, while Roth lets its presence drift menacingly throughout *The Ghost Writer*, without trampling. The questions evoked, the trauma's felt, the lessons learned all form themselves from the Holocaust. Its ghostly presence is felt more strongly than any writer's presence. The startling lessons gleaned by Zuckerman in *The Ghost Writer* are lessons necessitated by the Holocaust.

Arthur A. Cohen calls American Jews who were spared the Holocaust "the generation that bears the scar without the wound, sustaining memory without direct experience" (Berger 11). He continues: "It is this generation that has the obligation, self-imposed and self-accepted (however ineluctably), to describe a meaning and wrest instruction from the historical" (Berger 11). The Ghost Writer is such an attempt of immersion in an unexperienced past.

The Holocaust is felt like a soft mist by Zuckerman; it never vacates his mind entirely. Amidst the comforts of Lonoff's home Zuckerman watches the beautiful, as yet unidentified, Amy Bellette sorting papers on the floor and he tells himself that her bones looked "to have been worked together by a less guiless sculptor than nature" (26). Without a clue to her identity Zuckerman's mind turns immediately to images from a concentrationary universe. He soon recognizes, in Amy, an "unharmonious relation between body and skull," which tells him of "some early misfortune, of something vital lost or beaten down" (34). He comes to Lonoff for release from history but in his reconstructing mind he turns again and again to pictures which have suffused his early years. All Zuckerman needs is the knowledge that Amy is a "refugee" (71) to lead him to complete the puzzle. "I wondered," Zuckerman recounts, "if the dark refugee girl with the curious name Bellette could be Jewish, and in Europe had suffered from worse than starvation" (71). Zuckerman's obsession leads inexorably to this conclusion, and from this to his recreation of Amy Bellette as Anne Frank. It is from very vague details that Zuckerman injects the Holocaust. Zuckerman would have fit any pieces he had encountered to construct the same completed jigsaw.

Zuckerman is a post-Holocaust Jew in more than chronology. His life is tied to the facts of the Holocaust. His lucky history is always being balanced against the horrific history of those victimized in Europe. He lives in, as he sees it, a fallen world, "functionally Godless," as Richard Rubenstein describes it (Berger 91). Zuckerman's earnest search for a center, for a figure of authority and innocence, springs from his knowledge of the now-centerless world. Lonoff is described as being "oblivious of the major currents of...society" (17). He lives in a world seemingly separated from time, from history. Lonoff's home "is a haven from the totalitarian Nazi terror of twentieth century history" (Baumgarten & Gottfried 160). When Zuckerman promises himself that he will emulate Lonoff's life he is fantasizing about a life outside of history, a life underground. Lonoff seems hermetically sealed against the trauma American-Jews faced after 1945.

Scholars have commented on this tremendous angst which permeates the post-Holocaust generation. Some contend that all Jews "whether or not physically present in the death camps, are survivors," doomed to remember, and doomed to suffer the pangs of surviving, pangs born of the fear of the Holocaust's imminent return (Berger 11). When Zuckerman, in argument with his mother, exclaims, "We are not the wretched of Belsen," he makes evident his need to escape from the angst he would inherit from his family (133). He adds, "We were not the victims of that crime!" (133). Refuting the basic premise of the post-Holocaust Jew Zuckerman is here attempting to unlearn his parents' lessons. His need to break with them is a need to break from their interpretation of history. Zuckerman doesn't want to be a survivor, to carry the baggage of the death-camps. He wants, more than any-thing, a divorce from his roots, from the pain of remembering. However, his mother's response carries with it the sources of terror that are impossible to abandon. She tells him, "But we could be [the victims] - in their place we would be" (133).

It is the fact that cannot be ignored. With that indelible knowledge Zuckerman is forever saddled. His parents emphasize his position as sur-vivor. "I wonder," his father tells him, "if you fully understand just how very little love there is in this world for Jewish people?" (117). The question is, of course, intended to resurrect the fear that Zuckerman has tried to bury, the fear of a departed world which the elders still inhabit. Towards that same end Judge Wapter writes Nathan his ten questions. "If you had been living in Nazi Germany in the thirties," Wapter's first question reads, "would you have written such a story?" (129).The question, as Roth points out, "is impossible to answer. The answer is neither a simple yes nor a simple no" (WAJ-D 16). The question, though, is intended to be unanswerable. By invoking "Nazi Germany" at the top of his list Wapter hopes to intimidate Nathan, to compel him to recognize his status as survivor. The Holocaust is used as a bludgeon to force acquiescence without discussion or argument.

For Wapter, as for Doc Zuckerman and Mrs. Zuckerman, the Holocaust is the sole touchstone for one's work and life. One is judged by his allegiance to their conception of how to remember the Holocaust. As Lonoff's voice is stymied by its avoidance of history, so their voices are stymied by their sat-uration in history. They live in fear, afraid to act, to move, to speak freely. They are censored by the past, and they try to impose that same censorship upon Zuckerman. In their view, to portray Jews in anything but a sacrosanct manner is to play into the hands of anti-Semites, to invite a reprisal of the pogroms. Wapter's question, "Do you believe Shakespeare's Shylock and Dickens's Fagin have been of no use to Anti-Semites?" suggests this terror of furnishing anti-Semites with ammunition (129).

"This is not," Roth argues, "fighting anti-Semitism but submitting to it; that is submitting to a restriction of consciousness as well as communica-tion, because being conscious and being candid are too risky" (RMAO 219). Instilled with terror they would pass on that terror. Frightened by freedom they would subjugate the next generation. Fearful of victimization they vic-timize themselves and their children. The Holocaust is as much a poten-tiality as a memory. They live in its shadow, awaiting, fearing, its return, par-alyzed. Roth notes their "Timidity - and paranoia," symptoms of their trau-ma, their failure to move on and to grow (RMAO 221). The Holocaust holds power over these survivors, cementing a belated victory for Nazism. They see the world from the vantage point of the defeated, and so their lives are never their own.[10] Zuckerman understands what his parents cannot, that to portray Jews as only paragons of virtue and only as passive victims of injus-tice is, in effect, to classify and categorize Jews much in the way that the Nazis did. Its implication is that Jews are all this and only this, that Jews are not individuals, not human. For his parents and the Judge, Zuckerman's story is a way back into the Holocaust while for Zuckerman it is a way of confronting and surmounting the Holocaust, of escaping the ripples that engulf the others.

Zuckerman manages to move beyond the fear of his parents; he manages to not allow the Holocaust to hold him in check or to censor him. And he also, with great effort, frees himself of the feelings of guilt and of responsibility that his parents have instilled in him. The guilt of surviving, Bruno Bettelheim remarks, is a "guilt about having been spared" (26). He argues that "Being one of the very few who were saved when millions like oneself perished" furnishes one with an "irrational guilt," a guilt that tells one that his life was spared at the expense of others" (26). Bettelheim tells of the subterranean voice that echoes within the post-Holocaust man: "You rejoiced that it was some other who had died rather than you" (27). With this guilt comes a formidable responsibility, a responsibility "to justify one's...very existence, since it was permitted to continue when that of so many others exactly like oneself was not" (Bettelheim 26). The survivor feels "he has an obligation to prove he was worth saving" (Bettelheim 27).

When Zuckerman creates his fiction of Anne Frank he is not acceding to his parents' condition, rather, he is, for the first time, imaginatively exploring a subject that had been deemed off limits to him. In transforming his own complex, often contradictory emotions onto Amy/Anne he is able to investigate more fully than ever before his own relationship to the Holocaust, lessen his inherited guilt, and redefine his notions of responsibility, while, at the same time, he is asserting his individuality in the face of formidable restrictions. When Zuckerman writes of Anne, "If she was going to be thought exceptional, it would not be because of Auschwitz and Belsen but because of what she had made of herself since," Zuckerman's voice can be heard asserting his own refusal to be defined by the past, defined by the Holocaust; his voice can be heard resisting (164).

In "Femme Fatale" others try to induce in Anne a sense of guilt and shame. "Why is it," Miss Giddings asks her, "that for centuries people have hated you Jews?' (163). The question places the blame squarely on the victim. It, as Berger argues, asks "the victim to account for the behavior of the victimizer" (159), and harks back to Heinrich Gruber's contention that "Europe's Jews had - somehow - deserved the Holocaust," that they had let it happen, that they had collaborated with their killers (Berger 27). The contention is parallel to Zuckerman's father's assertion that Nathan's story can do damage, that he will be responsible, guilty, for its effects. Zuckerman and Anne suffer survivor's guilt but they ultimately reject guilt as an appropriate response to the Holocaust. Zuckerman has Anne respond to Miss Giddings, "Don't ask me that....Ask the madmen who hate us" (163). Anne insists on her own innocence. She insists that she is "not ashamed" (164). "That's the point," she adds (164). It is the point Zuckerman has been trying to make, too, if only to himself. Ladened with guilt since childhood Zuckerman, in his fiction, exorcises that guilt. He, too, becomes not "ashamed of anything" (164).

Zuckerman is also able, through his fiction, to dismiss the idea that he must somehow prove that he was worth saving. He recognizes the nefariousness of that claim in that it implies, as Bettelheim argues, "that those who perished were not worth saving" (27). Zuckerman comes to accept his status as un-victimized Jew "as a stroke of unmerited and unexplainable luck," owing nothing to his own uniqueness (Bettelheim 27). When Amy tells him that she missed the war through "Luck" Zuckerman must admit, "I suppose that's how I missed it too" (207). To accept luck as the only divergence between the victim and the survivor is to release oneself from a fruitless and pointless feeling of responsibility. Anne's story, as created by Zuckerman, with its picture of the "chaos" of the war, makes clear, as Alan Berger notes, "that anyone who survived the camps did so for inexplicable reasons" (159). In Anne's decision to let the world think her dead she undermines, once and for all, this need for proving the worth of survivors. In allowing herself to "vanish" she leaves undeniable evidence of the worthiness, the uniqueness, and the wisdom of a victim (183). She offers proof that victimization was undiscriminating, that survival had nothing to do with self. She tells the survivor that he need not spend his life attempting to discover his own specialness, to justify his life. He is not responsible for his survival or for others' deaths. Her death exposes the choicelessness inherent in the concentrationary universe.

Anne's responsibility is not to a conception of herself but to the memory of "the dead" (82). She hears their voices. "Oh Anne," they call, "Why have you deserted me? Help, oh, help me, rescue me from this hell" (172). Her decision to "vanish" is made "for them," meaning "all who had met the fate she had been spared and was now pretending to" (183). She views herself as "the incarnation of the millions of unlived years robbed from the murdered Jews" (186). Zuckerman's responsibility, too, is not to prove himself authentic or worthy to himself or to Wapter or to his family. His responsibility is not to the fears of the living but to the memory of the dead. For Zuckerman, honoring their memory means not submitting to coercion, not proselytizing stereotypes, and not stifling creativity in deference to the victims. Both Anne/Amy and Nathan memorialize the dead by rejecting the concepts that dehumanized them, and by insisting on living their own lives in a manner which will expedite a time, as Anne writes, "When we are people again and not just Jews" (177).

Anne, remaking herself as Amy Bellette, and Nathan remaking himself as Anne, both break free from parental strictures and initiate a celebration of the self, the unconstrained, unstigmatized self, the Jew that is a person and not one of a category. Anne declares her desire to recreate herself. "I wanted," she says, "my fresh life and my fresh body, cleansed and unpolluted" (190), a sentiment not unlike Nathan's wish for a "pure and incorruptible spirit" (42). Like Nathan, she wants control. Sitting upon a bench, her long awaited manuscript on her lap, she purposefully acts out "a preposterous display of unruffled patience" (166). Almost in rebuke to the forces which attempted to transform her into hollow flesh Anne exaggerates her "Forbearance," much as Nathan does in not responding to his father or to Wapter (166). They exercise choice to battle repression. They recognize their responsibility to the dead entails a refusal to submit.

The difficulty in this stance resides in the force with which the Holocaust demands acknowledgment and remembrance. Though Anne declares her intention to "forget her life" (150) she still feels a "seething passion" to "avenge the ashes and the skulls," and Zuckerman feels he cannot banish the voices of its spokesmen from his mind (183). The dilemma becomes how to recognize the unbreakable link with the Holocaust without allowing it to subvert the will. For both Anne and Nathan the answer returns to the concept of doubling. Anne admits to feeling "flayed" after the war, broken in two (189). "I felt as though," she says, "the skin had been peeled away from half my body" (189). She becomes, in effect, a new person, a double. She tells Lonoff, "their Anne Frank is theirs; I want to be your Anne Frank" (191).

Her condition is not exceptional. Many camp survivors comment upon this need to construct or recognize a double-self. "The Double of Auschwitz," Charlotte Delbo explains, "doesn't disturb me or mingle in my life" (HT 6). It acts as a separate and distinct individual. Doubling is necessitated by the experience of the Holocaust at the same time as it is a procedure for living with and battling the memories of the Holocaust. As Delbo remarks, "Without this split, I wouldn't have been able to come back to life" (HT 6). Doubling allows the survivor to separate what Lawrence Langer calls "deep memory" and "common memory," memory of the camps and memory of one's post-Holocaust life (HT 5). It allows the survivor to remember without falling victim to those memories. Doubling presumes duality, presumes what Nazism rejected, the notion that each Jew is an individual. Doubling, then, becomes a way not only to rejuvenate a debased or degraded self but a way to philosophically reject the ideological basis of the Holocaust. When Amy Bellette tells Nathan that she experienced "Somebody else's" childhood she is celebrating her own doubleness, her own malleability, (207). No one, she is telling Nathan, will label her again.

The attempt at labeling, though, continues beyond the Holocaust. Anne Frank becomes, for a generation of readers, the epitome of martyrdom, the quintessential and representational victim. Her story is appropriated to salve the wounds of the horror. Bettelheim explains the attraction to both the diary and to the various plays based on it, suggesting that it "found wide acclaim because...it denies implicitly that Auschwitz ever existed. If all men are good, then there never was an Auschwitz" (BWA 201). The play, furthermore, according to Sidra Ezrahi, "succeeded also in avoiding the issue of Jewish identity" (BWA 202). The diary, she goes on, "was transformed into a work of art which comprises both a litany of human suffering and a declaration of ultimate faith in universal goodness....In the emphasis on Anne's faith there is an implicit denial of her fate" (202).

This uncomplicated and shortsighted version of Anne Frank's story is the one that Wapter and his wife advise Zuckerman to see, calling it an "unforgettable experience" (128). They believe, argues Berger, that "if Nathan would do this...the young writer would refrain from writing anything potentially harmful to the Jews" (159). They want Zuckerman to submit to the stereotype, the cliche, the uplifting, the cathartic, and ultimately superficial version. But Zuckerman, as he tells his mother, "will not prate in platitudes to please the adults" (135). He will not adhere to a preordained interpretation. His fiction refuses to anchor itself in the universal verities, in the ultimate goodness and hopefulness of man.

In Nathan's fiction Anne Frank is not only an innocent girl who dies believing that "people are really good at heart," but rather she is, instead, a complicated young woman, at times frightened and at times brave, filled with desire and with shame (181). She is not a saint but a girl who feels "murderous rage" (182), who admits, "I wanted their Christian tears to run like Jewish blood, for me" (190). She is anything but a universal victim, a sacrificial lamb. Zuckerman, in reinterpreting Anne's story, restores her as flesh and bones, saves her from the dehumanization of the comforting legend that her diary has spawned; he saves her from a second annihilation.

When Zuckerman fantasizes about marrying Anne Frank he at first believes this marriage would "exonerate" him before his "outraged elders" (210). "Indifferent to Jewish survival?" he thinks. "Brutish about their well-being? Who dares to accuse of such unthinking crimes the husband of Anne Frank" (210). Critics maintain that this fantasy of Nathan's is an attempt, by him, to win the approval of his elders. James Young argues that in marrying Anne Frank Zuckerman is "becoming the kind of 'authentic Jew' his parents wanted in their son" (110).

But what Young and others fail to recall is that Nathan's Anne Frank is anathema to his people's Anne Frank; she is not their princess of innocence and forgiveness. His imagined marriage to his Anne Frank would only cement the division already apparent. It, then, can more accurately be read as a further challenge to his parents and to his world. Though ostensibly wishing for exoneration his deeper need is for escape (It is a testament to Nathan's ever developing individuality that even in his infantile dream of forgiveness he acts out a rebellion). "Indeed," argues Pinsker, his parents' Anne is "anything but the complicated woman Zuckerman invents, and then falls in love with" (MAF 54). Nathan's Anne is created not in subjugation to but in rebellion from the stereotype. Nathan has allowed his imagination to roam free, to construct beyond his parents' perspective and outside of their strictures. Freeing Anne Frank Zuckerman has freed himself.

The birth of the unconstrained imagination acts as the birth of a complementary self for both Anne and Nathan, the birth of the writer separate from the social or historical man or woman. Ezrahi points out that the writers who attempted to tell Anne Frank's story all "failed particularly in the representation of the secret duality of Anne's character' (203). Where they failed, Zuckerman succeeds. Zuckerman's growing awareness of the separation between the man that he is and the words that he writes gives him new insight into the sainted Anne. He writes, of Anne, that, though she remembers her life, "of the fifty thousand words...she couldn't remember writing one" (167). Her words appear "new and strange to her" (167). Sitting in the sun-filled Common two people come together in conversation, the reader and the writer, two separate beings altering each other's words.

Zuckerman's power as a writer comes from the strength of his imagination surmounting a formerly implacable barrier - in this case the barrier of the traditional representation of Anne Frank - and is consonant with Anne's ability to use her imagination to survive her ordeal. Anne, in her diary, speaks of "being able to see myself through someone else's eyes" (168). This imaginative faculty accounts for her uncanny resiliency. "The diary," she thinks, "kept her company and it kept her sane" (169). Writing, then, becomes a way to survive for both Nathan and for Anne, a way to empower the self. "Recording it was enduring it," Anne realizes (169). Similarly, Nathan's writing gives him access to formerly untapped knowledge.Writing releases the imagination, and the imagination is the source of strength for both of them. The imagination allows them to escape the self's condition, escape the limits imposed upon it.

"In the camp" Delbo explains, "you could never pretend; you could never take refuge in the imaginary" (HT 4). The resuscitation of the imagination is, like the assertion of duality, an undermining of the Nazi assault. To write, then, is not so much to triumph but to enact "a defiance of the anonymity of life in the shadow of the Swastika" (BWA 4). Zuckerman, through his imagination, finds his voice, his double, a double which provides no sure transcendent answers but does allow him some freedom of movement, some hope, the means to defy the shadow.

The difficulty that Zuckerman faces in relinquishing adherence to the canonical picture of Anne Frank is a difficulty all writers must contend with when imagining the Holocaust and its heroes and victims. The Holocaust is a daunting subject to take upon oneself, a subject which demands acknowledgement but which resists language. Theodore Adorno contends, in his famous words, "After Auschwitz to write a poem is barbaric" (SW 427). Roth comments on his own difficulties recreating Anne Frank's story: "Just what Zuckerman was fighting against," Roth tells Hermione Lee, "I was in fact succumbing to - the officially authorized and most consoling legend" (CWPR 183). Roth describes his first attempt at narrating her story: "It was taking a high elegiac tone....It was the tome appropriate to hagiography. Instead of Anne Frank gaining new meaning within the context of my story, I was trying to draw from the ready store of stock emotions" (CWPR 183). Roth's dilemma was how to disabuse himself of the "cliches" so easily latched onto, so ingrained within (CWPR 183). The Holocaust not only invites cliche but acts as a bulwark against the imagination, forcing the artist to hold back, to measure his words.

Rather than turning away in silence or repeating mantras of previous writers, Roth chooses to confront the Holocaust, not by representing or recording the events themselves, but by exploring the philosophical causes and existential effects of the destruction. As noted, Roth understands ideology to be the most heinous force behind the Holocaust massacre. Lucy Dawdiowitz explains that "Final Solution was a new phenomenon in human history," wherein "one people made the killing of another the fulfillment of an ideology" (Berger 19). David Hirsch notes that "The historical uniqueness of the Nazi genocide lay...in the systematic dehumanization," developed from a "German racist ideology" (255). *The Ghost Writer*, then, revels in all that ideology rejects; ambiguity, contradiction, irony, doubt. Zuckerman rejects simple narrow truths, single interpretations of history, single notions of art or of the artist. Zuckerman moves from being drawn to the ease of ideology to being repelled by it.

The language of *The Ghost Writer* is the language of irony, a language Zuckerman adopts for himself at the close of the book. "Irony," explains Milan Kundera, (to whom the novel is dedicated) "irritates. Not because it mocks or attacks but because it denies us our certainties by unmasking the world as an ambiguity" (AON 134). In an ironic novel, Kundera adds, "truth is concealed, undeclared, undeclarable" (134). Zuckerman comes to see the world in ironic terms, as unknowable and unclear. Irony is reversal: Everything Zuckerman assumes in the evening is turned on its head by morning: The master becomes the helpless husband, Hope seems hopeless, the life of ease and simplicity shows itself as eerily destructive, Anne Frank, the icon, becomes Anne Frank the woman, and Zuckerman in search of one true self finds duality instead. Entrapment becomes enlivening, imagination both freeing and restrictive, desire both awakening and subjugating. Ambiguity thrives, making certainty difficult but hopelessness equally so. The language of contradiction, once so hard to comprehend, becomes the language of the young writer.

The contradictions which assault Nathan become more visible to both Nathan and to the reader: Nathan tells himself, "the greater the effort to be sincere the worse it went" (13). Of Lonoff, he notes, "His openness about himself [was] so at odds with his formal attire" (28). Of Andrea, Nathan thinks, "the briskness of the handshake was in disarming contrast with the soft voluptuous appearance" (79). Confused and bothered, initially, by contradiction Nathan now welcomes it. "Convinced," he thinks, towards the end of the novel, "that that wasn't so...I persisted in believing that it was" (216). Recognizing the possibility of two divergent beliefs occupying the same single mind, Nathan sheds the skin of certainty.

Released from the unappeasable search for truth Nathan becomes steeped in all that ideology rejects. Truth and certainty are revealed as components of a dangerous and limiting ideology, an ideology tied ineffably with that which spawned the Holocaust. As Langer argues, anyone who attempts to write about the Holocaust must "be wary of formulas and single truths" (VOS 4). To deny definitive truth, to accept the ambiguous world, to deny any one to one correspondences, is to deny anyone's categorization as *Untermenshen*. Roth's novel draws forth the humanism of ambiguity as a bulwark against the antihumanism of ideology. In this light E.I. Lonoff and Hope Lonoff can be viewed with greater clarity and insight. Their marriage acts out the battle between humanist-individualistic values and conformist-anithumanistic values.

In one of the oddest readings of Hope and Lonoff's relationship, Martin Tucker asserts that Hope "is bereft of everything but her chores for the great writer, and yet not bereft, because the tasks she performs are valued by Lonoff in a ...fulfilling manner" (39). Rather than "fulfilling," their relationship is devouring. It devours not only Hope's dreams but also Lonoff's self. Lonoff, the once "ironic" writer has undergone a "ruthless...metamorphosis" over time (19), and Hope has the appearance of a "frontier survivor" (43), consumed by lifelessness. However, Hope's essential duality, her fire for life, her disquiet, her ties to Tolstoyan faith allow her to retain a certain promise, while Lonoff is left helpless and, finally, (H)hopeless.

The clue to Lonoff's antihumanism is discovered in his study. Searching through Lonoff's books Nathan notices, "There was more German philosophy than I had been expecting" (100). Two philosophers are mentioned, Heidegger and Wittgenstein, and they offer the key to Lonoff's psyche. The mention of Wittgenstein is instructive in that it links Lonoff to a philosophical position, Logical Positivism, that is ultimately self-abnegating and circular, a philosophy which undermines philosophy's usefulness.

Heidegger's name makes it clear that in his effort to escape the devastation he has embraced a philosophical position linked to Nazism. "Hitler and Heidegger," argues Hirsch, "shared a world outlook" (262). He continues: "We cannot fail to be struck by the close parallel between |Heidegger's| beliefs and the Nazi program of aggression, genocide, and enslavement" (259). It was Heidegger, after all, who stated unequivocally, "The Fuhrer himself and he alone is the German reality and its law, today and henceforth" (Hirsch 259). That Lonoff stacks his shelves with Heidegger's work and that his life acts out Nazi-like regimentation suggests not that Lonoff is a Nazi but that his failure to interact and understand history has led him down a dangerous and familiar path. Heidegger, Hirsch maintains, like Hitler, "sought to implement" his philosophy "by rupturing that fusion between Hellenism and Hebraism that constitutes European humanism" (262). The unnatural rupture of the natural division in man, whether using the terms of Arnold and Hirsch, or the Greek terms Dionysian and Apollonian, or Roth's Lonoffian and Pipikian, dehumanizes man. Lonoff's singularity is necessitated by his adherence to Heideggerian antihumanism. By freezing a part of himself, and by freezing himself from history, Lonoff is able to learn nothing.

Nathan's initial desire is to latch onto Lonoff and to his philosophy; to live Lonoff's life. It is a desire not only to escape history, as Lonoff has done, but to revel in Lonoff's Socratic surety, in a world without division. But, Lonoff, worried and reduced by his life, sets Nathan free. Having recognized his personal failure to unleash his own double, having recognized that his blood is diseased by history and by time, Lonoff offers Nathan his "rites of confirmation," displaying himself as an example of how not to live and how not to write (222). Zuckerman, having wanted to emulate Lonoff, finds the unlooked for knowledge that his own history offers him a more compelling and insistent voice, a voice in which echoes from the Holocaust are ever-present.

Unlike Lonoff, Zuckerman learns to reject any philosophy that ties him in any way to the intellectual roots of Nazism. Unlike Lonoff, Nathan, rather than turning his back to the altered world, learns to find the means to create from that world. Zuckerman discovers a restorative stance with which to begin his writing life, a stance which Roth utilizes in *The Ghost Writer*. Rather than surrendering to the ambiguity and unsurety created by the Holocaust, Roth uses those conditions to breath new life into his fiction. A fiction of searching, of grasping, and of questioning rather than of finding, holding, and answering is created from the ruins. It is a fictional universe in which closure is impossible. Langer argues that in this new universe "There is no closure, because the victims have not survived...have left no personal voice behind" (HT 21). Roth's fiction, then, revels in its rejection of closure, using it to suggest not defeat but possibility. As Pearl K. Bell argues, "When morning comes, nothing has been settled" (73), and as Patrick O'Donnell notes, Roth's fiction is "ever-unfinished" (374). Nothing is ended; the voices are not lost but still to be found, meaning is not dead but still to be located.

Language, in Roth, becomes indefinite, dialogic, playful. The doubling of words, rather than holding back, allows more freedom, more possibility. Language is made able to move off in varying directions, to suggest varying readings, to allow for varying interpretations. Language becomes ironic, ambiguous, carnivalesque, vibrant. It is unharnessed from the brutalization it underwent at the hands of the propagandizing Nazis, whose "Bureaucratic manipulation of language" made words into instruments of condemnation and calamity (Berger 30). Language becomes, as Zuckerman says of the slick road, "deceptive," "slippery" (39). This slipperiness of language is celebrated in Roth's text; a text which attempts to reinvigorate language after its debasement.

James Young's thesis in *Writing and Rewriting the Holocaust* is encapsulated as, "What is remembered about the Holocaust depends on how it is remembered" (1). In *The Ghost Writer* Roth concentrates, too, on the how of memory. He employs a style that inverts the conditions of the Holocaust world. The world of anxiety, of choicelessness and fear, of ideology and judgment, of unambiguous language and definitive truth, is rewritten to become a world where choice is reborn, where ideology is indefensible, where language thrives in rich play of meaning, and where truth remains elusive. Roth's text emphasizes the doubling of words and of men, the contrapuntal motion of time, the commingling of one time and the other, of text and text, Roth and Zuckerman, and James, Joyce, Babel, Chekhov, and Kafka. The pre-Holocaust works become open to new and unanticipated interpretations, interpretations which free them from the rigidity of history. The past and the present enter into a conversation with one another, mutually informing one another. The past must be addressed, but it must not be allowed to submerge the present.

Nathan Zuckerman learns, at the close of the novel, that the search for order is a fatuous search. The altered world is too diaphanous to find truth or surety in. Zuckerman is allowed to give up all the monist beliefs he came in search of. When Lonoff goes down the mountain of art all temples, all altars, all mountainous pedestals set above man are discredited. O'Donnell claims that in the end Nathan's will "is subsumed by a spurious parental authority" (375). The truth is that Nathan is not subsumed but awakened.

Roth claims that The Ghost Writer is an exploration of "the surprises that the vocation of writing brings" (CWPR 111). Zuckerman is surprised to have all he believed in and hoped for taken out from under him and to, nonetheless, feel reborn because of it.

With the Holocaust as a reference point Zuckerman is able to reject those forces that lead to the nightmare and to find a way to subsist intellectually in a world stripped of meaning, a way to negotiate between the demands of the Lonoffian self and the Pipikian self, letting both sides of his self come in contact with, and spark, the other. Zuckerman is a paradigmatic figure for Roth's major protagonists, men forever in doubt, forever battling outside forces and their own drives and longings, men who both reject and battle entrapment and who at times long for it, men who want to escape history and who are bound to their history, bound to remember.

As Zuckerman and The Ghost Writer act paradigmatically for Roth's oeuvre so too this chapter acts as a paradigm for the following study. The study will follow the same pattern blue-printed in this exposition of Roth's eleventh novel.The chapters which follow will explore, in the remaining Roth works, the questions discussed in regard to The Ghost Writer, questions of parents, of authority figures, of need and purpose, of autobiography, of literary precursors, of critical responses, of style, and, most importantly, of the Holocaust, to which all previous questions return. The concentrationary world deforms all relationships, to others and to one's own body and mind. The ambiguous world Zuckerman and Roth embrace, and create from, is a world they simply cannot ignore; it is their palette, the background for their one chance at creation

The Ghost Writer presents a portrait of the quintessential Rothian man, a man reified by the picture that adorns the paperback edition of the novel. The picture is simple, but in its very simplicity it tells the story. A man, presumably Zuckerman, stands in the midst of a long, ill-defined landscape.

His arms are crossed to the cold as the wind blows his scarf away from his body. Snow surrounds him, mixing with the sky, presenting the illusion of an endless horizon. Above him hovers the face of a young girl. The face is larger then his whole frame; it seems to form itself out of a darkening sky. The face is colorless, distraught, but sensual in its mysteriousness. The picture tells first of the heat of sexuality in the midst of cold, the intermixing of desire and pain, of need and of purpose. The face is god-like in its size and placement amidst the distant heavens, a reminder of authority, of powers that overwhelm a life, powers which send the coldness to the earth and watch in disinterest. The face is also that of the past, the face of history, of Anne Frank, of victims marched sullenly and barbarously, systematically, to their unexpected end. The face registers nothing, no pain, no joy. It is a melange of faceless faces, reminiscent of dehumanization. But, it is also, strangely, a solitary face, the face of one separated from the multitude, the face that even in its union with all the other victims maintains its singleness, it uniqueness.

The man is Rothian; man separated from the world, man left in the coldness of an earth he cannot understand, an earth changed unalterably in this century, an earth where meaning has been put in doubt, where certainty is lost. Like Crane's poet, whose voice asks for the universe's acknowledgement, he does not receive a satisfactory answer; he is left to puzzle out the world on his own. What surrounds him is barrenness, images of impotency, emptiness, the white endless snow, the dark endless sky. What surrounds him, moreover, is the face of the Holocaust, of the victims, the face that is never out of his mind, the face that will not be erased and which must be remembered; the face warns against ideology, warns against totalitarianism, warns against absolute power, absolute answers: The face and the emptiness are all there is.

And it is cold.

The man waits, like Job, for answers, waits to be told why he was born into this debased world, into this debased time. But he receives no word. Only the face is visible. To go on, to move, to act, to search out meaning; these are his choices. But how to act, how to search, how to create without demeaning that face? Perhaps it is best to stop, to let the cold wash over him, to let the vacant landscape take another victim. But that too would demean the memory. A choice must be made, and by the footprints in the snow the decision is clarified. He will not stop. But, in his hesitation, in the moment of questioning represented here, the voice of the Holocaust survivor is heard: "We lost. The world lost, whether they know it or admit it. It doesn't make any difference. And yet we won, we're going on..." (HT 205). With loss the man is forever saddled, but that loss is not enough to hold him still. The loss is present, the doubt is present, the fear is present; And yet, "we're going on."

And into the wind the man moves forward across a landscape, cold, barren, wintry-white: Into the fading daylight.

Notes

1.   Mark Shechner recognizes the indecipherability of the text in his early review of the novel, complaining that Roth tells "us far less than we want to know," and stating in rebuke, "*The Ghost Writer* could have been bolder with its modest premises and taken a few more risks" (216). For others the novel seems clearer, allowing more definitive interpretations. For Judith Patterson Jones and Guinevera A. Nance the novel is an attempt to answer the question, "What must the artist be in order to create authentically?" (122). Marilyn Fowler emphasizes Nathan's learning that "the man and his art are one and the same..." (212). Saul Maloff argues that the novel is "about the nature and risks- and limits - of art and the imagination..." (631), while Hermione Lee suggests it is "about influence" (70) Disagreements continue in decoding Roth's title. Adeline R. Tintner claims that Henry James is the ghost writer of the novel, suggesting that "James is directing Roth's pen," and that Roth's imagination is being "reined in by the Master" (Hiding Behind James (HBJ 49). Joseph Voelker puts James Joyce in the role of ghost writer, claiming that "the book is a *Bildungsroman* with a Joycean theme" (91). John Leonard emphasizes the ghostly presence of Chekhov (48), while Frederick Karl argues that the ghost writer is Anne Frank (American Fictions 540). Pearl K. Bell mentions "Kafka, Chekhov, Babel, Flaubert, and ...|Roth| himself when young" (72). To her, "this suggests what the title, with its sly play on words, means: that the imagination and craft of a writer are nourished so directly by the masters of the past that they become, in no invidious sense, his 'ghost writers'" (72). Fowler, too, views the allusions to former writers as Roth's "contemporary tribute to them" (154). Voelker views the dead writers' presence less benignly, describing them as "Oedipal obstructors," standing in the young writer's way, holding him back, causing a Bloomian belatedness to descend upon him (Pinsker CE 90). The most accurate evaluation is made by Jack Beatty, who writes, "There is no end to the clever variations on the title" (37). The title is ambiguous; it offers no answers. The limit of interpretations is the limit of the inventiveness of the reader, who adds his own ghostly voice, who becomes another ghost writer of the elusive and allusive text. Roth's text encourages this kind of active readership, and Roth claims, happily, "When you publish a book, it's the world's book. The world edits it" (CWPR 111). When Zuckerman approaches E.I. Lonoff's lifeless home he is unable to accept this knowledge. For him ambiguity is impossible; he wants surety, acceptance, he wants to believe, to find in the religion of art a stable base from which to begin his life, and in Lonoff a father to give him a priestly blessing.

2.   To surrender to desire is, for Nathan, to "lapse," to fall victim to forces he cannot contain (141). And yet like much else this lapse is not solely negative or

destructive; it is also cathartic and inspirational. It is cathartic in that it releases Nathan, momentarily, from his obsession with his father and, when completed, releases him from his lustful thoughts of Amy. The lapse of desire inspires because it initially focuses Nathan's attention on Amy, the stimulus and subject of his fascinating fiction. The guilt, moreover, of the masturbation leads him back to James, back to literature (141). Masturbation is both an uncontrolled and controlled act at the same time. The choice to masturbate is unconscious, visceral, with Zuckerman; it impels him. But the act itself is an act of supreme control and power, it is an act of potency and narcissism, an act outside others' domain. Masturbation is two-sided; it both entraps and liberates (141).

3.   When Zuckerman has Anne describe herself as having "wrought" her diary he acknowledges the doubleness of creation (175). The word "wrought" can be defined as "carefully worked or artistically done" (Compton's Encyclopedia Dictionary 2642). With this definition in mind Anne's diary is viewed as a work born of serious and concentrated effort, born of purpose, diligence; a work carefully and meticulously ordered by a controlled, contemplative, and resolute mind. "Wrought" can also mean "beaten into shape," or "a person possessed of an excited state of mind;" "a person stimulated" (2642). With this definition in mind Anne's diary is a work born of pain, anger, and desire, a work created by an exuberant, driven, excited mind; a mind acting on orders of the heart. Neither definition adequately describes her writing process; the work springs from both the heart and head, from both cold concentrated effort and unconscious heat.

4.   Dan Isaac argues that the action of the novel "precisely represents that moment in Roth's life immediately after the publication of the stories that were to make up his first book, *Goodbye, Columbus*" (47). He calls Zuckerman "Philip Roth, the younger" (47). R.Z. Sheppard suggests that the novel has "the look...of [Roth's] autobiography (70). Pearl K. Bell asserts that *The Ghost Writer* is Roth's salute to his youthful courage in defying Jewish family pieties" (73). Alan L. Berger pronounces boldly, "Nathan Zuckerman is...Roth himself in the late fifties," and he sees the novel as Roth's attempt "to give himself legitimacy in the Jewish community" (157). Saul Maloff, too, calls Zuckerman "the Roth character" (628), and Robert Towers sees Zuckerman as one of Roth's many "fictional stand-ins" (1). In conversation with Roth, Alan Finkielkraut tells him, "This young writer, Nathan Zuckerman, has just published a group of stories that remind us necessarily of your first work, *Goodbye, Columbus*" (CWPR 121). He adds, "I took it for granted that you were the younger writer Nathan Zuckerman" (129).

5.   Adding to the confusion is the apparent similarity between Roth and Lonoff. Though most critics have associated Lonoff with Bernard Malamud, J.D. Salinger, or I.B. Singer Roth, himself, has been suggested as a possible model. Roth, by his own description, leads "a nearly perfect Lonoff life" (CWPR 109). He tells James Atlas, "I write all day, take a walk at the end of the afternoon and usually read at night" (CWPR 109). Atlas, having been given a tour of Roth's 18th century house in Connecticut, realizes that Roth "has only to look around him" to write the description of Lonoff's living room (CWPR 108). Roth is, like Lonoff, "the Jew who got away," the Jew living in "the *goyish* wilderness" consistently writing about Jews (9); the writer who has

been able "to say something new and wrenching to Gentiles about Jews, and to Jews about themselves" (21). Finkielkraut states directly to Roth, "I see now that, not unlike Lonoff, you live like a semi-recluse in New England; you seem to write and read most of the time - in other words, to spend most of your life, in Lonoff's self-descriptive phrase, 'turning sentences around'" (CWPR 129). In another interview, this time with Sara Davidson, Roth is asked why he teaches. His response is a restatement of Lonoff's "This way, at least two afternoons a week I have to stop, no questions asked" (30). Roth tells Davidson, "It gets me out of the house (and out of writing) one day a week" (CWPR 107). What separates Roth and Lonoff is Lonoff's narrow philosophy of art, his inability to escape the prison he has constructed.

6.   She mentions the similarities between Nathan's "childhood scenes" and Stephen's "park visit," both of which are "happy childhood scenes which nonetheless prefigure later conflicts" (177), and Nathan's masturbating and "Stephen's wet dream," both of which lead to the creation of a written work" (Stephen's 'Villanelle' and Nathan's 'Femme Fatale') (176). Finally she reads Stephen's "Non Servium" as a precursor to Nathan's "I will not prate in platitudes to please the adults" (135).

7.   Adeline Tintner also suggests the influence of James's "The Author of Belltraffio. She views the two plots as parallels. She elucidates: "Both young men describe the country house thy are visiting with a good deal of envy" (50). Tintner notes an echo of James's narrative's metaphor of Mrs. Ambient "as like a work by "Sir Joshua Reynolds" to Zuckerman's description of Amy Bellette "as a Velasquez" (50). Besides the obvious similarities between Ambient and Lonoff Tintner recognizes that "Both Mrs. Ambient and Hope Lonoff suffer from the seclusion their husbands require for working," and that both are "genetically and temperamentally alien" to their husbands (50). Finally, Tintner argues that both stories tell of a hero who is "treated to a vision of domestic turmoil triggered by his own worshipful visit to the house of a great writer" (50). However, though their plots overlap James's story offers little illumination of Roth's text. If anything can be gleaned from the comparison it is that Lonoff becomes more nefarious when placed beside Ambient, and Zuckerman appears more heroic: He achieves the same awakening as James's narrator without causing a similar tragedy, the death of a child.

8.   She points out that "The cast of The Ghost Writer is similar in composition to that of 'The Middle Years,'" and that "Each of the Jamesian characters bears some strong resemblance to the equivalent character in Roth's work" (28), emphasizing the similarities between Lonoff and Dencombe, the established writers, and Zuckerman and Dr. Hugh, the young admirers. Edwards notes that both tales begin "with the setting" (28), and that Zuckerman rewrites "the opening image of Dencombe holding the new copy of |his| book" in his fiction of Amy Bellette (31).

9.   Several critics have attempted to link Malamud's novel with Roth's, and indeed there are parallels. James Atlas points out that both Dubin and Lonoff "dream of going off to Italy with a younger mistress" (CWPR 109), and Fowler adds, both elder writers are "fifty-six years old," both are "self-conscious about the bulge of their bellies," both "diet to control this bulge," "both men must consider whether to eat a scrambled egg, both wives scold them to ignore their diets," and both are

participants in a scene where a "younger woman disrobes…and receives no response" (188).

10.   Their view is so obscured by fear that they assume that it is prejudice, simply, which lead to the gas chambers. In this they bespeak a fundamental misunderstanding of the Holocaust. Roth argues that "Between prejudice and persecution there is usually, in civilized life, a barrier constructed by the individual's convictions and fears, and the community's laws, ideals, values" (RMAO 218). That this barrier disappeared "in Germany cannot be explained only in terms of anti-Semitic misconceptions" (RMAO 218). The Holocaust's truth rests on more complex grounds. Zuckerman's knowledge of the Holocaust is more sophisticated than his predecessors. As noted earlier, in his fiction he explicates Anne's diary making clear that Anne and her family displayed few traits that would label them as stereotypical Jews. "But that was the point," he explains, "that was what gave her diary the power to make the nightmare real….How could even the most obtuse of the ordinary ignore what had been done to the Jews just for being Jews?" (179). Prejudice becomes only a facet of the Nazi equation. Categorization of Jews of Jews as "the degenerates whose contamination civilized people could no longer abide," Zuckerman realizes, coupled with a merciless, unbinding, and inhuman ideology conspire to create a unique horror (180). Men are sentenced to death for no other reason than "the biological fact of their ancestry" (Ezrahi 11). "It took nothing," Zuckerman writes, "that was the horror" (179).

CHAPTER TWO

Abraham and Isaac

Dear Parents, I have always loved
you, all the same...

- Franz Kafka
- The Judgment

In March 1993, reading a selection at the poetry center of the 92nd Street Y
from his memoir of his father's last year, *Patrimony*, Roth relates, of an
evening's concert at his father's condominium community in Miami Beach:
"The performance was as alarming as it was heroic" (57). Roth's performance, too, spanned that vast spectrum, alarming for it spoke of death's
relentlessness, of the body's fragility with unusual candor, and heroic
because it was his own father, not a fictional construction, being revealed
that night, a father only recently departed and most clearly still achingly
present to the narrator.

In an otherwise perfectly controlled reading, Roth hesitates slightly as he
comes to the close of his oration. He has revealed his affection for his
grandfather's shaving mug and his desire for it as a final bequest from his
father. The mug had allowed him to see his grandfather "as an ordinary man
among men," and now would presumably allow him to remember his father
not only as a father but as flesh and blood (27). The mug comes to evoke
not only his father's distinctive face and body but his history as well, the
"blood bonds" which tether son to father. (91). Roth concludes his reading
recounting the end of a sad visit to his father in New Jersey. It is clear to all
that Herman Roth has, as he puts it, reached "the last chapter" of his life
(118). As the son leaves he is presented with "A couple of brown bags...sav-
agely twisted about to accommodate" a package (118). On the wrapping his
father has written, "From a Father to a Son" (118). Roth intones: "'Here,' he

59

said, 'Take this home.' Downstairs in the car I tore off all the wrappings and found my grandfather's shaving mug" (118).

It is with this last line that Roth chokes on his words, a moment of exquisite emotion interrupting an otherwise flawless soliloquy. Perhaps the enunciating of that so personal moment is too much for Roth; in recreating it its preciousness returns to him. Perhaps there is, in the reader, a shudder of loss, as if by reciting aloud such a private experience it is somehow taken from him. Or perhaps it is not the story or the recollection of that moment at all that humanizes the performer; perhaps it is the palpable sense that in completing his long reenactment he has once again lost his father. While he reads the father lives, his voice impersonated, his words spoken as though for the first time. The reading ends and once again the father is gone, the magic of literature and of drama departs leaving Roth alone on stage.

His composure regained, Roth takes his bow. The audience has witnessed a quintessential Rothian hour; the vertiginous movements of feeling and of performance, of art and of life, the movements of the writer and of the man. Roth's locus shifts back and forth between the peripheries of man; his fiction's life springs from that interaction, that tense balance and that frightening imbalance that so many of his characters feel and either battle against or accommodate themselves to.

And that shifting begins at home, with birth, with the vicissitudes of the father and the mother. Barbara Koenig Quart, in her short essay on fathers and sons in Roth's works, argues that "Philip Roth's canvas has always been just the size of a room or, at the most, a house - domestic, personal, the family as frame" (R 590). Actually, Roth's canvas stretches far beyond the domestic settings, far beyond the battle of children and parents, but certainly it does begin there, as the seeds for Roth's broader concerns. The father and the mother conjure images not only of the pastoral formative years which serve as a nostalgic reminder of all that has been lost, nor only of a battleground for future rebellion, but images of history, tradition, and memory.

Childhood is a time of restless oscillation, of protean changeability, of conforming and rebelling, of stability and discord, of peace and of anarchy. The father and the mother introduce and construct the world from which the sons and daughters rebel and to which they cling. They are the first narrative voices heard, they tell the first story. They introduce love and power.

They grant the child a reprieve from the concentrationary world, from the culture of death the children have been born into, and then they force that world upon the child, as though it were the retribution for their childish days of ease and safety, the nightmare in payment for their blissful daydreams. With love they guard the child from knowledge and with love they burden them with knowledge. They use their power to teach the child the necessity of individuality, the tyranny of forgetting, and with their power they threaten that individuality; they become what they have warned against.

Three powers hang over a child's life: the father dogmatic and vulnerable, dogmatic in his effort to remember, and vulnerable because of that memory, the mother, seductive and controlling, the victim and the victimizer, and an unknown, indefinable authority beyond the parents' nest, both comforting and terrible, comforting for it offers order in an orderless world, and terrible because its power is always a potentiality and a blight. The dichotomies of Roth's fiction are set; they form the broad base background to the puzzle that is to be constructed.

PATRIMONY

"Everything you learn just opens up six more questions," Roth says, speaking of his father's history (CWPR 268). "You discover that what you know is so partial, so small," he continues (CWPR 268). Writing *Patrimony* has not closed the book on his father nor on fathers as a subject. The last word can never be said. The father's role is so vast and differentiated, so mired in ambiguity and in feeling that it can never be clearly classified. Herman Roth remains always an enigma, always kept at some unbridgeable distance.

"You also discover," Roth adds, "just how deep the bond is between father and son, the totality of it - cultural, personal, biological, historical" (CWPR 268). The child is bound to the father's past, bound like Isaac to Abraham's altar. The story of Abraham and Isaac is reinstituted and reinterpreted in Roth's post-Holocaust world. The sacrifice of the son is no longer an act of beatific faith, an act that sanctifies. Now the father, Abraham, is at once a murderer and a slave to ideology, a killer and an automaton. As the first true practitioner of power he reveals the poles of the Holocaust-psyche, and as the source of memory he introduces the child to the flawed reactions to life in the concentrationary universe. In Roth the father occupies two distinct spheres, like the voice Roth creates in his memoir. Roth's fathers go beyond Lonoff and Doc Zuckerman; they are at times savagely dictatorial and at times weak, inarticulate, and slavish.

In *Letting Go* Roth delineates quite orderly the two types of fathers who will inhabit and define so much of his fiction. Gabe Wallach's father, Mordecai, lives to a strictly Pipikian code. He is "wholehearted" (37) and "turbulent" (42), a man of "passions" (41). "Whatever terror he saw in life," Gabe believes, "whatever turbulence gave him inward hell, he was unable to answer it with reason. So he took to magic" (41). But even his magic exists only as a momentary tourniquet to his "atheism" (40). His codes of conduct are all visceral and fleeting. He believes only in moments, in connections with others, in feeling. His concentrationary universe is empty and to battle that emptiness he need only submit to it, to turn away from any order. His life is a letting go, an expunging. Barbara Quart calls him "horribly helpless," but that helplessness is his strength (200). The Pipikian father accedes to vulnerability to confront and exist within the painful, aleatory world.

This is the legacy Mr. Wallach leaves his son, the patrimony Gabe inherits. Gabe is, in many ways, his "father's child," so terrified by savagery that he cannot act, made impotent by life's apparent meaninglessness (5). But what Mr. Wallach does not comprehend is that that very savagery was built, in good measure, on a nihilism of spirit not unlike his own. To not become the father, to "resist the old man," Gabe attempts to exorcise those qualities he disdains, to rebel against his father's ambivalence, his uncertainty, his teeming sentimentality and emotionalism, his anarchy.

He submerges his heart to submerge the father. He looks to rationalism to take him beyond the past. His father looks at Gabe and Gabe senses in his father's sad eyes the question, "how far down had I hidden my heart?" (33). Marge Howells screams at him, "You're heartless" (38). Libby Herz thinks of Gabe, "the cold-hearted rich bastard!" (335). Martha Reganhart sees him as a man of such little feeling that he always gets "away unscathed" (539).

Gabe tries and fails again and again to hold his hands and his heart in check. But it is that very failure that points him towards a more promising future than anyone in the novel. Having locked emotion away he finds what has been repressed returns, not to mock him, or to unman him, but to free him. For unbridled rationalism is a remnant of the Nazi mind. That Gabe does not eradicate all of his father's influence, that he eventually lets some of that magical tempestuousness back into him helps him to find a kind of tentative freedom with which he concludes the novel. What he has most wanted to escape eventually saves him.

Even Mr. Wallach, that most benign of fathers, refuses to disappear from the child's soul. If the slovenly, almost silent, misanthropic, unimposing man can overwhelm a son what of a Lonoffian father, a dogmatic and domineering father, a didactic father who is clear and forthright, a father who can condemn and who will accuse?

In *Letting Go* Paul Herz's father acts the role of the father as tyrant, the absolutist whose belief system will not countenance difference.[1] Mr. Herz "has a terrible heart" both metaphorically and physically (168). Feelings have been squeezed from him after the wreckage of his century. Unlike Mr. Wallach, his heart is stone cold and dying. His is an inversion of Mr. Wallach's nihilism, an inversion, though, no less discredited by the purveyors of genocide. For Mr. Herz Paul's marriage is a "wound" he "will never forget," an unforgivable breach (169). After throwing the newly wedded pair from his house he turns his back on them, referring to them only as "he" (167) and "her," their names unspoken, like an obscenity or a sacrilege (168).

For all his physical weakness a "certainty" resides within his deracinated body (167). His movements, unsteady as they are, remind Gabe of an "umpire," a judge making the definitive call (166). When he is told of Paul's job as a teacher of English he thinks only of "spelling" and "grammar," rules; his mind is closed to creativity, spontaneity, style (167). He wears his blinders proudly, unwilling to even contemplate a peripheral view. While these blinders provide their wearer with a halo of security, they inhibit and restrict in direct proportion to their protectiveness. "Maybe I can move my bowels," says Mr. Herz, but his bowels will not relent (166). His is a bottled up and blockaded self, a man obstructed and closed off, impotent in the face of life's vivaciousness, life's variety. The Lonoffian father is as inherently impotent as the Pipikian father. Where Pipik hides in emptiness unable to act because unwilling to believe in acting's efficaciousness, Lonoff is unable to act because he is closed off by the imposition of a self-constructed certainty that dismisses deviations.

It is that ideological perspective that pushes his son away. Paul attempts to alter the father's pattern, to let go of all patterns. He says to his uncle, "It's not easy, Asher, giving birth to yourself all over again at twenty-seven. I'm cutting plenty of bonds, don't kid yourself" (418). Giving birth to yourself is a psychological patricide from which there is no turning back.

Paul is about to set himself free on the day of his father's entombment. Refusing to appear at Mr. Herz's funeral will be the culminating act of liberation; the promulgation of a new life. "There were several choices open to Paul that moment," he realizes, while watching the funeral ceremony from a hidden distance (422). "He could have run away, or simply walked away" (422). He is given his chance, his one great chance, and instead of acting to free himself he edges closer to his own enslavement. "Instead of moving out, he moved in" (422). The power of the father reasserts itself, forces him inward. Images of death mark his movement towards the death-like life he is about to conjoin himself to: "In and in and in, past all kinds of tombstones, fancy ones, plain ones, old ones, past memorials to cherished mothers and beloved fathers, faithful husbands and dutiful wives, and even little children, whose dates told the whole miserable story" (422). Paul moves in toward his dead father, towards a reconciliation and a relinquishment. He becomes what his father was, what his father taught him to be, a man of duty. He fulfills the pattern, falls into it.

The chapter ends:

> For his truth was revealed to him, his final premise melted away. What he had taken for order was chaos. Justice was illusion. Abraham and Isaac were one. His eyes opened, and in the midst of those faces - the faces of his dream, the faces of the bums, all the faces that had forever encircled him - he felt no humiliation and no shame. Their eyes no longer overpowered him - He felt himself under a wider beam (423).

Critics have read this scene as an epiphany for Paul, a hopeful preface to a new life. Far from heroically letting go, Paul relents, gives up expectations for his own justice, his own meaning. He becomes a servant, a congregant, a victim forever locked beneath some other, some patriarchal power. "The text," argues Irving Feldman, "is from Kierkegaard" (35). In Kierkegaard's *Fear and Trembling* Abraham is celebrated for his emotions, for his divided self, whereas in *Letting Go* Paul's vision calls for an end to division, a surrendering of the son to the father. To Paul, Abraham and Isaac do not represent a vision of "the joining of the man of duty (Abraham) and of feeling (Isaac)," but a final rejection of feeling (Feldman 35). Paul sees no difference, no separation between the father and the son. They are one and the same, no independence for the child for he is merely the double of his progenitor.

Paul and Gabe turn, early in their lives, from their fathers only to have their father's image and influence reappear. In *Letting Go*, the Pipikian father, though oppressive, offers the son a means of salvaging his life, while the Lonoffian father, even after death, oppresses and controls the son's every movement, every choice.

Though *Letting Go* does introduce the two kinds of fathers which permeate Roth's works, the results upon the children do not always follow in the same pattern. The Lonoffian father does not always succeed in thrashing and dehumanizing the son, nor does the Pipikian father always have such a restorative effect on the son. Yet, the image of the father, in Roth, is consistently an echo of one or the other of these formative fathers; he is either a Mussolini "hanging by his heels" (ZU 199), or a weak man who "beshat" himself (P 172). He is either the reminder of Lonoffian authoritarianism and its results, or a reminder of the victim, not only the dead millions but the victim of history whose burdened memory enslaves him. To study both of these images is to see how they inhibit and inspire, provoke and emasculate, how they, most of all, can never be pushed aside or forgotten, how these average men forever etch themselves upon their sons and daughters, how they come to inhabit and shape their children's minds and destinies.

In an unsent letter to Diana Trilling in 1969 Roth writes about his "preoccupation with the warfare between parents and children," specifically in *When She Was Good* and *Portnoy's Complaint* (RMAO 26). His protagonists, as he aptly stated in 1969, are "bent on tracking down the source of " their sadness, their "grievances" (RMAO 26). They invariably turn their eyes backwards, towards their first years to find causes or place blame. Often they take on the "role" of "enraged offspring" (RMAO 26). Their rage springs from two directions. Where the Lonoffian father is present the child's rage screams against the dictates, the rules, the blindness of the father. But where Pipik is concerned the rage is for all that isn't said, isn't dictated, isn't taught, rage for the father who will not take on the full meaning of the word "father."

No character in Roth's fiction is more enraged, righteously enraged, than Lucy Nelson. Not even Portnoy with his howls of discontent manages to express the hateful and unforgiving ire that Lucy lets loose against her fathers. Though Duane, her biological father, is most often understood as her most profound adversary, it is her grandfather, Willard, Daddy-Will, who acts as the primary father-figure, and as such the primary scapegoat for Lucy's animus.

Lucy Nelson views the failure of her grandfather as a failure of language. "You never say! Never!" Lucy yells, infuriated at his inability to assign blame (258). His is a language of denial, of indecisiveness, silence. "Not to be rich, not to be famous, not to be mighty, not even to be happy, but to be civilized - that was the dream of his life," begins the novel, from Daddy-Will's point of view (3). Willard describes his dreams in terms of negatives. He starts his story of movement towards the civilized life by expressing the things he does not insist upon having. Even his stated dream, "to be civilized," is vague. Nothing, for Willard, is stated with surety, with fullness of meaning.

"What the qualities of such a life were he could not have articulated" (3). The first trope of language is indicative of Willard's limits. Throughout the text he is unable to get his words out, to say what he wants to say. His mind, intent on what it does not need and what it does not want, what it does not know and cannot express, remains in an anarchic state of uselessness. All that Willard "knew for sure" was "what he didn't want" (3). His words betray him as a man without hardened values, a man whose philosophy is formed from exclusion. Willard is, as he says, "open to opinion from all sides," holding no opinion of his own (9). His silence, instead of allowing an exchange of ideas, leaves a void in the family's life, leaves them bereft of a father who wields any real power. "What could Willard do but be silent," the reader hears again and again (14). "I only got so many words," he admits, "and so many different ways to say them, and after that -" (23). The father, the man who expresses a deep and abiding responsibility to care for and understand his children is unable to fulfill that responsibility because he is afraid to cast judgment, to pronounce edicts, to use his authority, because he is afraid to speak.

Where Willard seeks resolution in avoidance and silence, Lucy envisions language as a sacred realm of meaning and clarity. Hers is a "dream of language," argues Donald Kartiganer, "restored to a prelapsarian fullness of expression and action" (97).[2] Hers is the dream of purity, the dream Hitler promised to make real. Hers is the dream of meaning and purpose, the dream Kessler lost himself to. From the beginning Lucy searches unceasingly for a realm of pure union of word and action. Early in her adolescence Lucy "refused ever to tell a lie again, to anyone about anything" (75). Her words, from that moment of epiphany, are words as clear professions of truth. "People can call me all the names they want," she tells herself, "I have nothing to confess, because I am right and they are wrong" (85).

Lucy becomes lost, deaf to all but her own thoughts. As her husband, Roy, gives lie to his words Lucy's self-righteousness grows by leaps and bounds. She soon finds it impossible to hold her voice in check. She criticizes Roy's storytelling to Edward, "Oh, I know Roy," she says, "every Sunday of our lives you tell him! Because that's all you can do!" (261). "Every word you speak," she says, "it's awful. You're nothing, and I will never forgive you" (262). And it is not only to Roy that this is addressed:

It is first to Duane, Whitey as he is known, her estranged father, whose drunken frenzies and irresponsibility disgust and frighten her. His lack of control has torn her childhood apart. Duane is without substance, a man who exists from moment to moment, a Pipikian malcontent to whom words are just a useful way of getting by, of escape.[3]

Lucy's words also fly outward towards Julian Sowerby, Roy's Uncle Julian, another failed Pipikian father. Julian is exposed by "the kind of language he used" (92). His is a patois of patriotic cliches and obscenity. For Lucy, after hearing of Julian's extra-marital exploits, he plays one part and one part only. He is "a cheat of a person" (134), "a wicked man" (278), "a whoremonger! A philanderer! An adulterer!" and there is no salvation for his sins (279). She points her zealotry at her enemy, another demon father, to disempower and denigrate him, to extinguish his strength.

The rebuke spoken to Roy accuses him of being in league with Julian and Duane, of being another Pipikian father. Her anger at him is so vehement because it expresses her final failure, the failure to create at least one father to take her beyond the tragedy of her past. Were Lucy to change Roy she would, she believes, have a chance at life. But when Roy becomes a recreation of Whitey and Julian she sees herself condemned to live out her life with deceitful and capricious fathers, to reenact the primal scene, the confrontation at home that has set her ideological search in motion.

It is Willard, though, who carries the greatest burden, for it is he who had the authority and the power to change her fate, and so it is to him that her rebuke speaks loudest. Willard and Lucy are joined by the very form of the novel. The first chapter, Roth states, "introduces the character of Willard Carroll, the grandfather in whose home the angry heroine is raised" (RMAO 27). "The chapter," Roth continues, "proceeds then to enlarge Willard's idea of 'civilization,' revealing through a brief family history how he has been able to practice the virtues of courage, kindliness, and responsibility, as he understands them" (RMAO 27). Willard has attempted to exorcise his own father, his own past, the father who had "not a single human thing to say," whose pagan barbarism hangs over Willard's head as much as his own nullity hangs over his granddaughter's head (12).

"Only after Willard's way has been sufficiently explored," Roth explains, "does the focus of the novel turn in stages toward Lucy, and to her zeal for what she takes to be a civilized life, what she understands courage to be and responsibility to mean, and the place she assigns to kindliness in combat" (RMAO 27). The center of the novel, then, moves from Willard to Lucy, each attempting to remake a past contaminated by a rejected father. It is Willard's fear of repeating the savagery of his father that turns him toward silence. His is an anti-morality founded on his father's betrayal. Lucy, having defied her first father, grasps her grandfather for solidity but he offers none. She, in turn, rebels, adopting an antipathetic doctrine from her grandfather.

Instead of seeing Willard's failure as a failure of the doctrine he espouses she sees it as a failure of implementation. She exists, as does Willard, as a response to fathers. She is enslaved by her need for a imagined father and by her hatred for her own fathers. It is Willard's journey that parallels and portends Lucy's. As his response to his father was bound to fail, because it was a response and only a response, so, too, his granddaughter's fanatical answer to Willard is doomed to repeat that failure. The patrimony runs for four generations, from the barbarous great-grandfather to devilish Lucy Nelson.

Lucy ends her life not railing at the moon or the stars, at the community's petty morality, at America, or at God; her complaint is a complaint directed at fathers: "Farewell, farewell," she thinks, "philanderers and frauds, cowards and weaklings, cheaters and liars, Fathers and husbands, farewell" (303). She craves a world "without men" (302). All men become guilty, all fathers forever responsible for her particular misery.

The Pipikian father - his very impotence - navigates the child's life. That the child can or cannot eventually take control of her own trip is a clue to her ability to both accept and move beyond her father, her desire to cut some of the bonds that hold her and light out for her own territory, without the father as guide or as anti-guide. Lucy finds herself surrounded by Pipiks, voices without substance, fathers without power, words without meaning. Detesting their weakness she finds solace and righteous indignation in a refutation of them. She sees no attributes in the Pipikian life. For her Pipik is merely a failure, a failure in words and in deeds.

But Pipik can attract, can impel. When David Kepesh is given a choice between the absolute Lonoffism of his father or the absolute Pipikism of his surrogate father, Herbie Bratasky, he finds himself attracted initially by Herbie's seemingly joyful, effortless, blitheful life. Herbie's Pipikism is an ideology not founded on terror, as it was for Willard, but founded on acting and play. Herbie clings to evanescence as a means of enjoying the child's life. Kepesh is so influenced by this second father that even as he moves boldly forward, desirous of the kind of wholeness his father personifies, he does so in Herbie's terms. Herbie's influence precludes any advancement, any awakening of self.

Kepesh's interlocutor into the world of "temptation" is defined not by who he is but by the roles he plays (3). He is a "social director, band leader, crooner, comic, and M.C." (4). An elderly vacationer calls Herbie a "showman," and adds, "His whole stock in trade is that he's crazy enough for anything - that's his whole act" (5). Anything goes, this is Pipik's phrase. Under Herbie's tutelage, Kepesh understands "acting" as the facilitator of meaning, the way to uncover who he is. Role-playing, a Pipikian trope, is to be the means of establishing a Lonoffian structure. Beginning his search within this contradiction Kepesh's pursuit of uncontradictory stability must be fraught with peril.

Though he claims to be attempting "the solemn undertaking I call understanding myself," understanding, for Kepesh, is merely the appropriating and discarding of roles (8). In the course of the short novel Kepesh describes himself variously as, "Joe College" (20), "Casanova" (21), "Lord Fauntleroy" (22), "Romeo" (24), "Bluebeard" (26), "Don Giovanni" (26), "Johannes the Seducer (26), "Maupassant" (26), "Raskolnikov" (35), "Pudd'nhead Wilson" (35), "K" (65), a "sultan" (38), a "fallen priest" (39), "a naughty boy" (36), "Birgitta's pimp" (52), a "slave," a "slaveholder, an arsonist" (61), "a Victorian schoolmaster' (77), a "good boy" (189), a "man of feeling and conscience" (100), "Herbie's pupil," "Helen's suitor" (252), "Birgitta's accomplice, Baumgarten's sidekick, Gogol's berserk and mortified amputee" (261), and as a "wayward son" (252). He is also, by turns, the lecturer, the teacher, the man of literature, the Jew, the child. Kepesh looks to role-playing for identity. In that way he is more Herbie's son than anything else. Instead of looking within Kepesh looks without, instead of delving into the deep layers of self he remains fixated on the top layer. He remains amorphous, without qualities, to his audience, an imitator, an actor telling a story, revealing and understanding nothing.

In his dream of Prague Kepesh hears Herbie say, "You have denied yourself too much as it is" (193). Herbie is the voice of voraciousness, even in dreams, the voice that allows everything, encourages a continued dalliance with ever-changing, ever enticing roles. In that same dream Herbie promises Kepesh to "make you finally you, David dear" (193). The promise of wholeness through role-playing, through costumes, fictions, stories, is Herbie's dreamy promise. But acting is protective, not enlightening; it distances Kepesh from vulnerability, it hides the dangers of life, shields the performer from reality, from true choice. What Kepesh needs to do, the first step forward, is to stop, as he puts it, "all that cloying acting" (11). But when one is suckled on acting, when one sees in one's teacher and alternative father the blessings of the life of the actor, it is difficult to desist. The father, as a joyful, hearty spirit, manipulates and demeans the son's independent spirit. He introduces a misleading vista and points out the loveliness of the deceptive view, the false view, the sanitized vision where forgetfulness is a palliative that dissolves a horrible past.

More romantic spirits than Kepesh would be fully seduced by this vision, by this abundance, a spirit less experienced, younger. It is such spirits Roth invents in his breakthrough novella, "Goodbye, Columbus," spirits easily lured by the Pipikian household created by Mr. Patimkin, a house he rules not with a firm hand but with leniency, bribery, and seduction. Neil Klugman is "wooed and won on Patimkin fruit," on vastness and laxity, on superficiality, on the kind of grotesque world that Kepesh, eventually, learns to distrust (77). "Oh Patimkin," Neil declares, "Fruit grew in their refrigerator and sporting goods dropped from their trees: " a strange, inverted paradise, but paradise nonetheless (43).

Mr. Patimkin is the patriarch of this world of surfaces, the king of this Pipikian castle. Patimkin reigns over the "bacchanalian paraphernalia" scattered amidst his home (41). His is a world of "money and comfort" (96), a "plentiful" world where everything is designed to assuage fear, to calm nerves, to aid an escape from time (41). "He's not too smart," says Brenda of her father, "but he's sweet at least" (26). Sweetness, capriciousness; these are the qualities of the father, the qualities with which he controls his children. Mr. Patimkin is a "ferocious eater," a carnivore who attacks his food with animal relish (21). He consumes, takes in, accumulates.

The Patimkin home thrives in its sallow triviality, its members concentrating on frivolous detail to distance themselves from a world harsh and unrelenting. The children are stripped of depth, stripped of a past by a world "heaped with fruit" (53). "They're goyim, my kids," Mr. Patimkin tells Neil, "that's how much they understand" (94). They understand nothing because they have been sheltered from understanding, nourished on forgetfulness. The curse that comes with knowledge is veiled from them, but so is the independence that knowledge allows.

"The life [Mr. Patimkin] had managed to build for himself and his family" is a life isolated from history (94). As he has so noticeably separated his family from Newark so too has he separated them from the past. Murray Baumgarten and Barbara Gottfried argue that even the Patimkin's "suburban house" with "its specialization of functions by room make it possible to hide the past" (31). They call Short Hills "the suburbs of forgetfulness" (21). Like the forgotten storeroom in the Patimkins' house, the past is pushed away, discarded willfully. Mr. Patimkin has pursued and garnered wealth and with it comfort, but the price he and his family pay is the price of dissolution, the desolation of spirit. They have lost their history, and it is in the children in whom this is most devastatingly reflected; they are denuded figures, isolated and insulated, "programmed" (3). Forgetfulness increases with prosperity, this is the equation throughout Roth's first broadside attack on upper-middle-class morality.

"Maybe I could learn to become a Patimkin with ease," Neil thinks, seeing his eventual union with Brenda as a union with Patimkin blood, as if it were not a marriage being contemplated but an adoption (28). Indeed, Neil imagines himself not in his and Brenda's home but in Mr. Patimkin's business. Brenda tells Neil, "You know, you look like me" (70). On some intuitive level Brenda recognizes Neil's slow submersion of self, his transformation into a Patimkin. His identity begins to merge with Brenda, to assimilate much in the same way that Brenda's identity has been assimilated into her family.

Assimilation is an image that moves in many directions. Assimilation is not only a cultural project but a familial and personal one. As Ben Patimkin has assimilated willingly into the American culture, so too he assimilates his children into his way of life. Assimilation is a merging of self and a loss of self. As Ben cannot hold onto his own religious and cultural roots under the beguiling pressure of post-war avaricious America, so too Brenda and her siblings cannot hold onto their individuality under the convivial pressure of their generous father. Mr. Patimkin illustrates Michel Foucault's concept of "panopticon," the means by which a seemingly democratic power enslaves its subjects; for Roth it is a method with sinister implications after the Holocaust. When Neil takes over for Mr. Patimkin in a basketball game and Ben tells him, "You're me," we have witnessed a clear indication of Neil's assimilation (28). Slowly the new son becomes the father, his first self erased.

But with Brenda's rejection, like a cold hard slap in the face, Neil becomes himself again, regaining his duality and his distance, losing the dream of Eden but escaping the claws of Ben Patimkin's insubstantial world. The end of their relationship signals a start for Neil and an ending for Brenda. She gives herself to her father, is entombed by his Pipikian power. "Damn it, Brenda," Neil says, "you're guilty of some things" (132). Her father has taught her just the opposite, and so she turns to him. Guilt, pain, history, memory, meaning, time, sadness, death, are hidden behind surfaces, behind the green of cash. She becomes fully assimilated, all dissonance and depth encased in family. She returns to her father when Neil turns out to not be his recreation. The image of Paul Herz running back towards the arms of his family is appropriate here. But here the father wields his power not through forms and dictums but through comfort and consolation, superfluity. The Pipikian code proves entrancing to the child. Amidst the carnival provided by the adoring father the real world is obtruded. The price the child pays for domination is the price of imprisonment.

Neil describes this Pipikian power to whom he loses his love as, "tall, strong, ungrammatical" (21). Tallness and strength are evidence of Mr. Patimkin's pose of confidence but it is his grammar that reveals him. Grammar is everything Ben disassociates himself from. Grammar is study, meaning, difficulty. To Ben Patimkin language is his to use as he pleases. There is no grammar to which he must subscribe, no rules he must adhere to in his evanescent life.

His tallness and his purported strength distance him from the typical Pipikian father, but they are just shells hiding a vacant self, a self as listless as Mr. Wallach, as terrified as Willard, as unreal as Herbie, and as weak as the most memorable Pipikian father in Roth's canon, Jack (or Jake) Portnoy. Ben's grammar ties him distinctively to Jack, who his son compares unfavorably to the "grammatical fathers" (145), who "never use double negatives" (145). Beyond their language there would seem little to unite these two fathers. Ben controls while Jake is controlled. Ben succeeds in the new American world while Jake spends his life slaving for "The Company" (6). Ben buys his way into America while Jake's company's insignia, "the Mayflower" (6), is a tell-tale sign that he is "forever on his way to America and can never arrive" (Guttmann 180). Ben assimilates while Jake divides the world into "goyische and Jewish" (75). And yet for all their dissimilarities they suffer from the same Pipikian weakness, the weakness that Ben hides with a false facade and which Jake reveals with every movement. They have no sureness, no truth, no consistent strength they can grasp to or impart.

Jack Portnoy is, as Quart explains, "an ambassador for the bounded life" (R 593). He is a victim and only a victim, a victim of history, of persecution, of anti-Semitism, and of bodily malfunction. "Here he is," Quart argues, "constipated, servile at work...and all the while, through, harboring deep rebellious strains, strong resentment toward the Wasps in authority that he serves" (593). But that rebelliousness is barely spoken, and never is it acted upon. Jack Portnoy's rancorous words, his bitter condemnation of "The Most Benevolent Financial Institution in America" (6), and its leaders, who Jack refers to as, "the whole pack of them up there in Massachusetts, *shkotzim* fox-hunting! playing polo!" resound no further than the living room (8). As Portnoy explains, "no sense demeaning himself by knocking them in public" (6). His words are exhortations into an abyss. Alex witnesses the weakness of his father's words, the dread that defines his father's life. Words are only impotent attempts to ease a moment of pain; for Jack, as it was for Ben, words are spoken and then they disappear, misfired blanks doing no harm and providing no help, echoing only for a moment.

It is in response to this that Alex Portnoy seeks to rearm language, to reinstate power in the spoken word. His soliloquy to Doctor Otto Spielvogel is more than a reiteration of childhood complaints, more than an expression of the debilitating effects of the inner battle between need and purpose, more than the comic expression of an Oedipal nightmare; it is an attempt to do with words what his father could never do with them, to make them mean something, answer the questions of his life.

Words, to Alex, are "galvanic;" they contain a hidden importance that need only be uncovered (20). The "silver tongues" of the Christian fathers beckon to him, promising salvation (42). "I am afraid," he admits, "to open my mouth for fear that if I do no words will come out - or the wrong words" (149). In Portnoy's lexicon there are right words and wrong words, and his session is, in good measure, an earnest attempt to unearth the right words, to make them his own.

Toward that end Alex tries to define and categorize all that he comes in contact with, to bring order to the disorder of life, an order that seems beyond the powers of the impoverished father. Headlines run through his mind, bold-faced and clear: "ASS'T HUMAN OPP'Y COMMISH FOUND HEADLESS IN GO-GO GIRLS APT" (181), "INSURANCE MAN'S SON LEAPS TO DEATH" (193), "ASS'T HUMAN OPP'Y COMMISH FLOGS DUMMY" (197), "JEW SMOTHERS DEB WITH COCK" (240). Though these are projections of infamy and humiliation, they are also the signs of a mind craving cold, hard facts, words which announce truth, which confidentially speak a meaning.[4]

A new language, precise, accurate, measured, is the means to attain that surety, to recreate life as the embodiment, the continuation, of a game, of a false construction. But that language proves as strangulating as its precursor. Chasing that false dream to Israel Portnoy finds his impotency more virulent than ever. He finds himself becoming the father. "Doctor," he says, "I couldn't get it up in the State of Israel!" (291). His adventure has led him back to the start. His movement away from the father has been a movement towards the father; he runs forward only to come full circle, into an unexplored past.

The scream which ends the novel marks a transition from a belief in language's perfectibility to an acknowledgement of its imperfectibilty. It signals not closure but the start of a new search, a search in which he will both rail against the father and attempt to redeem the father. Portnoy admits to both the patricidal drive and the drive for the father's renewal. "Christ," Portnoy yells, "I could strangle him on the spot for being so blind to human brotherhood!" (169). Balanced against this anger is an equally powerful affection, and an urge to uplift the floundering father. "In my liberation," Portnoy explains, "would be his - from ignorance, from exploitation, from anonymity" (8-9). The competing voices drive him forward. Still attached to the father and still reaching beyond, Portnoy acts as the quintessential Rothian man, pulled this way and that, back and forth, enlivened by the very complaint that enrages him.

Jack Portnoy neatly brings together the Pipikian fathers, unifying this disparate group of failed but, as Quart says of Mr. Portnoy, "very real and sympathetic" figures (592). Jack is, like Mr. Wallach, a man of heartfulness and terror, stymied by trepidation. He is, like Daddy-Will, a man whose language has failed, who resists speech, resists all conflict. He is, like Herbie Bratasky, an untrained teacher who sets his pupil in a false direction. He is, like Ben Patimkin, greedily protective of his child, resistant to reality, hesitant of structures for grammar or for behavior. And Alex responds in a manner consonant with each of his peers. Like Gabe, he rebels but finds the rebel's stance as barren as the father's. Like Lucy, he seeks to topple and reinvent the father. Like David, he searches for a definitive role, a headline, and is led astray. Like Brenda, he chastises and mocks the father only to admit to a deeper bond than heretofore confessed to. And, like Neil, he ends somewhere in between one world and the next, not a recapitulation and not yet his own man either. He ends, like Neil, trying to gauge the self from a "reflection in the glass," still trying to know exactly what he is, what he owes and what is owed to him (GC 135).

A Pipikian father, in truth, would sound like an oxymoron to the ears of any son or daughter in Roth's fiction. For everything that a father should be, according to a strict definition, is contradicted by these fathers. Potency, didacticism, unwavering truth, law, meaning, are embodied in the male form. As Portnoy complains of his father, "Who should by rights be advancing on me retreating....Who should be scolding, collapsing in helplessness" (41-42). And as he later remarks, "Who should run the show, Poppa, is us" (88). The cliched father is the rule for these children and when the father does not live up to the conception the child is overwhelmed, thrown loose. Some, like Lucy, can never turn away from a limited categorization, while others, like Portnoy, Gabe, and David, are left to remake their conceptions, to evolve a more multi-dimentional perspective. But for all the ideal father begins as a fiction, a portrait not of Pipik but of Lonoff, the patriarch who tells right from wrong, who makes rules that cannot be broken, whose brazen confidence acts as a clear anchor in a churning whirlpool.

An anchor, though, works in two divergent ways; it protects the vessels from spasmodic motion, from drifts towards disaster, and it holds the vessel in place, rescinding motion, allowing the passengers no alternative siteline. Its very power to keep the boat calm postpones an interaction with the turbulence. Its power is falsely calming. Few can, or want to, look beyond the anchored waters to view the unknown sea.

Protective at first, restrictive over time, the Lonoffian father is this anchor and in both his postures he effects the child in contradictory manners. Shielding the child and providing her with a clearly demarcated rule-book for life, the father offers a paradisical youth while he obscures the child's ability to create her own rules, to question rules handed down. By restricting the child, hampering him with boundaries and barriers he must not cross, the father boxes in the child but provides, at the same time, an unambiguous authority to battle, an ideology to resist, to form his own individuality in response to. The child's progress is a matter not only of the father's real or imagined strength but the child's will. There can be, in Roth, no single figure of blame pointed in any direction; choice remains the prerequisite of the child, his to take up or to surrender.

Peter Tarnopol, in *My Life as a Man*, runs from choice, flaying it in a worldview inherited from his own Lonoffian father, the father Quart describes as, "old and Jewish, full of support and embrace" (R 596). Quart's use of the word "embrace" is insightful, for like "anchor" "embrace" presumes two meanings.The embrace first comforts but as it becomes firmer and less elastic it encloses and smothers.

In "Salad Days," Tarnopol's first attempt to assess his failed life, he invents Nathan Zuckerman, a fictional surrogate of himself, to allow him the distance to revisit the past. His exorcism through writing begins, naturally enough, with an invocation of the father, the "shoedog" who "gave him Dale Carnegie to read" (3). His father's reverence for Carnegie's paradigm for living is derided by Zuckerman, but reverence for words written, for authorized and verified literary works becomes inscribed on Zuckerman's psyche, becoming as much a part of Nathan as Dale Carnegie's cliched words are a part of his hardworking father. Here, in the first lines of his first "useful fiction," Tarnopol hits upon the orienting event for Nathan which propels him towards his disastrous courtship and marriage of Lydia Ketterer (a substitute for Tarnopol's own mismatched wife, Maureen). Though it is not to his father's book that Zuckerman turns to for knowledge it is to the world of words: "Nathan would read a book called 'Of Time and the River' that was to change...his attitude...toward Life itself" (12). Looking for a model to substitute for his father's model he chooses to look in the same direction. Woolf's elegiac and romantic pages become Nathan's first guide book, the Dale Carnegie of the intellectual, the road-map for the literate boy. His father suggests a code of conduct and he rejects that code but not the idea of a code; following his father's lead he searches for that real code that will lead to meaning, to success, truth, transcendence.

Zuckerman becomes less his own man than the progeny of literature. He imagines himself "like Dilsey" enduring the hardships of life (15). Language is Zuckerman's sacrament, his palimpsest, as his father's simple ethic of hard work was for him. Jay Halio contends that "By the time young Nathan enters college as an English major, he fully asserts himself" (127). Far from asserting himself, Nathan submits himself to literature's authority. From his indoctrination at Bass College where, "the ivory on the library walls...could be heard on certain moonlit nights to whisper the word 'tradition'" (11), to his assignment as a "clerk typist" - a transcriber of words - language remains his one source of certitude (18). His faith in language is so strong it refuses to slacken even in his most carefree salad days.

Zuckerman's father, in "Courting Disaster" is a bookkeeper rather than a shoedog, and the description of him begins to crystallize in this story. As bookkeeper Mr. Zuckerman is typically "precise" and "colorless," intrigued with the beauty of the "arithmetical solution:" "thin, austere, and humorless" (36-37). Solutions, answers, are the father's creed, and the son, while running from arithmetic, regards literature with the same clinical, austere eye, looking for answers, proofs, in celebrated words. As Mr. Zuckerman is precise with his numbers, so Nathan tells his writing students to "try to be precise" with their efforts (66). Nathan is the bookkeeper's son, trying to add the sums to find meaning. "Sometimes I think that underneath all that 'maturity' you're just a crazy little boy," says Sharon Shatzky to Nathan (74). Little boy he is, his father's boy, entranced by the clarity of his father's lessons, attempting to impose that mathematical simplicity on his own life.

Behind Zuckerman's two stories stands the author, Tarnopol, who, in his fiction pronounces his attachment to his father but fails to recognize the deleterious effect that attachment has had on his own decisions, particularly his most profound decision to marry Maureen Johnson. "I read books and I wanted to write them," Tarnopol claims in his autobiographical narrative, "My True Story," the work which, in conjunction with the two fictions, allows him to wean himself of his father's influence and achieve a more distanced picture of his father's early teachings (174). Books occupy, for Tarnopol, the same sacred place they occupy for his creation. Tarnopol is longful of a "Flaubertian transcendence," an epiphany brought on not by experience but by literature (231).

As the initial event for Zuckerman is his father's mandate to read Dale Carnegie, the initial event for Tarnopol is a similar injunction, narrated in Zuckerman's story, hidden in fiction. The father is shown a signature of Nathan's. The indecipherable name looks to the man of order "like a train wreck" (4). Incoherent, it points forward to Tarnopol's manuscript, which sits in a "liquor carton," and is "defaced with x's and arrows of a hundred different intensities of pen and pencil, the margins...tattooed with comments,

reminders, with schemes for pagination" (238). The message of his manuscript, Tarnopol declares, is "Turmoil," the same message of the signature,
two signs of the self out of control (238). The father looks at the signature
and yells, "Goddam it, boy, this is your name. Sign it right!" (4). To sign his
name right, to find the words that will solidify himself, becomes Tarnopol's
exercise. That there is a right way is never in doubt. Language promises definition for those capable of exhuming it.

As his life becomes ever more complex, as definition proves more and
more difficult to uncover, Tarnopol begins to leave his "semen" in "places"
(211). "I go to the bathroom. I leave it somewhere," admits Tarnopol (211).
"Your signature," reveals Spielvogel, referring directly at the original image
that has pushed him to this point (211). The power of the father's words, so
easily overlooked and repressed, returns. The "small-time haberdasher" is
only small-time in the world; at home his power is ineluctable (198). "The
reverential bonds of childhood" are not easily transgressed (219). Tarnopol
assumes that Maureen, for all her duplicity, would not lie about "something
as serious as fatherhood" (192). Fatherhood retains it magisterial aspect for
Peter. It both propels his writing (his first novel is titled A Jewish Father) and
undermines his life. It fosters a belief in certainty which leads him into
Maureen's tormented arms.

Maureen, creative and manipulating, takes advantage of the weakened
and naive son. She promises so much - depth, surety, drama. Her words are
"uttered wholly ingenuously" (196). She means them to be "believed" (196).
They are clear signifiers linked to clear signifieds. Maureen presents herself
as the muse that will ennoble Peter. She becomes a substitute father, the
patriarch for the adult Peter. She calls him "Peppy," his childhood nickname
and promises to "make a man out of" him, taking over the role of the neg-
lected father (285).

With the death of this second father Tarnopol is given a chance to reconsider the father's role in his life. Maureen's death leaves Tarnopol mumbling
to Spielvogel, "I don't know anymore....Now the whole thing doesn't make
any sense" (327). Maureen's death, senseless, empty of thematic meaning,
challenges Tarnopol's conception of life as inherently interpretable and of
Maureen, in particular, as a vessel of meaning. She had promised truth and
structure, events leading in a codified and identifiable direction, like a work
of traditional literature, with an underlying and discernible plan. Her unexpected and violent end turns these concepts on their head. Peter says he is
"free" but freedom come not quite so easily (327). He has, in Spielvogel's
words, been "released" (327). He is now ready only to begin to answer the
stranger's question in the bookstore: "I mean - what ever happened to you?"
(236).

"My True Story" provides clues to Tarnopol's reconception of literature
and language, a reconception that leads back to the father. Towards the end
of his story Tarnopol reads Faulkner's "Nobel Prize speech from beginning
to end" (322). He thinks, "And what the hell are you talking about? How

could you write *The Sound and the Fury*, how could you write *The Hamlet*, how could you write about Temple Drake and Popeye, and write that?" (322). Faulkner is knocked from his pedestal. The former Tarnopol would never think to question one of the immortals of the literary pantheon. But Tarnopol's reverence for literature has been chastened. He no longer seeks the perfect signature, the faultless guide book.

"Maybe all I'm saying," writes Tarnopol, in an imaginary letter to Karen Oakes, "is that words, being words, only approximate the real thing" (231). Words have lost their talismanic power. And if the longing for language can be reevaluated so too the impetus behind that longing, the father's lessons, can be reinterpreted. The book ends with a long conversation between Peter and his parents. "At least now listen to your family once," says the father, and Peter answers, "Okay, I will" (330). But his acquiescence is followed by a quick "hanging up" (330). He listens but he now makes his own decisions. The father's words are not to be ignored, but neither are they words of scripture. Peter becomes "his own lord and master" for the first time, neither slave to his father nor in complete rebellion from him (330). A middle-ground has been reached: Literature is just literature, the Father only a father.

Tarnopol is, like Kafka, a son who might cry to his father, "My writing is all about you; all I did there, after all, was to bemoan what I could not bemoan upon your breast" (POD 166). His cries, whether for Maureen or in the guise of Zuckerman, have been cries to the father.

Kepesh recognizes his own attachment to this Kafkaesque image of the son - he visits Prague to commune with its spirit. Like Hermann Kafka, Mr. Kepesh is the Mosaic dad" (8), the man of rules who has led an "exemplary life" (245), who can tell the Pipikian father, Herbie, "it's simple - the shofar is for the High Holidays and the other stuff is for the toilet. Period, Herbie. Finished" (6). David admits to an affinity for his father's steadfastness, admits to "a feel for the rules and preferences of society" (8). Structure seems as promising as desire and role-playing for the developing professor. Kepesh wants a role as tight-fitting and right as his father's perceived role as father.

Kepesh's relentless motion is surely a "solemn undertaking," for it is rooted in a desire for closure (18). Towards that end Kepesh focuses on one distinguishable characteristic of his associates and stamps them as this one thing. Birgitta is the "whore," the representation of "The mythology of the Swedish girl and her sexual freedom" (29). Elizabeth Elverskog is the epitome of the vulnerable, the "weak" (33), the "innocently simple-minded" (32), "pliable" (35), "trusting" naif (43). Helen Baird is an "unbelievable character," with a "corny and banalized mentality deriving from Screen Romance" (56), "a dramatic young heroine" (64), a "Carmen" (57), a "Cleopatra," and an actress in a "trashy grade-B thriller" (92). Claire Ovington is the "shy," "supremely innocent and guileless" (151), "devoted girl" (241).[5] Their onedimentionality is directly attributable not to their actions but to Kepesh's vision.

David wants to be able to say simply and with confidence, "All this is wrong, son. It is no way to live," as his father does (114). He wants clear pictures, clear judgments, clear roles, a clear notion of self. Abe Kepesh hears the young homosexual yelling in the intercom and says, "I'll crack his head open," while his son is unable to make a move to remove the intruder (155). When his wife dies, his son is sure that "In a few days he will be himself. He has to be, that's all there is to it" (117). So simple and straight forward and yet difficult for David. "You tighten your belt and you go on," says the father, as son languishes, desperately, frantically trying on roles, reading, traveling, talking, writing, moving from woman to woman, and all to find a seamless sureness similar to that which his father has always possessed (117).

Sureness, though, keeps its distance from the striving son, ever receding and then reappearing. Only while lecturing in the classroom does Kepesh approximate his goal. If he cannot find fixed meaning in the world, he can impose one upon the classroom.[6] For Kepesh the role of Professor is simple and undeviating; the Professor is the interpreter, the disciplinarian, the authority, the figure at the exact center of the hierarchy of the classroom. To be a professor is to control the language of the students, control the syllabus, to move dialogue toward a declarable goal. To be Professor, then, is to be the father, but for Kepesh it is a title more wished for than owned, for it does not transcend the one-hour duration of the class; it disappears with the closing of the books.

A more durable order settles on Kepesh on Labour Day weekend. In the last fifty pages of the novel all its elements have come together, reconciling, momentarily, all the tensions Kepesh has felt. For a moment the contradictions are subdued; they merge together and enact for Kepesh a preview of where the longed for clarity will lead. Abe is present, Helen has appeared, Claire remains by his side. David asks himself -watching a parade of the past wander through his mind - "And whose next, I wonder? When I sit down at my place for dinner, will there be an extra place at the table for Birgitta?" (249).

The images come together, the voice reaches its most perfect pitch, its most heartfelt and sincere. There is, in that instant, a felt sense of satiation and closure, as if everything had at last formed a perfect wholeness. But what does this wholeness confer on David? Not fulfillment and joy but fright and terror. "Why should I feel as though I have lost a bloody battle when clearly I have won?" Kepesh asks (250). He sits in a veritable garden of Eden, with "apple-smooth, apple-small, apple-shiny, apple-plain, apple-fresh" Claire, the "perfect young woman" and "the most livable of lives," and what does his mind turn to - death (251): "I wait to hear the most dreadful sound imaginable emerge from the room where Mr. Barbatnik and my father lie alone and insensate, each in his freshly made bed" (263).

Closure becomes consonant with death, satiation equals irretrievable endings, wholeness means life is done. When all is reconciled there is not bliss but emptiness, when there is no more to search for there is no hope. David has found the inevitable end of the Lonoffian ideology, an ideology that can only lead to stagnancy, to the end of questioning, the end of movement, to death. It is of the father's death he first thinks because it is the father who he has followed to this end. The sterility of the belief in absolutes, in definitiveness, in the self as an absolute and sturdy figure who does not change and cannot grow, shows itself in all its horror to Kepesh as he lies in Claire's arms aware, finally, where his father's path must lead.

Ideology pulls the needy son promising him so much, presenting the distinct image of a paradise found, a paradise not unlike the remembered childhood when doubts disappeared with a father's look. The self is smothered, lost in Truth. "Me no longer exists out here," Henry Zuckerman tells his brother in Israel, explaining his decision to abandon his family and join a Jewish settlement in Judea (CL 118). Another son desperate for the potency of the lost father, Henry finds a replacement in the nationalist ideology of Mordecai Lippman. "There isn't time for me, there isn't need of me," he tells his secular brother in *The Counterlife* (118). "Not me - we. That's where Henry's me had gone," thinks Nathan (118).

Sexual impotence propels Henry deeper into the heart of the Lonoffian darkness. The "single terrible side effect" of a medication he is taking for his heart is impotence (1). Henry experiences impotence as an exile from self, from his life lived as the "father's best son," the dentist son of the chiropodist father (126). Potency, "never seriously questioned" before, is stripped from him and he feels disinherited (5). The desire for surety, for a center like the one imposed upon "a dutiful and acquiescent child by a dogmatic, superconventional father," becomes his sole desire (84). To regain his lost potency he is willing to risk everything, risk even his life in a dangerous bypass operation. "You can't leave them fatherless," cautions Henry's wife, Carol (7). But in that very sentence she leads him towards the operation and subsequently his death. To leave the children fatherless, her words imply, is to leave them without a center to hold their lives together. That Carol, too, views fatherhood in this very narrow, traditional, way convinces him that a father is not a father without his potency. If he cannot provide them with the image of the father - the image of his own father - he need not exist for them.

Henry wishes to be a "tabula rosa," to be a child again, no longer plagued by time, or questions, or meaninglessness (9). He longs to "Bring it all back...the sixties, the fifties, the forties" (8). He longs for a return of "his most innocent years," years following the dictates of of the father (8). Nathan recognizes the reason for his brother's entrancement by Lippman. "It's Dad," he tells Henry, now renamed "Hanoch" (121), as if given a second birth, "but the dream-Dad, supersized, raised to the hundredth power" (155). Henry has recreated the father, "the omnipresent Victor Zuckerman," and has "enslaved" himself to him (125). He moves into "Abraham's bosom," becoming the son who subsists on the dogmatic authority of the father, who nourishes himself on his father's potency (125).

"There is another world," Henry/Hanoch tells Nathan, "a larger world, a world of ideology, of politics, of history" (117). And it is to this ideological world that Lippman promises entrance. The liberal Shuki explains Lippman's movement as tinged with "fascism," and it is to this fascist element that Henry is drawn (84). The fascist longing, the longing to be part of a whole, to be led, is the child's dream. To gain control one gives oneself to another's control. To attain potency Henry relinquishes his potency to Lippman, to find his self Henry makes his self vanish. The son is devoured by the father.

Kepesh uncovers one result of the Lonoffian quest and Henry reveals its converse. If Kepesh finds stagnation, death, and impotency, then Henry finds the possibility of murder, potency in action. The gun that Henry carries, and that Nathan cannot take his eyes off, tells us where Lippman's ideology will inevitably lead. The Lonoffian dream makes murder a viable option in the march towards salvation. Once someone or something is designated "enemy" or "worthless," or "inhuman" he can be guiltlessly extinguished. From Joseph de Maistre, who Isaiah Berlin deems the originator of fascism, till now the ideologue has found little reason for not using his rightness to wipe clean those categorized as filth, degenerates, or unworthies. Following the father's creed, latching himself to a new, more powerful father, Henry straps on his gun and gives his fidelity to someone who might direct him to use it.

Vibrancy and hope are denied to Henry who obfuscates his vision, turns his eyes from anything that raises doubt. The subservient son, still, Henry will never grow. Nathan - angry, voracious Nathan - with Maria's aid, comes to a more open, more enlivening view of his world. He comes to accept the relentless movement back and forth between security and vulnerability. "Things don't have to reach a peak," Maria tells him (218). "They can just go on" (218). Though Nathan is as entranced by the certainty of his father as Henry, he can never give himself firmly to it, can never silence the questions. His is the stance of the combatant who both loves and hates his father. Nathan learns to let his life flow and recede, to countenance the disharmony and live within it. "It isn't necessary," Maria tells him, "to give things a shape" (218). Never to know the ideological fullness of his brother or father, Nathan, from his initial realization in *The Ghost Writer* to his more profound theorizing in *The Counterlife*, grows into an autonomous self, longing for authenticity but more conscious of the creative and humanizing gifts of unauthenticity.

The Henry of "Basel" and "Judea" ends his story as stagnant as the body in Barry Shuskin's cryonic fantasy, "frozen like a lamb chop" (49). Though Nathan grants him a new narrative in "Gloucestershire," it is an alternative existence the ideologic Henry could never anticipate or recognize. Nathan concludes one of his own narratives aware of and alert to "transition" and transformation (371). The last image invoked is that of his "erection, the circumcised erection of the Jewish father" (371). But, for Nathan, the image is no longer of fatherly potency. Having discarded his "innocent vision of fatherhood" (309), having declared himself "not one of those Jews who want to hook themselves up to the patriarchs" (365), the circumcised penis no longer represents the father's limitless, undeniable strength, the father's inherent promise of "redemption" (369). Instead, "Circumcision makes it clear as can be that you are here and not there, that you are out and not in" (370). Unity is impossible and finally anathema to Nathan who sees its malignancy in his brother's fate.

Circumcision, Zuckerman adds, as a coda, makes it clear "also that you're mine and not theirs. There is no way around it: you enter history through my history and me" (370). His is not an outright refutation of fatherhood and tradition but rather an acceptance of its strengths and limits, of the structure it provides and of the submission it demands. His patrimony, he knows, cannot be thrown off, nor can it be worn like a protective cloak. He reaches an accommodation with the dead father in "Christendom," a balance first discovered while standing on E.I. Lonoff's mountain over twenty years earlier.

In *Zuckerman Unbound* Nathan is suffering from a deep need to leave his past behind and find a new "Home" (ZU 171). Zuckerman is the marginalized Jew, marginalized by history and by the desire to forget that history; exiled from both his past and the contemporary world. Home, for Zuckerman, is something in the future, something new and unconnected to all that stands behind him, personified by Victor Zuckerman, the dying father who, Zuckerman is told, "was always there behind you" (ZU 67). His concerted effort to leave behind whatever once ground him down, whatever once restricted him, leads him to this vast purgatorial wasteland. "From what," Zuckerman asks himself, "in God's name are you in flight?" (56): From fame, from art, from the father's history, the bitter admonitions, from death.

Death becomes the central obsession for Zuckerman as he concerns himself more and more with the unforgettable image of his father lying unconscious in his bed. It is Victor Zuckerman, his body and his Lonoffian philosophy - "all that he was dead to" - leading Nathan toward death (197). On his deathbed the oppressor lies mute, nothing left of the formidable foe Nathan has described. He is the picture of all Zuckerman wants to renounce; the face of the tormented and airless past and the face of the decrepit and morbid future.

"You are no longer any man's son," he reminds himself (223). The past is past, his father gone, presumably to be pushed from memory. "Enough of fathers and sons," Zuckerman announces, exhausted, liberated (192). He feels as "exultation" leaving Miami and his father behind for good (197). Feeling as though his entrapment has ended forever, Zuckerman tells himself to "Forget fathers....Plural" (198). All fathers, all figures of stability and purpose are rejected. They are not even objects to contemplate. They simply cease to exist with the one father. "All that respectable moralizing," Zuckerman remarks, "all that repressive sermonizing, all those superfluous prohibitions, that furnace of pieties, that Lucifer of rectitude, that Hercules of misunderstanding, extinguished" (196). The god-like father is vanquished and all barriers incarnated in his worn body are are overturned. Zuckerman is fully free, he believes, fully unbounded.

The symbol of structure laid to rest, Zuckerman turns his back on all structure. What has made him an artist, the tense, painful pull between the claims of the father and the claims of the son, is put aside in a relentless search for freedom, freedom from "the grip of time" which "seizes everything finite just the same" (96). He runs from the father, runs from death, and in that flight he finds that he has run from all that made him an individual and a writer. He is left with no deity, no center, no hope, left without a subject, an identity, a vocation, left only a fragile body. Unbound he is but with nothing to hold onto and with nothing to remember.

Nathan is left to "drift, just drift," to "surrender to surrender," and we find him adrift in *The Anatomy Lesson*, his body, the last vestige of his former self, aching in undiagnosable pain (AL 37). Without terms of meaning a cure cannot be found, a reason for the incapacitating agony that leaves him prostrate on the floor of his apartment. He is a nonentity, "No longer a son, no longer a writer" (41). His father, for all his hard-headed dogmatism, has fascinated the son, written the writer, and without him Nathan feels himself a "nothing fellow" (67). "He had begun to believe that if it hadn't been for his father's frazzled nerves and rigid principles and narrow understanding he'd never have been a writer at all" (40).

Roland Barthes argues, "The Death of the Father would deprive literature of many of its pleasures" (47). For Zuckerman the father's death weakens his creative drives; with nothing left to fight, argue with, combat, and with no one acknowledged power to submit to or to confound, with no past to pull one's nightmares from or to exorcise the writer is left without a "subject," without even the desire to create (AL 39). Nathan's body collapses upon itself, the puppeteer's strings, which manipulated and controlled it, gone and there is nothing left to hold him up.

Nathan has entered his "second life," but a second life with no origins, no memory (109). The vacuity of his new life reeks havoc upon his blood and bones demanding a return of the father, a return of meaning. One by one Nathan tries to invent new fathers: Dr. Kotler, who is "sizable" and "weighted" (113), Milton Appel, the tormentor who is addicted to "scolding" and to "verdicts" and "judgments" (165), and finally, Mr. Freytag, "the last of the old-fashioned fathers," who becomes, in the cemetery, the very embodiment of Victor Zuckerman (280). In what is ostensibly an attempt at symbolic (or indeed real) patricide, Zuckerman "pounced upon the old man's neck" (261), yelling with all his tremulous ardor, "Freytag! Forbidder! Now I murder you" (263). The pathetic figure of a young man so weakened by his own hand is not a figure of fury but of resignation. His outburst is an acknowledgement of the father's ubiquity.

"Honor thy Finkelstein! do not commit Kaufman! Make no idols in the form of Levine! Thou shalt not take in vain the name of Katz," screams the son, satirizing the self-importance of the elder Jews, their imagined power (263). They treat themselves as idols not to be destroyed or disobeyed; they are the prophets of the law. Their power subsists beyond the grave. "These bones in boxes," exclaims Nathan, "are the Jewish living. These are the people running the show!" (262) But it is less a cry of remonstrance than it is a cry for their return, as if the words he speaks make the sentiment true. The father is returned.

For Nathan's next move is not an expiation of the past but a return to it. He sees himself, now, as a doctor roaming "the busy corridors of the university hospital" (291), submitting to a "clear and practical" profession, dealing in stories with a "definite, useful, authoritative conclusion" (109). He finds peace in the "unassailable solidity of a medical vocation" (110). Having imagined himself cast off from the father, he reimagines himself enfolded back within the Lonoffian arms of the dead Doc Zuckerman. He becomes the new Doc Zuckerman. Updike argues that Zuckerman's demons are "not exorcised," rather they are reclaimed (OJ 372). Updike declares Zuckerman's aspiration "to become a nice good-doing doctor" as "knuckling under" (OJ 372).

Being Nathan and not Henry his failure is not complete. Unlike the brother he imagines locked away in his box of marriage, or his box of messianic religiosity, or the actual box of death, Nathan's great virtue is his awareness of his defeats. In *The Prague Orgy* Nathan's questioning voice returns to retrieve him, in the tones of a diary writer, the innocent form of Anne Frank, the ghost which ranges through *Zuckerman Bound*.

As Anne Frank's legacy made plain to Nathan the insidiousness of his critics' attacks, the shallowness of his own longings, and the impossibility of the Lonoffian aesthetic, so too Prague's preposterous history, its fantasy-like reality, returns Nathan to himself.[7] All preconceptions are undone in Prague. Here, Nathan thinks, "there's no nonsense about purity and goodness" (470). It makes a lie of the Lonoffian quest, and gives evidence of where that quest must lead, has led, how ideology has deracinated a world. To follow the father's mold is to become one with the "sleek, well-groomed, dark-eyed" authority whose power is masked with a "smile," and who has the ability to decide if one is "fiction or fact," to decide if one is human (471-472).

Like Anne Frank's memory, Prague awakens the slumbering boy, turns him both towards his past and away, enables him to accept it without dissolving into it. "One's story isn't a skin to be shed," he thinks, "it's inescapable, one's body and blood" (470). In his diary Zuckerman begins a retrieval of the freedom he found on Lonoff's hill, a freedom he can now name, using his new-found knowledge to understand and write his past.

His desperate need for his father's approval is gone. He can turn back without shading his eyes and see his father in all his weakness and in all his intractability. He can address his father's ghost not as the guiless upstart of *The Ghost Writer* who flees on a bus, nor as a slave aching for the blessing of the dictatorial father, but as an individual torn between love and hate, admiration and fear. He doesn't want, he claims in *The Counterlife*, to chain himself to his father, but nor "is it my intention to simplify that connection" (370). He has decried the "innocent (and comical) vision of fatherhood," and has come to a more sophisticated and ambiguous vision (369). He is "divided," but division is not a sign of "mental illness" but of "health" (365). Division implies possibility, fission, tension, not a pandering to an image, nor an effusive and complete withdrawal. The father is reintegrated and reappraised by the son whose complex interrogation gives new life to both.

To reach and accept a balanced picture of the father is no easy task for Roth's sons and daughters. The fathers are almost wholly envisioned as Pipikian or Lonoffian with little room for variation. Even as Nathan learns to accept the father he still understands him as a particular type of man. Even as he balances dual yearnings within himself he sees the father as singular. Even as he recognizes the positive aspects of both - the Lonoffian fathers' tenacity, their "Never say Die" attitude toward the world of anomie, and the Pipikian fathers' heartfulness and warmth, their seeming freedom - he fails to see the father as differentiated.

The father image, in Roth, must be studied as divided into two segments, but a full study cannot end there. Roth's weakness, in his very eloquent study of fathers and children, is his inability or unwillingness, as yet, to create a narrative with the father as the mediating voice. Even in *American Pastoral*, Roth's eloquent exploration of the mistakes of a father, Swede Levov, he requires Zuckerman's imaginative intervening to tell the story. Roth's novels are novels of children, not of fathers, and as such the father always is blocked from the reader by the son's words. The son is loathe to see the duality of the father. And yet there are moments when the father breaks free from his set role. In a novelist as earnest and ambiguous as Roth, as set against absolute interpretation, even the father manages to escape his confines.

Victor Zuckerman, he who disclaims his son's achievements, his betrayal of Jews, who castigates his son for his besmirchment of history, is said to have "always defended" Nathan to others (ZU 70-71). Their relationship, Nathan asserts, was surfeit with "tender emotion" as well as animosity (AL 40). Kepesh states clearly his own misreading of his father. In *The Breast*, he admits, "My father's behavior has been staggering. I don't know how to account for it, except to say that I simply never knew the man" (29).

The father is more than a Lonoff or a Pipik; he is also the interlocutor of language. His is the voice of poetry and of the vernacular. "Take a good deep breath," Jake Portnoy tells his son, "Take in the piney air all the way....good winter piney air" (29). For Alex the words bring forth a transcendental sensation. "I couldn't have been more thrilled if I were Wordsworth's kid," he remarks, dreaming of his father's poetry (29). And in his ungrammatical moments he teaches his son the beauty of speech, the language Portnoy uses to surmount his anxiety. Of his own father Roth writes, "He was the vernacular, unpoetic and expressive and pointblank, with all the vernacular's glaring limitations and all its durable force" (P 181). And is not *Portnoy's Complaint*, and so much of Roth's oeuvre, an attempt to merge the vernacular and the poetic, to bring together the written and the spoken word, the language so reminiscent of his astounding father?

The father remembers his own past and creates his son's past. The sons are inscribed by Newark, by their first homes, by the world discussed over the kitchen table. "I felt a deep knowledge of Newark," Neil Klugman states, "an attachment so rooted that it could not help but branch out into affection" (31). Newark is the father's domain, where he "remains" while the rest of the Portnoy family goes to the country in the summer (29). And the degradation of Newark echoes the degradation and decline of the father.

"The past dies these days, does it," the father asks disdainfully, feeling his body slip away, evidence of time's deadening strength (POD 244). The father is the most palpable symbol, in Roth, of this degeneration and of death. Mr. Herz is said to be "within an earshot of eternity" (166). David Kepesh buys "portable oxygen units" to prevent his father's death, and then lies awake listening for the the noise of dying (POD 263). Victor Zuckerman's incapacitated body surprises Nathan with the knowledge of how "utterly helpless his protector could be" (ZU 183). Jake Portnoy reminds his son, "you'll get old" (110). And in *Patrimony*, Roth's most elaborate and beguiling portrait of a father, Herman Roth seems to ask both the doctor and his son, "Why...should a man die at all?" (134). There is no answer, not for the son or the father: The father is the harbinger of the son's death, the constant reminder, foretelling the future as he shaped the past.

Only memory can battle death and time, only memory can save the past, but even its power is limited. "My memory is no good anymore," says Herman to his son (P 84). Memory dissolves with the body, but it is memory that can be passed on, that can bind son to father. And it is memory that Herman teaches his son; that is the patrimony. "You mustn't forget anything - that was the inscription of his coat of arms," Roth writes (P 124). "To be alive, to him, is to be made of memory - to him if a man's not made of memory, he's made of nothing" (P 124).

Roth's writing sings with memory, with the son's need to record, to hold onto his own past and his father's past, to use literature as an accessory to remembrance. "I must remember accurately," Roth tells himself, "remember everything accurately so that when he is gone I can re-create the father who created me" (P 177).

In *The Anatomy Lesson* Zuckerman thinks, "A first generation American father possessed by the Jewish demons, a second generation American son possessed by their exorcism - that was his whole story" (40). Not

Zuckerman's and not Roth's whole story, the remembrance and exorcism of a dark past does reverberate in Zuckerman's adventures and in Roth's writings. Roth's father's repertoire of memory is said to have contained only three items: "Family, family, family, Newark, Newark, Newark, Jew, Jew, Jew" (TF 16). Each provides identity but is equally surrounded by darkness and pain. It is the last item, though, that overwhelms the others. "To me," Roth writes, "being a Jew had to do with a real historical predicament into which you were born" (TF 126). That predicament has less to do with assimilation and tradition - the pull of America versus the pull of religious identity - then it has to do with history, with the world crumbling while the young boys in Newark do their homework, argue, masturbate, survive. Zuckerman locates only "two points of reference in all the vastness" for his father: "the family and Hitler" (ZU 199). Hitler's Holocaust instills terror and the determination to remember into the sons and fathers. Herman Roth's cry to memory is not only for the memory of his streets and his compatriots but expands beyond, as does Roth's novelistic memory.

Like Eli Peck, in Roth's early story, "Eli the Fanatic,"the father compels the son to remember a particular past. "I'm your father," Eli tells his newborn son (297). Wearing the clothes of a concentration-camp survivor, he promises his little boy, "And when you're old enough, I'll get you one, and you'll walk with me" (298). The son will, if not become the father, salvage something of the father's identity. "You can go some place that makes Woodenton look like a slum, but you'll wear it. And you'll make your son wear it, wherever he goes" (298). As the distance grows between father and child only an act of memory returns the father, only an act of memory can keep the past intact. "Remember," cries Eli, "Remember," cries Herman Roth over thirty years later.

Memory is the tissue of Roth's fiction and the tissue of the father's life. It cements a connection not only tragic but joyful. Memory implants the contradictions of life. The father's lessons are of the satisfaction of hard work balanced against the inevitability of failure, the beauty of the quotidian balanced against its pain, the simple tranquility of a single moment balanced against that moment's disappearance, laughter balanced against contemplation, the past balanced against the present, resistance balanced against capitulation. It expresses the very attributes one needs to survive intact in the concentrationary universe.

"Little by little, I took everything back," Roth writes of his father's trifles (P 90). *Patrimony* attests to the reclamation not only of relics but of the father and his story. *Patrimony* is a memoir of how that story becomes the author's own. The father is "omnipresent" in life and in death, his presence deepening even as he disappears (TF 16). Roth quotes I.B. Singer's remark about his brother, claiming that like Singer's brother his father's "presence becomes greater and greater with each passing year" (CWPR 269). Like the Holocaust, which even as it recedes in time retains its hold on memory, the father, the bastion of that memory, continues to tell his tale through the son.

"God, you are your father's son, aren't you?" asks Philip's mistress in *Deception* (83). "Whose should I be instead?" he responds (83). The son's bond to his father is everywhere apparent in Roth. It repels and propels, holds back and sets free; it creates the son and allows the son to create himself, letting all the dichotomies and complexities merge together, leaving the son to construct his world from that melange. "My history still takes its spin from beginning as his Roth," the son admits (TF 19).

"Well," says the bemused mistress, "it's just all a bit of a surprise, after reading your books" (D 83).

"Is it?" asks Philip - answering for Gabe Wallach, Paul Herz, David Kepesh, Lucy Nelson, Neil Klugman, Brenda Patimkin, Peter Tarnopol, Nathan Zuckerman, Henry Zuckerman, and Roth himself - "Read 'em again" (83).

THE MOST UNFORGETTABLE CHARACTER

Olenka, the heroine of Chekhov's dazzling story "The Darling" is defined always by her relationship with some other. She is daughter, niece, student, wife, widow, and finally surrogate mother. She has few ideas of her own but a seemingly inexhaustible capacity to give love, and her life takes on meaning from the objects of her love. To understand the world of "The Darling" is to peak inside the minds and memories of the sons and daughters of Roth's books. No cliched liberated mother occupies center stage. Mrs. Patimkin, Mrs. Kepesh, Mrs. Tarnopol, Mrs. Portnoy, and Mrs. Zuckerman exist on the perimeters of the social world. They are reliant upon another, prisoners of connection.

Mrs. Patimkin sits in her fruit-filled home, free only so far as her husband allows her to be free. Mrs. Zuckerman lives as a compilation of her sons and husband: Sitting in a restaurant, surveying a menu "she would have thought: 'This is what Victor would order. This is what Nathan would order. This is what Henry would order.' Only then would she order for herself" (AL 48). Her life evolves from her men; she is the sum of those she loves. "My husband," she would tell the waitress, "loved ocean scallops. If they're fresh, and nice big ones, I'll have the ocean scallops, please" (AL 48). There is a certain forlorn beauty in that scene, the resiliency of what is gone and yet still remembered, the voice of the dead revived, but it mostly speaks of a condition of enslavement that one must recognize to understand the portrayal of mothers throughout Roth's works. Of his parents Zuckerman remarks, "Once a year they quarreled....Otherwise she never opposed him; however he did things was right" (Al 174). This subservience is not a product of an individual weakness but is part of a cultural pattern which harks backwards in time.

In *When She Was Good*, Willard's mother, "could never conceive of wanting anything other than what she had; or if she did, it was really other than she seemed, she felt it was not prudent to speak of her desires in front of her husband" (3). The tradition moves from the old-world of Chekhov's servicing darling to the new wilderness of America. And it is inherited - like the memory of the father - passed down from woman to woman, from mother to daughter.

Willard's wife longs for the "old days," the old ways, the times of ease, when a mother's role was simple and sure (251). Mrs. Tarnopol is virtually drowned out by her husband's loquaciousness; she "listened in silence" as he advised Peter (328). In *The Professor of Desire* David's mother is early described as the victim of a "slave driver" husband (15). "Once she marries," her son declares, "she is brought "to the brink of nervous collapse by the end of each summer" (15), a summer in which "she yelps and yipes like a sheep dog whose survival depends upon driving his master's unruly flock to market" (16). Mrs. Herz, in *Letting Go*, is ordered to serve and stand by her dying husband even in his most absurd pronouncements, and is only able to reconcile with Paul after Mr. Herz's death. She has a "bitter, drawn " and "spiritless" face, her color a "brownish-gray;" her pallor evidence of the disease of servitude (166).

Like Hope Lonoff, these mothers are victims of their confinement, their lack of worldly transaction, their voicelessness beyond their four walls. Their silence is consonant with their position as representatives of the concentrationary-world: disempowered, dispirited, marginalized. Even Sophie Portnoy - the oppressor, the mother who would seem to give lie to the supposition of the mother's secondary status - even she, who seems to take on the father's role ("But what a mix-up of the sexes in our home," Portnoy whines (41)) exerts little power outside the the confines of the kitchen, the bathroom, and the bedroom. It is the father who goes out into the world, the father who, though he fails, is allowed the possibility of worldly success. If the world has overwhelmed him he is at least within the world, in battle, fighting on. Barbara Quart recognizes Alex's "pride in the maleness of his father's body, the size of his forearms, of his genitals" (215). The father's thickness is an inversion of the mothers femaleness, her eternal link to the ephemeral.

Sophie, when first introduced, appears to be "between incarnations" (3), "making herself emerge, limb by limb, out of an invisible state and into her apron" (4). It is this semi-visible state which defines the mothers, a personage present and absent, never consistent, never completely there. She is, as Zuckerman says of his mother, "diaphanous in recollection," first "a breast, then a lap, then a fading voice calling after him, 'Be Careful.' Then a long gap when there is nothing of her to remember, just an invisible somebody" (AL 47). The trope of invisibility moves from *Portnoy's Complaint* to *The Anatomy Lesson*, the mother held back by her liquidity, and when transformed merely into an apron, the cloth of the homemaker.

Chekhov's 1898 portrait serves well Roth's America. Mothers born twenty years later, and in a vastly different continent, come to define themselves in the same terms as Olenka, the sweet and solicitous caregiver. And yet, dependent, submissive, weak as she is, Olenka is resilient and persevering, using her limited role to exert whatever power she can. Thomas Winer and Karl Krammar locate a certain "despotism that Olenka exercises in her relationships" (112). In Roth, the mother, too, has a despotic side, the despotism of the powerless and the aggrieved, the despotism of the victim.

The mother assaults from an unexpected angle. "If not for me, how could you do that to your father" Mrs. Patimkin asks, shielding herself behind the bulky figure of her husband (129). "You are my son and whatever you decide is right. However you live is right," Mrs. Zuckerman tells Nathan, adding, "As long as you know what you're doing" (ZU 73). Quietly, almost without notice, as an afterthought, the mother makes her disappointment known.

Virtue, goodness, love, the warmth of food, the soft touch of healing, are turned on their heads, used not only to administer but to impede. "Upon my shoulders was the velvet touch of my mother," the young narrator of "The Fence," a college-story of Roth's, remembers (14). But that touch is not only soft and comforting, it is also a grasp that holds back, keeps the boy away from the children on the other side of the fence. Olenka's ward, Sasha, feels her love as an aggression even into his sleep wherein he cries, "Get away," to the sheltering mother (22). Her ability to control is commensurate with, indeed it is dependent upon, her ability to express love. "I picked a virtue early and hung on to it," Mrs. Wallach writes (2). Virtue is used not only to heal but to "push and pull at people" (2). Mrs. Portnoy says she is "too good" (123). Her goodness is also her tyranny and it is a tyranny not easily routed for it is rooted in that very goodness, in virtue itself, in care.

Care begins at home, with food; food, that most innocuous and necessary substance, forms an essential tie between mother and child. Aunt Gladys, in "Goodbye, Columbus," seems a slave to her kitchen, preparing "four different meals" each night, but cooking is far from servitude; it is, in fact, her one exercise of strength, the kitchen her provenance of authority (4). In the kitchen she is the master. "Twenty years I'm running a house," says Gladys, sure in her lair, before the stove, more confident here than anywhere else (5). During Neil's meal his aunt sits over him, criticizing his eating habits, making sure he does justice to her food. Neil eats as if under surveillance, feeling the "heat of the food in my face" (5). The heat tells the reader of a "warmth," as Jonathan Raban puts it, between Neil and his aunt (923). Warmth, though, also connotes the suffocating closeness Neil wants to escape.

Mrs. Zuckerman and Mrs. Kepesh, sweet and noiseless women, show their own willfulness with food. "What violence she practiced," says Zuckerman about his mother, "went into making dinner" (ZU 175). Food becomes an opportunity to transform marginality into power. In *The Professor of Desire*, Mrs. Kepesh brings her son "some two-dozen round plastic containers of cabbage soup, matzoh-ball soup, Kugel, and flanken, all frozen and neatly labeled" (106). A gift, a last expression of love from a dying mother, it is also a controlled act of aggression. Its message is a criticism of his inability to fend for himself. Looking into his refrigerator "she groans as though her throat has just been slit. '"One this and one that, and that's it?' she cries" (106). He has failed as a man, her words of loving concern imply. He is still a boy. She gives to take away, provides in order to say what she is barred from speaking.

"She cooked for you," David's father says, after her death, "and then she went away" (117). Food is her inheritance to him, a sign of her love and of her disappointment, of her weakness and her hidden strength. David returns home, after the funeral, with a "half-dozen containers each bearing the same typewritten label: 'Tongue with Grandma's famous raisin sauce - 2 portions'" (117). Food draws forth the past; it is memory made tangible, expressing continuity and absence at once just as it expresses the mother's fealty and her tyranny; its ambiguity leaves the son with a mixed legacy, a mixed remembrance of the mother.

No mother, in Roth's work, is associated more with food than the eponymous Sophie Portnoy. Food is the first principle in Alex's relationship with his mother, and it inaugurates his more sophisticated complaints. "Invariably," Portnoy tells Spielvogel, at the start of his session, "she was already in the kitchen by the time I arrived, and setting out my milk and cookies" (3). The set table is always miraculously there and ready to be used by the indulged and beloved son. "What is more thrilling," asks Alex, "then to hear 'Aunt Jenny' coming over the kitchen radio and to smell cream of tomato soup heating up on the stove?" (173).

The comfort, though, is supplemented by a feeling of Sophie's diabolical control. Sophie's power manifests itself, through a child's eye, in food. Her setting of the table "intensified my respect for her powers," Portnoy explains (3). "She could make jello," he relates, still amazed, "for instance, with sliced peaches hanging in it, peaches just suspended there, in defiance of the law of gravity. She could bake a cake that tasted like a banana" (11). Alex remembers his mother "expertly bleeding the chocolate in and out of the vanilla;" nothing less than a "miracle" in Alex's eyes (44). He sees himself as a "total slave to her kugel and grieken and ruggelech" (96). Mrs. Portnoy is, according to the son, "God's mouthpiece on earth in matters pertaining to food" (90). And what does this culinary omniscience do to the child? Does it offer him a surfeit of warm memories of a mother's slavish devotion to a child's health and pleasure, her great care in the kitchen only for him? Certainly it offers that, but at the same time it takes away something. It turns the child, Portnoy says, into a "Fruitcake," a weak and impotent son reined in by the mother's goodness (125). Symptomatic of Portnoy's illness he uses the language of food, his mother's tongue, to denounce his mother's actions. Always in her domain Portnoy finds little avenue for escape, if full escape is indeed what he wants.

Alex is overwhelmed by food and all it connotes. "Food," as Mark Shechner points out, "is the first medium of love and authority" (123). Portnoy feels it as a noose around his neck which fits comfortably at first but tightens with time. To resist its power, and consequently the mother's power, Alex looks in two directions. First he refuses to eat, closing his mouth, expressing his own "willfulness" (15). But not eating offers him little solace. It only intensifies his mother's ruthlessness, as she stands over him with a "long bread knife in her hand" (16). And yet that abuse is remembered as an attempt at beneficence. "She is only asking me to do something for my own good," Portnoy tells his doctor (16). Like the "kosher laws" which introduce "limits" but only for the good of the practitioner, the mother's seeming violence is for the child's betterment (82). It is this dichotomy, goodness holding a knife not to hurt but to heal, danger clothed in saintliness, that throws Portnoy into his fits of madness.

The second method of rebellion can be called chazerai ingestion. For Sophie chazerai is an abomination, a cancer. Chazerai, junk-food, is pronounced "just as she might say Hitler" (33). Any breaking of a rule brings to mind a betrayal far more sinister. Chazerai is danger: "There are plenty of good things to eat in the world, Alex," his mother warns, "without eating a thing like a lobster and running the risk of having paralyzed hands for the rest of your life" (94). For the son, as Shechner argues, "chazerai symbolizes freedom," an assertion of self (124). But that assertion is still in Sophie's milieu. Breaking a rule gives credence to that rule; disobeying the food-injuction is only effective as long as that injunction has validity.

And, for Alex, chazerai is not simply a means of freedom. It is also associated with loneliness, with parentlessness, squalor. Smolka, who "lives on Hostess cupcakes," who "drinks coffee and eats donuts" for breakfast is not a person to be envied but to be pitied (173). Alex finally asserts the same contemptuous attitude toward chazerai eaters as his mother. He sees them not as freedom-loving individuals but animals unable to control or put limits on what they ingest. The strictness of his mother and other Jewish mothers compares favorably to the "idiocy of the goyim" (144), who "know absolutely nothing of human boundaries and limits," who eat and eat, without any regard for health or morality, who would devour his past (182). Chazerai offers no escape, but rather a return home to the laws and language of Sophie's kitchen.

Food gives way to sex, but sex is tied to that same kitchen and that same mother. Masturbation, Portnoy explains, took place "Before meals. After meals. During meals," the point of reference still the table where the earlier battles raged (19). Portnoy's masturbation takes place to the sounds of Sophie deriding him about "Harold's Hot Dog and Chazerai Palace," eternally connecting his lusts with eating and with the voice of the concerned, overbearing mother (23). Portnoy's masturbating excursions revolve consistently around artifacts of food: He can be found "squirting my seed into the empty wrapper from a Mounds bar" (18), falling upon a "cored apple that I banged silly on that picnic" (18-19), fantasizing to the voice of an "empty milk bottle" (19), and violating "the maddened piece of liver...behind a billboard on the way to a bar mitzvah lesson" (19).

Masturbation is the road to liberation, his penis "the battering ram to freedom" that will unburden him (33). But just as chazerai proved complex and multiform so to masturbation pulls Portnoy in two directions, toward release and towards restriction and terror, for just as eating chazerai ends with an uncontrolled sexual appetite and diarrhea, masturbation begins to be associated with disease and death. "All that pulling and tugging at my own flesh," thinks Portnoy, "all that friction had given me an incurable disease" (19). The fears implanted by the mother never are released; the terrors are transmitted from dinner table to bedroom. When Portnoy confesses to masturbating with a second piece of liver, one that "I had in the privacy of my own home, rolled round my cock in the bathroom at three-thirty and then again on the end of a fork, at five-thirty," when he, as he puts it, "fucked my own family's dinner" it is remembered not as a victory but as a defeat, "the worst thing I have ever done," a betrayal of "that poor innocent family of mine" (134).

When Alex matures from masturbation to women he looks only for "Shiksas" because "they will eat anything...And the terrifying corollary, they will do anything as well" (81). They strike Portnoy as creators of lubricious freedom and as destroyers of the mother. "SHE'LL EAT YOU UP ALIVE," screams Sophie about the mystical "BLONDIE," and surely that is what intrigues Alex, for the food imagery, the idea of unbridled eating works magically on Portnoy's psyche (189). Sexual boundaries join with dietary boundaries becoming confused in Portnoy's memory: "A terrible act has been committed," Portnoy recalls, "by either my father or me. Did he fuck between those luscious legs the gentile cashier from the office, or have I eaten my sister's chocolate pudding?" (87). Transgression travels from the world of food to the world of sexuality, both ministered by the mother's tongue.

"Maybe that's all I really am," Portnoy opines, "a lapper of cunt, the slavish mouth for some woman's hole. Eat! And so be it!" (270). To eat, to indulge in sexual frenzy has been his goal, his means away from childhood incarceration, from the "mesuggeneh rules and regulations" that overwhelm him, but eating still connotes something bestial, a betrayal of his best self, a crime, an allegiance with the first victimizers (34). Portnoy is caught between "phobic avoidance and insane lapping" Shechner argues, the first felt as a psychic prison the second as a devolution (124).

His attraction to The Monkey is as his attraction to forbidden foods, to that which is inherently bad for him, that which the mother warns against. The Monkey attracts because of her admission of wanting to "eat the banana" while her friends have sex (161). The act unifies Portnoy's twin obsessions, desanctifying both food and sex. The Monkey, the inhuman, grammarless, cartoon figure with the Neanderthal appellation appears a beacon of freedom, the object of complete rejection and dismissal of the mother. And yet, as far as Portnoy travels he returns home. The roads he seeks for rebellion are roads chosen by his mother. Linguistically, emotionally, gastronomically, intellectually, and sexually, Portnoy is tied to his ambiguous mother.

In Israel he finds a "mother-substitute," Naomi, and unable to have sex with her he pleads, "At least let me eat your pussy" (270). The image has come full circle, the son begging the mother for oral sex. Still in the posture of supine solicitation Portnoy has not come far; another continent, another time, but still the mother's formative power stands above him. He sees himself as someone who must "crawl through life then," after asking this question of Naomi (271). He is pulled back and forth, desirous and then censorious of those desires. He wants both to devour (eat) his mother and to love her, to withdraw from her prohibitions and to adhere to them. In his relationship to food and to sex he enacts his essential complaint: "torn by desires that are repugnant to my conscience, and a conscience repugnant to my desires" (132). In every way this complaint parallels the ambiguous relationship to the mother, the contradictory claims she makes upon him and the contradictory perceptions he has of her.

The son wants to merge with the mother's body, to have her become only a bastion of bliss, of infantile pleasure. Even Portnoy's earliest sexual fantasies, those performed in the shared bathroom, call for the mother as lover. He imagines a "mythical being who always called me Big Boy" (18). And who is that mythical creature, finally? In fact she is not mythical at all, nor is she Thereal McCoy. "Alexander is a big boy" (13) she says, this mother who teaches him to "pee into the bowl like a big man" by "tickling the underside of my prick (133)," this mother who "sits on the edge of the bed in her padded bra and girdle, rolling on her stockings and chattering away" about the son's love for his mother, this mother who is "so attuned" to Portnoy's "deepest desires," who makes him "want to growl with pleasure" (44-45). It is she who holds him in sexual paradise, she who promises sex and love combined blissfully together. Yet her promise is also denied in her every action, her every warning - what she gives she takes away, what she offers as seduction is later denigrated as filth and dirt.

Still the image of the infant suckling delightfully, unambiguously, on his mother's breast - no questions to be answered, no doubt to be overcome - retains its apostolic force. "What if breasts began to grow on me, too?" Alex wonders, imagining himself transformed "into a girl," a fear but also a fantasy, a final return to the life-giving body, a fantasy Kepesh lives out in *The Breast* (39). Zuckerman holds his mouth to a spot on his baby book where he assumes "His mother's milk had stained the page," trying for a moment to hold on to that time to which he can never return, that time that exists only in imagination, not even in memory (AL 65). The mother is "Not gone; beyond gone," Zuckerman thinks (AL 45). The great absence of the mother creates in the son an overwhelming, if hidden, need to re-enter the womb, hence Kepesh's compulsion to insert his nipple into women, particularly into Claire. As Freud writes, in "The Infantile Genital Organization of the Libido," "The vagina becomes valued...as an asylum for the penis; it comes into the inheritance of the mother's womb" (115).

But the urge to become the mother is not an urge so crystallized or certain for the mother is never just one thing. Kepesh's need for ultimacy is balanced against its impossibility. The mother cannot be understood as purely a nourisher or as purely an image of sexuality. She embodies both simultaneously, denying the possibility of any clear interpretation.

The murkiness of the mother, the bisecting lines of discordant emotions provided to and by the son create a mother who will not be slated as one image or idea. One is drawn towards and away in the same moment. It is in the divide, within the contradictions, that the child is entrapped. Shechner sees Mrs. Portnoy as an unreformable dictator, an oppressor who "wants nothing less than the annexation of her son, the full possession of and control over his manhood" (125). Portnoy's angst springs not from an impression of his mother as this all-possessing authority but as both a provider and a restrictor, a lover and an enemy, a suckler and a jailer. If she were just what Shechner describes her as she would be easily dealt with, easily loved or hated. But that she is both the one who offers magical love and the one who elicits fear she leaves the son with no method of response. The son who rails, "WE CAN'T TAKE ANY MORE! BECAUSE YOU FUCKING JEWISH MOTHERS ARE JUST TO FUCKING MUCH TO BEAR!" (PC 121) is, in spirit, the same son who upon hearing of his mother's death thinks languidly, "No woman alive thought of me, certainly not with love" (POD 120). She is too much to bear, the son exclaims, and too much to live without.

In that grey area guilt becomes a menacing presence, born not of pure rebellion or acquiescence but of ambiguity. Guilt can only be effected if a relationship is not clear. Guilt insinuates itself in the cracks between affection and anger. It can debilitate the adult sons who would seem to have little to fear from their tiny mothers. For Martin Tucker its power is the explanation for Kepesh's transformation. Tucker suggests that Kepesh has become a breast as a self-imposed "sentence of guilt" (36). Guilt, of course, is not a sufficient explanation for Kepesh's disaster but Tucker does illustrate how far-reaching and embedded guilt is within Roth's men and women, how metamorphosing it can be.

Portnoy feels guilt like a living creature. "Every place I turn," he admits, "something else to be ashamed of" (50). Alex's "shame" tails him like a private investigator, like a conscience, like a super-ego, all sent by the mother to keep him in line, to both watch and protect him. He feels shame for his misdeeds and that he views them as misdeeds makes clear his respect for the rules he breaks. "I am the Raskolnikov of jerking off," he says early in his session, describing himself as a criminal not as a libertine (20). From his earliest recollections he sees himself not as someone breaking free of unjust persecution but as a cowering criminal: He envisions himself variously "caught" and "not caught" (21). He imagines the "person who turns me in" getting his reward (39). "The culprit is me," he remembers of an incident at home (86). "What will become of me if I'm caught," he wonders masturbating discreetly on a bus (127). "They'll haul us in," he warns the liberated Monkey as she performs oral sex on him on the mayor's lawn (213). In Roth, as in Kafka, 'Guilt can never be doubted.'

Guilt is inborn, part of the tribal, concentrationary, heritage. To break away is to risk not only transforming oneself into a criminal but to risk losing the mother's approval and love, something no son in Roth's works, no matter how deep his bitterness runs, is willing to lose. To rebel is to be "A bad boy! A Shande to his family forever" (PC 201). "My mother is about to vanish," thinks Kepesh, "And her last memory of her only child will be of his meager, rootless existence - her last memory will be of this lemon I live with" (POD 108-109). Here guilt is not a product of a broken commandment but of an imagined broken heart. The disappointed dying mother can gain no satisfaction from her son's life. He has betrayed her by not succeeding, has displeased her by living a shabby life, by not providing her with the *naches* she deserves. Portnoy fails his mother by remaining unmarried and without a child, Tarnopol fails by marrying the crazed Maureen, who causes tears to fall on Mrs. Tarnopol's face when she asks her to clean her dirty underwear. Kepesh fails his mother by his loveless, sterile, barren life. And Zuckerman fails his mother by divorcing over and over again, by living, as Roth states, an "unhallowed" life, a life of shame (CWPR 188). "Ma, I'm sorry...that I'm compiling such a bad marital record," says Zuckerman, admitting his guilt, asking for pardon (ZU 73). And the mother's voice, which like Joyce's rhythmical verse in 'Portrait' mandates, "apologize, apologize, apologize" is not a voice easily satisfied or lowered in tone (PC 211).[8]

The mother is constantly "hocking us to be good, hocking us to be nice," Portnoy explains, and that interminable hocking has its desired effect; it instills a moral gauge that cannot be thrown down (122). It cannot be thrown down because with its absence so too the mother must be absent, she whose eyes are "the color of the crust of honey cake," whose eyes remain "still open" and seeing, whose eyes, Portnoy realizes, through everything, are "still loving me" (69). To renounce the guilt to to renounce the love. Every transgression is a desecration of the mother's image, a desecration of her loving eyes, a desecration of the voice that says, "You are my darling boy, and whatever you do is right," a voice unlike any other (71).

For each sexual tryst and moral failure Portnoy finds himself on the "rack of guilt" (107). When his mother's actual words no longer speak an invented mother comes forth and speaks her mind in the tones of the great judge who condemns Portnoy to "A TERRIBLE CASE OF IMPOTENCE. ENJOY YOURSELF" (272). The voice is Alex's - "DON'T BULLSHIT ME WITH LEGALISMS, PORTNOY" - but it is also his mother's - "YOU KNEW RIGHT FROM WRONG," and indeed the judge is a "she" (272). He ends proclaiming not his innocence but his guilt. He whines like the baby he once was, protected and warmed by the mother. His scream returns him to a pre-linguistic time when the only voice he could connect to was that of the nurturing and indomitable mother, the mother who is his fist accuser and his first love.

The debts the mother imposes, debts for birth, for love, for the amenities of life, for language, weigh heavily on the son's head. He thinks of them not only with gratitude but with sorrow, the sorrow of the victim unable to act freely for freedom often means a leave-taking of the mother and her history, a refusal to honor his debts. Zuckerman's literary success makes him less able to face his mother, less able to trust his own motives and emotions. "All this sentiment," he thinks, sitting alone in his mother's apartment, "He wondered if it was only to compensate for the damage he was reported to have done her with the portrait of the mother in *Carnovsky*" (52). Though he complains about the reading publics' inability to draw distinctions between art and life, and though he is assured of his mother's understanding and sympathy, he is ever-haunted by the ghost of that portrait, haunted by the knowledge that for all he owes her, for all her goodness, instead of honoring her, celebrating her, he disparaged her in front of the reading world.

Henry's eulogy feels, to Nathan, as an attempt at "undoing the damage of *Carnovsky*" (AL 56), Henry's effort to "cleanse from the minds of her Florida friends the libelous portrait in *Carnovsky*" (44). Dividing his mother's items with Carol Nathan waits for her to turn to him and say, "And this is the woman the world will remember as Mrs. Carnovsky, this woman who adored you" (AL 60-61). He waits and waits for censure, waits to hear, "that was her reward," waits to be told how his irresponsibility has fouled "this touching, harmless woman" (62). The words never come, not from Henry, not from Carol, not from any other person; they emerge only from within. The accusations are self-inflicted, springing not from others' misconceptions but from his own guilt. It is not what Carol says that he fears but the words he speaks to himself, the self-flagellating tones that he transfers to others. The debt he owed his mother has been ignored, has been trampled upon, the work that granted him freedom devours his freedom, leaving him with only regret and sorrow, guilt and loneliness, unsure of where he is or what he feels: "Not even when I'm in tears am I sure what gives" (52).

In "The Mistaken" a son writes a long letter of explanation to his mother trying to understand and alleviate the contradictions of childhood. "You told them the truth," he thinks, "and that hurt. You hid the truth, that hurt too. His own mother had loved him. That had made things better? Only worse" (7). Nothing is as clear as it was imagined to be. In protecting him from "the troubles, the ugliness, all the rotten things" the mother promised a world that didn't exist; protection became isolation (7). Contradictions swirl, ambiguity predominates, the mother is a representation of a world with no center, no surety. Portnoy's first line tells the story: "She was so deeply embedded in my consciousness that for the first years of school, I seem to have believed that each of my teachers was my mother in disguise"

(3). That 'seem' speaks louder than any other word, embedding his reminiscence in the language of doubt; the doubt that serves as the foundation of all that follows.

In *The Facts* Zuckerman offers a telling criticism of Roth's manuscript. Zuckerman reminds Roth how he began his narrative with a description of himself as "The little marsupial in his mother's sealskin pouch" (167). He then asks, "But where, by the way, is the mother after that?" (168). The mother virtually disappears from the text. "The fact remains," writes Zuckerman, "that your mother has no developed role in either your life or your father's" (168). "Why the omission?" Zuckerman asks, attributing it to a repression, a desire to rewrite the past as "serene" and "desirable" when in fact it "was more like a detention house you were tunneling out of practically from the day you could pronounce your favorite word of all, 'away'" (173). He envisions Roth's mother as a warden who surrounded and suffocated Roth's spirit, and Roth as a son who misremembers, purposefully, his difficult past. For if it wasn't difficult, Zuckerman asks, if his mother was indeed the "Jewish Florence Nightingale" (168), "how do you get from that to Josie," Josie being Roth's fictitious name for his first wife (169).

Zuckerman's observations are correct to a point. The absence of the mother as a concrete presence is surely curious. But a more likely interpretation of that absence is not due to a desire to sanitize his mother falsely but to the simple fact that his mother is a diaphanous form, similar to, though not necessarily a model for, the mothers of Roth's protagonists. Like his sons and daughters Roth has difficulty placing her, no matter how great his descriptive power. She has no 'developed role' because she cannot be packaged neatly into a role. His portrait is a testament not only to her inherent marginality in the social world but to a depth of character that still eludes deft and succinct interpretation. What is left out is what still can't be calculated or explained, the strange and illogical mother.[9]

Her very body holds disparate associations for the child, the "Feeding" breasts that begin life and proclaim "Sunny existence knows nothing of death" (AL 51) becomes the "corpse" that he cannot "place" or "connect" to (AL 43). Her very intangibility, her quick, unanticipated bifurcations and transformative power suggest a flesh that does change, that grows old, that dies, that cannot remain innocent or young, fresh and giving. The mother is the embodiment of time's passage, of movement and depreciation, of horror. Roth claims that *The Facts* is partly designed as a "palliative for the loss of a mother" (8), a surreptitious attempt to return to a past before death became an issue, a time, as Portnoy says, when he felt life "will be endless" (15). And yet, inherent in the mother's description, in all of Roth, is a sense of death's inevitability. The mother's very gaze, Tarnopol claims, declares, "You must grow up and you must go away" (151). In *The Facts* Roth describes her, from the outset, as the flesh "whose metamorphosed incarnation was a sleek black sealskin coat" (18). Even here, where by his own admission he seeks to write of the mother as a deathless personage, he turns back to the language of metamorphosis and change. In every act she performs the mother calls to mind its opposite, and so if she is the harbinger of life then she must be, too, the harbinger of death.

When Big John Baal takes Nickname Damure to visit the "world-renowned 'Cradle of Civilization,'" in *The Great American Novel*, they encounter the sundry dichotomies of the mother, dichotomies caricatured hilariously(150). "I'll get you mothered all right," Big John tells the excited Nickname, "I'll get you a momma who really plies the trade" (150). The mother is both whore and pure, both patient nurse and extortionist, demanding two dollars and fifty cents to sing "Alouetta" (157). She emasculates as she arouses. "Hey, that, there looks like fun," says John, watching his teammate bathed by one of the bought mothers (154). "Only it ain't," answers Nickname (154). The mother's seeming soft touch is felt as humiliation. The mother both elicits fear, causing mature men to "cry like they're going to die" and beg for the light to stay on all night, and calms those fears, promising to "clean you and oil you...put you in your nice jammies and feed you and read to you and put you to beddy-bye" (133). The regression into childhood brings back memories of comfort and protection and also brings to the fore childhood terrors long buried. The mother is the "Eternal Mom," seemingly immortal and a "grandmother," an aging figure nearing her end (153).

"She the one what does it to you," says Big John (152). She gives and she takes, promises and revokes, enjoins and dissuades. She remains forever an unknown essence while promising solidity. She heals and the healing becomes the wound. She damages and the damage is understood as benign. A miasma of contradiction, the mother engenders everything the son wants to overcome. "Why should emotions be mixed," asks Zuckerman, when clarity was promised to him "when he was a boy" (ZU 185). In his eulogy for his mother Henry Zuckerman depicts a mother all of "virtues" (56) Nathan thinks, listening to his devoted brother, "Chekhov, drawing on material resembling Henry's had written a story one-third that length called 'The Darling'" (56).

Like Henry, Chekhov designs his tale to tell a particular story, in Chekhov's case the story of the subdued powerless woman living only to serve men. But Chekhov, as Tolstoy understands, wrote a different story than the one he intended to write. Tolstoy argues, "The Balak of public opinion bade Chekhov curse the weak, submissive undeveloped-woman devoted to man; and Chekhov went up the mountain...but when he began to speak, the poet blessed what he had come to curse" (25). Tolstoy's reading, marred by his own ideology, is incomplete and finally as limited as Chekhov's conception, but it does allow a reader to see the ambiguity embedded in Chekhov's story, to note the lack of a clear, concise interpretation of his short story.

Similarly Henry's story is incomplete, though he, too, does not realize it. Though not a "ludicrously idealized portrait" Henry's is a portrait that dissolves the mother in surety, her image frozen by the eyes of a small and believing child (185). As Nathan points out, "the virtues were all hers. Yet they were virtues of the kind that make life happy for a little boy" (36). They are virtues that appease and calm before the contemplative and questioning man is born of the toddler. With growth, with the maturation of a desirous and individualized son those virtues change form, entrapping as they once soothed. Henry and Nathan stand as contradictory respondents to the dilemma of the mother, Henry subduing and indeed erasing one side of the mother, and Nathan learning to accept the more distressing, yet, in the end, more realistic and hopeful ambiguity of the mother, learning to accept her contradictory presence, her marginality and her authoritarian power simultaneously, and to grow from that acceptance.

Henry paints a false picture, a half picture, while Nathan finds a kind of equilibrium, tentative and always in motion. Trying to decide whether it is true that he has demeaned his mother in his book Zuckerman finally realizes, "In a school debate, he could have argued persuasively for either proposition" (68). Zuckerman has reached an acceptance of his mother's disharmony, and the disharmony in his own relationship to her. He has found out what can be pictured as a middle-ground between Chekhov's Darling and Tolstoy's, a ground of friction and debate, a ground constantly shifting and consequentially constantly developing in new directions.

The relationship to the mother, its very instability, is what awakens the son. "The whole point about your fiction," Zuckerman writes to his creator, "and in America, not only yours, is that the imagination is always in transit between the good boy and the bad boy - that's the tension that leads to revelation" (TF 162). The friction of contradiction leads not to impotence but to strength. The mother's voice is the voice of literature, the voice that Roth's fiction recreates, the voice not of perfection or of total anarchy, of Lonoff or Pipik, but in the conflict between the two; in the discordancies is the music. "Because," says Zuckerman, "the things that wear you down are the things that nurture you and your talent" (ZU 174). It is a lesson the good son, Henry, will not learn for to learn it is to enter into a world impossible to delineate neatly like a dentist's X-ray.[10]

The mother's flesh, the sign of life and of death, speaks of the ambiguity of the world, an ambiguity the child must eventually accept if he is to grow. To accept the mother is to accept the concentrationary world, to learn to live according to its unknown rules. The father is a model of one or the other vision of life, a model to accept and to rebel against. Growth comes from the rebellion and from the emulation, from the constant interchange between the child and father. But the father maintains his Pipikism or Lonoffism, rarely venturing into the chasm in between. The mother resides always within both worlds, shuttling forever and unpredictably between the two, never becoming one or the other. The father is a knowable entity, who rarely contradicts his code while the mother is fraught with contradiction. The father introduces and represents the twin evils of the Holocaust ideology, and the twin, insufficient responses to the Holocaust reality, while the mother holds forth as the emblem of the post-Holocaust world's ambiguity.

And if the father is of the world, of the streets, of Newark, than the mother must be associated with the country and its promise of respite from the noise and danger, the tumultuous grind and relentless pressure of the city. If a third of the father's mantra of life is "Newark, Newark, Newark," the mother's unspoken mantra must include tropes of the pastoral (TF 16). If the son is tied inextricably to the specifics of the father's "repertoire" of Jews, Newark, and family, he is as deeply tied to the generalities of the mother's repertoire that the word Eden seems to encompass.

While Mr. Portnoy stays in the city Mrs. Portnoy resides with her children "at the seashore," in a "breezy room," under the changing skies, the shifting winds, away from the consistent "humidity" of New Jersey (29). It is for the father to carry the burden of hard work in the anarchic city and it is for the mother to reign over a domain of pre-lapsarian perfection, to prolong the child's sense of innocence, to keep him a "boy-baby, and body-borrower-in-training," a "invulnerable animal" until childhood's unforeseeable end. (TF 18).

"At fifty-five," Zuckerman tells Roth, "you've begun to make where you came from look like a serene, desirable, pastoral haven" (TF 173). A haven it appeared to be in the eyes of a child, separate from the dangers of Newark, from the far-away world, from guilt and death. The sons and daughters remember a time in their childhoods, alone with mother, when they were "imagined to be pure" (POD 9). David Kepesh's winter years spent within the "cozy, fortified hibernation" (13) of the "mountainside resort hotel" (3), under his mother's leadership is reminiscent of Roth's childhood hibernation within his mother's "sealskin coat" (TF 28). Childhood is recalled as a protected time when one is "the apple of your mother's eye" (MLAM 201). "You and I know," Zuckerman tells his mother, "that it was very nearly heaven thirty years ago" (ZU 69) Heaven, Paradise, Eden, these associations resound in remembrance of the mother. Portnoy finds "Remembering radishes - the ones I raised so lovingly in my Victory Garden. In the patch of yard beside our cellar door. My kibbutz" (271). The natural world and home are integrated, a perfect agrarian splendor felt like a religious retreat, a taste of God. In Zuckerman's mother's home there hangs a painting with "hills of a lilac-colored island by Gauguin" (AL 51). Gauguin's paradisaical Tahiti is a vision of "Tropical Eden" to Mrs. Zuckerman (51). For Nathan it is a perfect illustration of his impressionistic memory of his former world. As it is a dream of some future bliss for the black boy who visits the Newark library in "Goodbye, Columbus," it is for Roth's more privileged sons an ancient representation of what was, of what life looked like from their child's eyes, of life before knowledge, before disaster; the life created, not by the artist, but by the mother.

It is her pastoral promise that the son binds himself to, that rekindles an "infantile veneration" to his"first provider" (TB 66). "You are/ The promised kiss of springtime," the mother sings to her son and in his naivete and idealism he believes it (AL 50). Helen, Kepesh's first wife, plays on this still smoldering memory: "If only," she says, "his wife could remember that when David had dinner in Arcadia, his mother always set the fork on the left and the spoon on the right....oh, if only his wife could bake and butter his potato the way Mama did in the wintertime" (POD 71). David does long for his mother's perfect touch, and the "bedroom vista of my childhood," with its "gentle green hills and distant green mountains," the greenness of fertility, of plenty, of the wilderness, the agrarian dream realized (192). For Neil Klugman, too, the dream of Eden is a dream of the green untrammeled landscape. The "Green Lane Country Club" in Short Hills calls to him as fervently as Brenda does (16). Short Hills is Neil's frontier, his western fantasy. He thinks, "the old Jews...had struggled and died, and their offspring had...moved farther and farther west" (90). West is not so much a direction as a state of mind, a movement towards the green trees and vast countryside of New Jersey, away from the hot and cloistered city, away from the real and towards a fiction.

Theirs is not an original dream but one embedded in the American consciousness. The search for "the little nooks of still water which border a rapid stream," as Washington Irving writes in his notebooks - a quote Leo Marx uses as an epigraph to the first chapter of his book excavating the pastoral dream in American culture and literature, *The Machine in the Garden* - is a search as old as the country. America, as Marx maintains, has been envisioned as a "fresh, green landscape," one unsullied and imbued with limitless promise (8). A new Eden, it once was to European dreamers and explorers, it became a new Eden to its colonists and citizens, as they moved farther and farther west, towards its heart (3). In the American imagination the frontier still brings to mind thoughts of "harmony and joy," of perfection embodied in the natural splendor of a wilderness uncontained, free from the contaminations of development and of memory (Marx 3). For Freud this privileging of the rural suggests a desire to escape "the grip of the external world" (Marx 8), to allay all fear and enter a "cocoon" dedicated only to the "pleasure principle" (Marx 28). It is a desire to become "as nothing" (151), as Portnoy expresses it, to disappear from the travails of culture, to become "a big brainless bag of...desirable tissue," as Kepesh describes himself; a desire to reattach to the umbilical cord, to become again a child with mother (TB 66).

Marx divides the pastoral impulse into two distinct types: the "sentimental" and the "imaginative," the sentimental being the most prevalent and the easiest to adhere to (5). For Roth's children the sentimental pastoral - "an inchoate longing for a more 'natural' environment" - coincides with the attempt to reclaim the mother's image from the deepest recesses of memory, to make her whole (Marx 5). The simple emotional pull of the landscape is connected with the simple magnetic pull of the mother. Willard looks at the "deeply green" "serene order" of Liberty City and sees his second chance at life, sees himself as a boy again (WSWG 6). Zuckerman, remembering his early life, contends that "He felt as though he'd come out from the East by covered wagon" (175). His language is that of the agrarian myth, the frontier myth, a myth less about moving forward than about reversion. Zuckerman becomes, in his mind's eye, only a "mouth:" "He sucked through a straw and he slept" (277). He becomes an infant, fulfilling his early pronouncement, "When he is sick, every man wants his mother" (3). His linguistic urge toward the frontier, westward, has taken him to this point, to this pathetic caricature of infancy. He lives in his bed forgetting everything "that had happened since he'd come out to go to school here the first time" (AL 282). He becomes the sixteen-year-old son "intoning...shantih, shantih, shantih" (282). The search for peace, embodied in his movement westward, is a search for the mother.

To recapture the Edenic bond of mother and child is at the heart of Roth's protagonists' program. Neil is attracted to the Patimkins not for their prosperity but for their green lawn, their bowls of ripe fruit, Short Hills itself, which Neil admits, "I could see now, in my mind's eyes, at dusk, rose-colored, like a Gauguin stream" (38). Kepesh finds in Claire the "artless and untainted" surrogate to live with him in the country (251). She is a "dream of a girl," her apple-like skin embodying the Edenic garden (262). In Sullivan County Kepesh will have his Catskills childhood once again. Paul Herz runs toward his wider beam, into his mother's arms, by extricating himself from the "cramped...bushes" into the oneness of the cemetery lawn (422). Surrounded by the natural world Portnoy shows his first signs of acknowledging the Monkey's humanity. He and Mary Jane are "two more rootless jungle-dwelling erotomaniacs...dreaming the old agrarian dream in their rent-a-car convertible" (186-187). They form a symbiosis only in this "idyllic" setting, "under red and yellow leaves" (194). Sam R. Girgus suggests that Portnoy's search for "the real McCoy" is a search for America. The Gentile women in the novel, he argues, "embody America" (130). Portnoy, like Roth's other sons, views his country as "a feminine pastoral image" (Girgus 129). To possess the woman is to possess the American Eden, to possess, finally, the first woman associated with this dream, the first woman with whom the son forms "the most passionate bond of a lifetime" (AL 239).

But the sentimental pastoral dream will not hold. Like Portnoy's sublime weekend it can not last, it will not sustain itself. In a "fallen world" the dream of paradise is inherently a false dream (TB 88). In a world post "Oswald, Ruby, et al," a world of unexplainable violence and untempered hatred, America can no longer be viewed as a mecca of innocence. To do so is to blind oneself to the real, to deny history. As Marx writes, "this ideal has appeared with increasing frequency in the service of a reactionary or false ideology" (7). The past offers too much evidence to the contrary to have faith in the "illusion of peace and harmony in a green pasture" (Marx 25). If one insists one becomes blind, one becomes an ideologue subservient to a myth. The dream of perfectibility has too many corpses in its wake for any contemporary man to give in to it. Neil Klugman realizes this as he dismisses the Patimkin world. His dream, he realizes, has always been an impossibility. Looking at the August sky Neil sees it as "beautiful and temporary" (78). He knows, even while under its spell, that it cannot last. The past no longer offers the memory of paradise. The dream the mother initiates is denied by the mother's history and indeed by her very flesh.

In his essay Girgus unknowingly locates another flaw in sentimental pastoralism. Girgus suggests that Portnoy is seeking "assimilation through sex" (132). He then argues that Portnoy's trysts are attempted "conquests of the virgin land" (131). Girgus argues that "Such penetration" of women and of land "equates psychologically to possession and domination" (132). His language vacillates between words of cohabitation and conciliation and words of militarism and aggression. Here is the contradiction at the heart of the pastoral quest. The search for cohesion, for paradise and innocence becomes mired in violence and degradation. It becomes an effort not only to discover Eden but to force it into being. The very terms of the quest preclude its success.

Contradiction becomes evident in the simple agrarian fantasy. That the country, the uncivilized wilderness, is always and only a haven of tranquility, a haven of consensus, is undeniably a false proposition. Marx reminds his readers that the Arcadian vision of America was at once overturned by observation of its "hideous wilderness," a dangerous, relentless landscape of predators and cannibalistic animalism (84). Not only sweet and sun drenched, the land was also barbaric and mindless. What the pilgrims of Roth's stories long for, the primal garden, is revealed as chaotic and frightening, without borders or boundaries, a nihilistic environment of malevolent beasts, the European world that their new America was imagined to replace and heal.

The unambiguous ideal is suffused with ambiguity. The attempt toward the merging of child and mother, the attempt to return to an unambiguous infant-life is rife with innate contradictions. When Zuckerman recollects his early freedom, as he moved westward towards Chicago, he thinks, "Eight-hundred miles between him and home" (174-175). For Nathan the pastoral is not only a dream of reversion but of escape of "removal" from the bond with his mother (175). The very urge to return to the mother's paradise becomes a means to escape her, to break away. When Portnoy, in the "mountains" of "Vermont" experiences an epiphanic love for The Monkey he enacts more than an unconscious desire to join his mother in Edenic union (187). When he celebrates with oral sex under the trees he is in fact flouting his mother's laws, rebelling against her restrictions on eating. His new freedom is not merely a conjoining but is a rebellion. As he tries to move nearer to the mother's original promise he also moves further away.

The sentimental pastoral must be replaced by the imaginative, or complex, pastoral, a notion which takes into account both the attractions and the repulsions of the agrarian ideal, which occupies a "middle-ground," according to Marx, "between the opposing forces of civilization and nature" (23). This "semi-pastoralism" is akin to the acceptance of ambiguity the child must develop in regard to the mother (Marx 23). The terrain of America is not Eden and it is not a terrain of savagery, the urge to move west is not wholly innocent nor is it wholly malevolent; the mother is not a perfected ageless bastion of beauty and truth nor is she only a disciplinarian, a figure who subjugates and controls the son, the urge to connect with her is also an urge to move beyond her. "In a sense," argues Marx, "America was both Eden and a howling desert" (43). So too the mother is both the creator of the child's Eden and its destroyer. She is the first victim and the first to transform victimization into power. She is the repository of the pain of their heritage and the source of a world that appears to challenge the truth of that heritage. She is always the only person with whom one has shared a body and as such she is representative not only of this togetherness and symbiosis but of its absence, the body whose distance tells the child he is ever alone. "There's nothing on earth that keeps its promise," say Mickey Sabbath, in *Sabbath's Theater*, thinking particularly of his mother (32). The image of the mother is now essentially concentrationary in Roth's work. She is a new form, a battered form, an unclear form, altered by the shadow of genocide.

In Roth's first novella and in a novel, *The Counterlife*, published over twenty-five years later, Roth tells the same pastoral story. Both Neil Klugman and Nathan Zuckerman learn to accept the ambiguous mother and to reject the pastoral myth. Neil's 'Goodbye, Columbus' is more than a goodbye to middle-America, or to suburbia, or to Brenda and her family; it is both a goodbye to a short-lived dream and to fantasy. In the end if Neil is disillusioned it is a dissolution compensated by freedom. And Zuckerman, too, rejects the "idyllic scenario," rejects the possibility of a "recovery of a sanitized, confusionless life" (CL 369). "We all create imagined worlds," he says, "often green and breastlike," but those worlds with their "virginal vision of Momma," offer no solutions (CL 309). They are blinders to life, false ideologies, the "therapeutic pastoral" of the failed and frightened man (CL 309).

"Well, that's over," Nathan decides, "The pastoral stops here" (369). In a novel about breaking free of ideology and structure Nathan rejects the structured pastoral dream and the structured vision of the mother. "Circumcision" leads to his epiphany (369). He suggests that it "gives the lie to the womb-dream of life, the appealing idyll of living 'naturally,' unencumbered by man made ritual. To be born is to lose all that" (370). Once the separation from the mother is complete one must begin to build his own self without a reliance on ancient myths or taught conventions. The mother, who seemed the only perfect solid object, is as ambiguous as the concentrationary world itself. But that ambiguity is not only a hazard but also an opportunity. Zuckerman holds on to the mother's ambiguous visage, grasping that ambiguity, and wearing it like the costume of freedom.

THE POWERS THAT BE

The possibilities of freedom dance in front of the child's eyes, mocking his imprisonment and his fear of leaving his cocoon. Freedom is always a risk, always a danger. In "The Fence," a story written for his college magazine, *The Bucknellian*, Roth juxtaposes the secure home the protagonist resides in, with the world outside his door, the world of the orphanage where children seem to play without constraint. A fence surrounds the orphanage, but the boy, Lee, feels that the fence surrounds him, that the green field the parentless children run upon is the free realm from which he is excluded. "I had wished," remembers the boy, "that when I was born again...I would be an orphan" (18).

To be an orphan is to be free. And yet what is the price for that freedom? The "mother's lips pressed" to his neck, the "hand" holding his "tightly" must be given up (18). The single bed, the sound of the father returning home, the sturdy four walls which create a child's singular world must be forsaken. And what does that freedom provide to replace the parents' stolidity and history? "I will be all alone," the boy thinks: Alone, with nothing to turn back toward (19).

The dream of being a unfettered orphan is a false and essentially barbaric dream, primal in it its very urge. To lay siege to the past, to systematically demolish the pillars of memory is nothing less than an act of desecration and destruction, particularly in this century. Instead of questioning and confronting, one simply demolishes. In *Patrimony*, a book that performs the opposite rite, Roth comes across a cretinous cab-driver, a "violent bastard," who tells him, "My old man's in his grave now without his front teeth. I knocked 'em out of his fucking mouth for him" (156). The driver goes on to tell Roth, "I didn't go to his funeral even" (157). For this son the father does not exist; he has been excised with a punch. "He actually did it," Roth tells himself, "annihilated the father. He is of the primal horde of sons who, as Freud liked to surmise, have it in them to nullify the father by force" (159). It is a nullification that does not ennoble or heal. What this son acts out is a barbarous "devouring" akin to a reckless pillaging of one's history (159). It leaves him not free or awakened but further dehumanized. He pulverizes himself with his hateful punch and with his battered memory. To forcibly enact, whether physically or intellectually, the orphan dream is to come no closer to its imagined promise, the promise the young Lee grasps to as keenly as he grasps to his fence.

The orphan dream is false, dangerous, and empty, and yet it thrives throughout Roth's works, garnering an incredible resiliency in light of its baselessness. While the attraction to ideology and to submission is evident, the attraction to nihilism and parentlessness is more obscure, more grounded in an often unexpressed fear, that basic, universal fear of aging and of death. The parent is the face of time made clear. In the parents' very eyes death is foretold. To escape them, then, to make them vanish, is to hide from death. To exist in the orphan's uncontained wilderness is to exist without walls, without a past, a future, to be eternally present and self-creating. No evidence of time's debasement stares at you. Nothing is believed and nothing is real. The Holocaust evaporates, the wound is healed. Death ceases to exist; it is just another lie told by an authority which cannot be trusted.

"Kaddish," Allen Ginsburg's ode to motherhood, supplements our image of Chekhov's darling. Now more than an ambiguous woman, both slave and master, the mother is a pure victim of her world and of her biology. And as such she tells her son more about his own future than he might want to know. "Strange to think of you, gone without corsets & eyes, while I walk the sunny pavement of Greenwich village," the poem begins (7). Naomi's end promises an eventual end to the sunny walks in New York. It tells him, unsympathetically, "What came is gone forever every time" (9). The comfort of the mother gives way to her promise of the end of the sun (son). "Forever. And we're bound for that, Forever - like Emily Dickinson's horse - headed to the END" (11). What these seemingly powerful figures finally reveal to the child is their own powerlessness. "I've seen your grave," Ginsburg writes, "O strange Naomi! My own cracked grave" (27). Death stares out from the father and the mother, and all the judges and teachers, and the child sees only his own end in their wizened features. "People," Roth writes, in *The Last Jew*, an early version of *Portnoy's Complaint*, "built things up, and got overexcited, and told each other lies and fairy-tales, and it all had to do...with the fear of dying" (9).

The face of death, though, is not exclusive to the parents or to those seated upon high. For in the very rebelliousness of the young the elders see their own end. As the power of the old deserts, the power of the young hovers like vultures around them. As the son sees his death in his father's wrinkles, the father sees his end in the son's round face and unblemished skin. As the son sees himself escaping his past, the father sees the past despoiled, the millions of dead forgotten, murdered anew.

Kaddish, the word itself, is traditionally applied to the first born son because he will recite the prayer of death at his father's funeral. At birth, then, the child announces the father's demise. Hostility between child and parent begins immediately. The battles that are fought, the deep antagonisms that are formed, and the creative heat that is produced begin with the collision of mortals who feel threatened by a new force, who see in someone else the dissolution of their own authority.

In the war of words between Irving Howe and Philip Roth, and later in the imaginative fictionalizing and elaboration of that war in *The Anatomy Lesson*, the anger that fuels the combatants is less an anger at a man or his work than the anger of a man as a representation of one's diminishing authority. Each reacts to a felt assault on his strength, an assault on his own vulnerable Holocaust-haunted self, and on the source of his individuality, his precious sense of identity. In Roth and Howe, and more fervently in Zuckerman and Milton Appel, two men become the Kaddish - the face of death - to each other.

When Roth published his first book, *Goodbye, Columbus,* Irving Howe offered praise in *The New Republic.* "What many writers spend a lifetime searching for," Howe wrote, " - a unique voice, a secure rhythm, a distinctive subject - seems to have come to Philip Roth totally and immediately" (SOB 17). For a young writer, already criticized for self-hatred, and labeled dangerous for the Jews, the touch of Howe's authority acted as a salve for the wounds others were inflicting. Yet even in his initial support, Howe expresses a criticism that will surface in each of his writings about Roth. He claims that Roth "is one of the first American Jewish writers who finds, so far as I can judge, almost no sustenance in the Jewish tradition" (18). Though he adds that "none of this should detract from Mr. Roth's achievement," it is to this point he will return to again and again (18).

Before continuing with Howe's complaint, it is necessary to ascertain the validity of his charge that Roth's works separate themselves from the Jewish tradition, the Jewish past. Are his stories of "Middle-class American Jews" not "drawn from memories of Jewish childhood and family life, from the values of the Jewish tradition"? (SOB 18).[11] Roth's Jewish roots are clear; his very rebelliousness is a tribute to Jewish history rather than a challenge to it. From his earliest works any reader can plainly see the Jewish past influencing the present action. The Jews in Europe stare at Neil as he eats his fruit, searching him for betrayal. Allusions to fascism and to "burdened" Jews in flight hark back to a past that cannot be fully hidden, even in Short Hills (GC 118). What does Ozzie feel if not the weight of Jewish history upon him? That he questions the canons of the past only validates their power. Is it not their unique ancestry that Grossbart and Marx share in "Defender of the Faith" that makes Marx's heroic action so difficult?

The Jewish tradition, the Jewish question, is rarely distant from Roth's concerns. Jewish mothers and Jewish fathers disclaim upon their children's actions, the son, Paul Herz, marrying a non-Jewish girl, the son, Portnoy, disavowing God and religion, refusing to attend High-Holiday services. Jewish writers and teachers, Zuckerman, Herz, Kepesh, are pulled toward Prague and Israel, towards a history that predates them. Roth describes *When She Was Good* as "my book with no Jews in it," making clear how aberrant it is in light of his usual concerns (SDII 61). In *Operation Shylock* Smilesburger tells "Roth," "What would you be without the Jews?" (388). Biblical images from Abraham and Isaac, to Job's trials, to Exodus are restructured in Roth's contemporary world. Yiddish seeps through these texts, the language of Singer, of the dead. If Roth's tradition appears different than Howe's it is due to a difference in generations and orientation, not in tradition.

Roth does not fastidiously seek out the Jewish past, he does not pursue vehemently allusions to Job or to Abraham or Moses, but that past finds him, occupies him like a ghost. It is infused in his body, it seeps out of his pen like blood. To run to it, to highlight one's indebtedness in order to impress the world with one's great Jewish conscience would be, for Roth, a false and debasing use of literature. The writer goes where he must not where he will find readers and praise.

Roth's is almost a memorial manner of writing, like Wharton's, a manner that both criticizes the narrowness of a world but nevertheless respects it beliefs, its solid culture. It is Roth who upon his father's death thinks, "He should be buried in a shroud...that was how his parents had been buried and how Jews were buried traditionally" (P 234). And Roth is surprised that his father would not pass his tefillon on to him, but rather to his grandchildren. "My nephews," he writes, "raised in a secular ethos, with no knowledge of Judaism, were Jews in name alone" (P 98). He is, he feels, different from them; though he questioned much he was taught he imbibed it and was nourished by it. The new world is somehow less for its freedom, for it is a freedom without awareness of freedom's cost. It has nothing, not even a tradition to reject. Roth is more the man in the middle, like his father, neither observant, unbudging Jew, nor apostate, forgetful Jew. His is a fictional stance that criticizes both these types, that finds its fruit in their interaction.

How Howe, an often wise and discerning critic, misses this aspect of Roth's work is hard to explain.[12] In "Philip Roth Reconsidered" Howe calls Roth "a writer who has denied himself, programmatically, the vision of major possibilities" (230). He chastises Roth for choosing an "audience" over "readers," and has nary a kind word to say for any of Roth's works besides "Defender of the Faith" (244). While his criticisms of Roth's style, his use of the skit, and what Howe sees as his need to score "points" (228) with "contempt and animus" (237) are arguable, what appears as the prevalent issue is Roth's disinterest in, in fact his antagonism toward, "tradition" (236). His characters, Howe argues, experience "little of the weight of their past" (231). Howe contends that, like his creations, Roth's historical and literary past effects him little. "Despite his concentration on Jewish settings," Howe maintains, "and his acerbity of tone," Roth "has not really been involved in this tradition" (236). Roth's satire, for Howe, is little less than a witty dismissal of the history of pain— laughter as a means of amnesia.

Howe claims that Roth's stories spring from a "thin personal culture," which he defines as "the ways in which a tradition, if absorbed into his work, can both release and control his creative energies" (236). "He lives at the end of a tradition," Howe states, "which can no longer nourish his imagination or that he has through an act of faith, chosen to tear himself away from that tradition" (237). The Jewish tradition, according to Howe, that Roth has departed from, denied forcibly, extends "in Yiddish from Mendele to Isaac Bashevis Singer and in English from Abraham Cahan to Malamud and Bellow" (236). This solid tradition "yields him no sustenance," Howe reiterates, "no norms or values from which to launch his attacks on middle-class complacence" (230). Howe sees not only disinterest finally but Oedipal anger at his precursors. "There is a parasitic relation," Howe concludes, "to the embattled sentiments and postures of older Jewish writers in America" (230). Roth is viewed as the last slayer of a wounded tradition.

It is for *Portnoy's Complaint* that Howe saves his bitterest bile, and yet after reading his criticism one sees its locus to be no different from the rest of his essay. *Portnoy's Complaint* "helps explain...what Roth's true feelings about, or relation to, Jewishness are" (241). The complaint against "Jewish guilt," "history," and, "inhibition and repression," "speaks in some sense for Roth" (240). Roth is once again the devaluer of tradition, the Jewish cannibal. He becomes not only the quintessential vulgar rebel whose own culture offers nothing to replace the culture he undoes, but the leader, the general at the head of the assault on tradition's edifice, of which Howe has become the gatekeeper. *Portnoy's Complaint* is for younger Jews, in Howe's estimation, "a signal for 'letting go' of both their past and perhaps themselves, a guide to swinging in good conscience, or better yet, without troubling about conscience" (243). Not only is Roth denigrating his tradition, he is the Pied-Piper leading a whole generation away. Roth is a representative writer whose critical and popular success "reflected the point at which the underground springs of both Yiddish culture and the immigrant experience had finally dried up" (WOF 597).

What Howe battles against is not Roth per se but what he seems a harbinger of. Howe's three essays suggest a malaise that is the opposite of belatedness. For Howe it is the tradition's demise, not its power that frightens him, the end of the world of his fathers, the world he has formed himself from. Roth is his Kaddish promising not only his usurpation as a Jewish authority but the eventual disappearance of all that furnished Howe with purpose. What Howe fears is the orphan world from which Roth is the messenger. Tradition gives meaning to his life, purpose to his writing, substance to his words. Tradition is cohesive force holding together the Diaspora Jews in the grim aftermath of tragedy. With tradition's collapse, foretold in Roth's every sentence, he becomes unauthentic and disempowered. Roth seeming nihilism, his ahistoricism, his irresponsibility foretell Howe's eventual ruin, his death, and the death of that which he holds sacred.[13]

Roth's fictional interpretation of their conflict takes us further towards an understanding of their mutual distrust and disappointment with one another, further towards an answer to the questions their conflict poses. In *The Anatomy Lesson* Zuckerman does battle with Milton Appel, whose curriculum vitae and criticisms echo Irving Howe's. "Milton Appel had unleashed an attack upon Zuckerman's career," Nathan remembers, fueled by his unexplained pain, "that made Macduff's assault upon Macbeth look almost lackadaisical" (68). Zuckerman "remained shocked and outraged and hurt" long after the requisite time he usually allowed for thinking about a negative review (70).

For Zuckerman Appel is more than a writer. He "had been a leading wunderkind of the Jewish generation preceding his own" (70), a writer deeply "cherished" by the young Zuckerman, a writer who allowed Nathan to feel that "He wasn't alone" in his alienation, in his distance from his own father, in his personal misanthropy (71). Even Appel's Yiddish anthology was felt not as the "prodigal son's return to the fold" but as "a stand against" "the assimilationists" and the "Jewish nostalgists" and "the prospering new suburbs" (74). Appel's early words helped Zuckerman to feel that he had been "Set free," that alienation meant the freedom to choose, to take from tradition and to deny tradition, to accept what one wants and to reject what one does not believe in (74). Appel authorized Zuckerman's individuality, his liberation.

And then, out of nowhere, he reclaimed them; this is the pain Zuckerman feels, the pain that Roth shows evidence of sharing. Appel's attack teaches the lesson of authority's power, for if one feels sanctioned by an authority that authority has the ability to retract that sanction at any time. The claws of Appel's power turn on Zuckerman and they sink deeper than any others for they are the same claws that initially set him in flight.

Both Appel and Howe and Zuckerman and Roth feel the sting of their antagonist's words; they feel them as definitive threats. The elders see their world falling to the deconstruction of the young, the structures of their temples collapsing under the salacious vocabulary of those who will follow them, while the young writers see the darkness of authority's censure as an attempt to stymie them with dictates. The elders see tradition as a means of holding onto memory, holding onto some continuity in life, while the youths see tradition as implicated in the Holocaust's fires, and their own rebellion as a positive assertion of freedom, an assertion which degrades the Nazi assault.

Though Roth and Howe, and their fictional stand-ins, share much in common (perhaps because they share so much), they come to represent the most profound attack on each other's place in the hierarchy of intellectual life.The slight authority a man attains for himself is all, at times, that gives him a sense of being, of limited but real power, and power is a diminishing resource in Roth's concentrationary world. Howe and Roth battle each other the way a man battles against various authoritarian forces. In Roth's works the threat to one's personal authority is constantly present, a legacy of the recent past. His men and women feel pulled and pushed, crippled and imprisoned, by various seen and unseen forces, forces which attack and threaten as surely and as persistently as these writers and critics attack and threaten one another.

History, most prominently, infringes on the authority of Roth's Jews, refusing them full autonomy. "Is this what has come down to me from the pogroms and the persecution," asks Portnoy, "from the mockery and abuse bestowed by the goyim over their two thousand lovely years" (37). History casts a pall over every decision, and yet forgetting history leaves one completely undone. The Americanized Jews of Woodenton are ineffectual louts because they have closed their pretty shades on history. They are victims of history as surely as Tzuref and his orphans are victims, though they cannot recognize it. It is forgetting, or not taken account of, history that both Howe and Appel accuse Roth and Zuckerman of.

Howe blames *Portnoy's Complaint* for signaling an "end to philo-Semitism in American culture" (PRR 243). "One no longer," Howe contends, "had to listen to all that talk about Jewish morality, Jewish endurance, Jewish wisdom, Jewish families. Here was Philip Roth himself...confirming what had always been suspected about those immigrant Jews" (243). The Holocaust's revelations had caused a wariness in authors to discuss the unseemly, human, side of Jewish life and Roth, in Howe's view, had broken that wariness, allowed the Jews to be desanctified and hated once again. He had played into the anti-Semites' hands, disregarding the lessons of the past. Zuckerman summarizes Appel's argument against him as, "Six million dead-six million sold" (95). All Appel's words, Zuckerman feels, are nothing less than a surreptitious judgment on his Holocaust sensibility, his inability to understand or act on the Holocaust's teachings. Both Howe and Appel use history to control, to cause guilt. Their fear of the Holocaust's reoccurrence has stripped them of their artistic honesty and they want a similar self-editing to pervade the next generation.

But Roth recognizes the danger in philo-Semitism at the same as he reads the Holocaust's pedagogy in a rather different way. Rather than allowing it to hold his creative energy in check, the Holocaust tells him to fight against the natural tendency to glorify Jews in order to counter anti-Semitic stereotypes. "I am trying to be truthful," Roth says, and truth, as he sees it, is more important than pretty pictures (SDII 60). Roth does not write books, he claims, to "celebrate the virtues of the Jewish people" (SDII 60). To subscribe to a written or unwritten program, whether celebratory of or denigrating towards Jews as a whole, is to give up one's integrity, to become an ideologue or a hagiographer, not a writer. One gives up one's authority to a greater authority, allowing someone else, Howe, Appel, to make his choices, allowing one interpretation of history to control one's present. "Zuckerman's in terrible history," Roth admits (CWPR 189). But it is how he reads and responds to that history that defines him, how he studies and survives that history that makes him a writer.

If history cannot chasten and contain, the contemporaneous world, a product of history, does its part to emasculate and lobotomize the individual. "Actuality," Kepesh thinks, "seemingly pounces upon even our most harmless illusions" (74). The real is a force as antagonistic as history. What Roth writes about in "Writing American Fiction" is just this dilemma, the real's arbitrariness, its ability to confound and belittle the imagination. A writer writes into the heart of history and then into the heart of the real. Zuckerman and Roth must come to terms with their past, with Howe's and Appel's warnings, at the same time as they must come to terms with the unpredictable now, the moment in time they move in and through. Desires and dreams, plans and goals, are usurped by the world's volatility. Howe and Appel are part of that unanticipated real, part of the unexpected roadblocks thrown in the way of the artist's and the individual's growth. And for Howe and Appel, Zuckerman and Roth are the facts of the new world they must accommodate.

The real hinders the traveler, it humbles the ambitious. It is what undoes Kepesh, what manhandles Zuckerman, what confounds "Philip Roth" in Israel. The real is everything most try to shut their eyes to, the blood and guts, the savagery of life. Howe notices, and then criticizes, Roth's awareness of the real's power in his first two novels. He claims, "Roth's two novels betray a swelling nausea before the ordinariness of human existence, its seepage of spirit and rotting of flesh" (PRR 238). Howe's critique suggests that the real should somehow be sweetened in literature, that disgust is not a proper perspective. It goes hand in hand with his suggestion that full portraits of Jews, faults and all, is improper. In Howe the fear of the real must be buried, in Roth it must be excavated. That which terrifies, the massacre itself, must be allowed into the realm of consideration, into the realm of fiction, or it will manipulate and control one's vision.

The real overwhelms but there is no substitute for it, and no avoiding it. To hide from it is to deny it. Repression becomes sin and shame in the concentrationary universe. For Roth the real offers more than just punishments. Every seepage of blood is, too, a sign of life. "Once you sidestep disgust," Roth says, speaking of *Patrimony*, "and ignore nausea and plunge past those phobias that are fortified like taboos, there's an awful lot of life to cherish" (CWPR 272). Through excavation, not avoidance, the blemished reality can be faced, if not healed. In *Patrimony* the father's embarrassing inability to control his bowels in Roth's house, and Roth's subsequent cleaning up after his father's accident, is transformed from a moment of ugliness to a moment of epiphany. The body's fragility is an expression of its humanity. To turn away from the real, to hide in some distant purified tower, is to miss the moments of connection that can be born only from an interaction with the real. When Maureen lies bloodied on the floor, in *My Life as a Man*, Tarnopol, inhibited for so long, held by his fear of direct confrontation with the real, residing too remotely in literature's segregated garden, feels the triumph of attacking the real evil in his life. "The real thing at last," he cries out" (280). "The real thing - and it was marvelous. I was loving it" (280). He feels liberated in his violence, freed from falsity, in touch with all that terrifies him. "In retrospect," he tells Spielvogel, "one of the high points of my life" (280). To turn away from the real is to miss life, Tarnopol and Roth discover; to accept it and explore it is to risk much but is to be alive.

The real and history are ephemeral powers in any one man's life, present but more relegated to the background in day to day living than the more recognizable and tangible presence of others who, in flight from their own terrors, attack and diminish those around them. Judge Wapter's edicts, Maureen's denunciations, Lucy's judgments, Mr. Zuckerman's last word, Helen's accusations, Baumgarten's caustic cynicism, Grossbart's machinations, Eli's lawerly requests, Bigoness's blackmailing are all attempts at control. If the real and history cannot be fought, one's anger is channeled towards that which can be fought.

Characters fight each other, like Howe and Roth, to secure for themselves some semblance of order. What transpires, then, is a constant back and forth motion of accusation and response. Howe's power play is responded to by a power play by Roth in *The Anatomy Lesson*. An unending cycle of attack and defense is inaugurated, with each action wedded to the other. The methods of both the attack and defense can be categorized in three ways: Naming, Desecrating, and Taking Control. Each method is suggested in the conflicts between Roth and Howe and Zuckerman and Appel, and each can be understood as a tentative, and usually unfulfilling, method at reducing one's sense of entrapment in the concentrationary universe.

To name an oppressor is to somehow contain him. When Howe calls Roth a "cultural case," he places him in a neat category (PRR 229). He is explained away as a "case," an inevitable result, not an original presence. When Zuckerman calls Appel the "Defender of the Faith" (106), and "the Charles Atlas of Goodness," he devalues Appel's words (167). He is no longer a singular accuser, but a representative of a type. Appel the man is transformed into "these Appels" (158). His criticism loses its sting, his words lose their value once they are deemed part of a predictable type.

The victim names his pain and thus domesticates it. When the residents of Prague look at each other and say, "It's Kafka," theirs is not simply a pronunciation of abject acceptance (POD 169) Even this communal naming in some way negates some of the pain, places under a label that can be understood, that can be spoken. Having a language to explain enslavement, as many Holocaust-poets believe, is the first step to overcoming it.

Kepesh repeats the Prague citizens' act of naming to harness the panic of finding himself turned into a breast. Naming is the first course he takes to overcome a new helplessness. Lucy Nelson ascribes her victimization to "men," and in this decisive labeling she finds some comfort, a port of blame to explain her misery (302). Maureen Tarnopol understands a man to be a "torture device," the cause for her unhappiness (317). Jake Portnoy and Alvin Pepler use the label anti-Semite to account for their own weakness. Pepler traces all his woes to the rigging of Smart Money to favor Hewlett Lincoln over him. His eidetic memory is no use to him in a world where anti-Semitism rages. He contends that there was a "limit for a Jew to win....To break the bank you had to be a goy....The bigger the goy, the bigger the haul" (35). And Korngold and Levy choose Korngold's son as the scapegoat for their depreciated condition. If Mr. Korngold would be "a good son" their "mess" would be alleviated (LG 108).

Alex Portnoy uses naming not only to quiet his fear but to subjugate others. He renames women with pithy titles to remove their strength as individuals. What begins as an act of self-protection becomes an act of oppression. Mary Jane Reed becomes "The Monkey," and later "The Cunt," and as such is dehumanized, made into a possession to enjoy and degrade at will

(107). "You, with all your big words and big shit holy ideals," says Mary Jane, "and all I am in your eyes is just a cunt - and a lesbian - and a whore!" (141). By classifying her he has taken away any distinguishing features, taken everything outside those all-encompassing words. (It should be added that Portnoy's job is a continuation of this tendency - by defining a group of people "disadvantaged," as needful of help, he, in fact, takes a portion of their humanity away; they are all one, all the same, children in need of Saint Alex). Naming is more than a defense mechanism; it is also a means of attack. The victim and the oppressor engage in the same fruitless technique and neither sees nor understands the other beneath the layer of tropes.

If naming is insufficient to fight the powers that be, many will turn to desecrating that which they are in conflict. Renaming history, reinterpreting the world one travels in, offers only short term release and soon the individual is drawn to a more aggressive and creative strategy. When Zuckerman's phone call fails, when he finds "that from phoning Appel and venting his rage, he was only worse," he redirects his anger by creating Milton Appel, pornographer (AL 168). As the editor of "Lickety Split," Milton Appel speaks words that the real Appel would abhor (181). While turning Appel from tormenter into victim, from the censurer to the censored, Nathan takes his revenge on the moralistic, sententious image Appel has developed for himself. More than merely creating an anti-self to let his imagination run wild, to free himself from his own "dwarf drama," Nathan, like Chaplin in "The Great Dictator," is desanctifying the authority who has devalued him (AL 145).

Peter Tarnopol, feeling himself like "Rudolph Hess" spending his "twenty years in Spandau Prison," writes angrily about "the army of slobs, philistines, and barbarians who...control the national mind" (58). They lose their stature in derision. Words rescue the victim from further victimization.Tarnopol tears away at the authority's superiority to ennoble himself. He employs the same formula his wife, Maureen, employs, lying prostrate in his kitchen. She defecates to rob Peter of his triumph, to diminish his moment of felt manhood. Smitty's narration, in The Great American Novel, is an attempt not only of retrieval but of demythologizing and disempowering the organization that has denied him his voice. His satire, outrageous and bawdy, rewrites the tired cliches that the proprietors of baseball have foisted upon a unknowing and naive public. It unmasks an authorized story, makes a mockery of the force that Smitty cannot overcome.

In Our Gang Roth mocks Richard Nixon with a similar satiric gesture. Roth parodies Nixon to expose and undermine him, to remove the skin of legitimacy he wears. Comedy, in Roth, is often an attack against those in control, those who set the agenda, who make the rules, who echo and reecho the worn banalities of the patriot, who control the tastes, who define the zeitgeist. He mocks the Jewish elders, the critics, the fathers and mothers, the police of Prague, the spies of Israel, the militants of the West Bank, in an effort to challenge their self-affirmed legitimacy, their power. Authority figures become the fodder for Roth's vindictive pen. With his words he levels the playing field, regaining a measure of authority for himself and his readers, for those who constantly feel a power enclosing them.

Roth gives an accurate picture of his parodic effort when describing a scene he witnessed while visiting Prague. Walking the streets, Roth hears laughter from a group of citizens. They are watching Milos Jakes, "the former first secretary of the Czech Communist party" in a "closed meeting of Party apparatchiks in the industrial city of Pilsen in October 1989" (CIP 15). Their laughter, Roth explains, is at Jakes's "dogmatic, humorless Party Rhetoric," the kind of language that kept them enslaved for decades (CIP 15). "Watching people walk back out into the street grinning," Roth writes, "I thought that must to the highest purpose of laughter, it sacramental reason-for-being - to bury wickedness in ridicule" (16). Their laughter reduces their former enslaver to a clownish figure; his power is howled away. Desecrating the bastions of power is parody's way of relocating power to those who are often its victims.

The method only goes so far, for it is, in the end only as lasting as the laughter it creates. And desecration is a flawed method in that it is employed, too, by the power itself to give impetus to its oppression. If subjects, people, become vermin, less-than-human, the power structure believes itself sanctioned to do as it pleases. When Dixon calls his citizens "sources of contagion," he linguistically allows for their destruction (120). In replicating the powers' methodology the impotent individual legitimizes it; he gains no lasting freedom from debasement.

The final course of action is taking control, assuming authority for oneself. Appel and Howe make themselves into figures of authority, judges of culture. It is they "who've whammied my muscles," Zuckerman declares (AL 158). "They push in the pins," he continues, "and I yell ouch and swallow a dozen Percodan" (158). They are granted power far in excess of their strength, like the lion-tamer over the lion. Assuming power is no original task. It is the obvious end-result of weakness.

"I know this place," exclaims Armando, in an early Roth story, "Armando and the Fraud," pointing with youthful ignorance at his imagined control of his store (32). Armando's benign words presage the more virulent pronunciations of authority. I am in charge, I know right and wrong, I control, says the new authority, ready to subdue all who cross his path. Authority's belligerence breeds new authority, as wicked and damaging as itself. Judge Wapter, Lucy Nelson, and Milton Lippman exude the confidence that comes with a delusional sense of authority, a knowledge that one's words stand above all others in veracity.

The power to control the story, to hold sway over the words, is the power most of Roth's characters long for. The author seems to hold this power, this god-like ability to decide fate, to create worlds, history, to map the earth to his own specifications. "When it comes to writing, it's you who's the authority," Pepler tells Nathan (AL 153). But Zuckerman denies his own authority.

His writing is victim to his life, to his parents, his world, to his body, even. He is no more authoritarian than any other character. In Roth's work the writer is implicated again and again. Perhaps this explains Roth's relentless mixing of autobiography and fiction. Everything is in doubt. Roth's stories are fictions and they are facts; neither world can be excluded, and neither world can be granted simple truth, simple authority. Roth's writers, himself included, are as victimized and powerless as his other characters. To become an authority, even in his writing, is to give up something of his self.

In *Deception* Roth creates the anti-writer, the voice that Pepler assumes for Zuckerman, the writer who commands and demands, who controls the words, controls the action, who is like Joyce's god, paring his fingernails while others expose themselves, writing what he wants, giving nothing of himself, risking nothing. "I'll write them down. You begin" (D 9). The voice is didactic and domineering. It is the voice of he who is in charge, he who demands action in response to his words. It is the voice of the accuser and the judge talking to or at the prisoner.

Roth's deceptive novel seems presented democratically, equally narrated by both parties: Each will ask and each will answer questions, each will reveal insecurity and vulnerability, each will speak forthrightly. But as the script unfolds only one participant bares her soul, only one answers with truth. "I look forward to your answers," says the voice of the man, the writer, Philip (11). And answers are what he gets, answers to a relentless inquisition. In just the first of seven sections devoted to pre and post-coital intimate talk Philip has asked thirty-four probing questions, while her few questions have been deflected. While his questions resound as accusations - "Why were you drunk?" - and personal invasions - "How unhappy are you?" (14) - questions designed to open up the subject, to arouse her to talk, to make her uninhibited, unshackled from propriety, her questions most often refer to herself - "Is that what I want? Is that it?" - rather than to him (25). He reveals little, she all. He asks, she answers. When she turns the tables on him and asks, "Why aren't you happy with your wife?" he responds with a question, "Why isn't your husband enough?" and suggests, "Perhaps we should give this conversation up" (48-49). He remains hidden in veils of language while she opens herself up like a corpse on a table, exposing her passions, her unhappiness, her pain, her history, her blemishes; even the lump on her cervix comes up for discussion. He shelters himself behind the mask of Philip, listener, friend, lover, all associative descriptions. If he deigns to tells anything it is in the guise of "reality-shift," a game of make-believe, a fiction (67).

Philip sits in his room and the voices come to him. He sits immobile, the assembler, the psychiatrist, the ear for everyone. He asks for truth but his game is fiction. He demands boldness and candor but claims everything is a lie. His is the smile of "power," as Zuckerman describes it, seemingly "benign," the false face that protects the manipulator from exposure (TPO 472). *Deception* is the portrait of the artist as dictator, as Nazi-like fiend, as purveyor of the lie. The other speakers are marionettes, held aloft by the puppeteer. Yet Philip, for all his power, is less a living presence than any other character. He loses the reader's sympathy early and slowly disappears like an omniscient narrator. In the process of pulling at others he loses his humanity. He is too sure, too right, too clear; he has too many answers, too much virtue. Philip remains a solid structure, never alive. He tells the story without experiencing it, a dispassionate automaton. The oppressor degrades himself in his oppression. He must withdraw from the world of men to control men.

The power over others then costs too much. It answers only one element of the terror he is attempting to extinguish. A partial solution, like naming and desecrating, it leaves the practitioner bereft, never allowing the release from the real, from history, or from others that one craves. Release is impossible from the powers which complicate life, which deny autonomy, which exert their pressure daily on the lives of even the most powerful of men. Time moves, history is inviolable, men and women will seek to possess and dispossess. Howe and Roth, Zuckerman and Appel, are allies battling each other in order to enunciate their rage at more implacable enemies. Howe sees Roth's use of his own words as evidence of their own plasticity, their use beyond his control. And Roth sees, in Howe's strange enmity, the unforeseen attack of an authority that towers over him. Howe sees the future grasping him and undermining his world and Roth sees the past impinging on and impugning his world. Howe fears what runs behind him and Roth what towers atop him. Each attempts, with various degrees of success, to name, desecrate, and take control, but each is left no more satisfied than Zuckerman is when he hangs up on Appel.

As Nathan tells himself, "Only Appel has nothing to do with this pain" (AL 159). The pain that all four combatants assert is a pain that transcends the conflicts with each other. Is not Appel and Zuckerman's battle only a consequence of their felt losses to the world? Both are sick, made decrepit by time and by unforeseen ailments. Roth argues that "If it weren't for Zuckerman's physical pain, there'd be no Appel in this book" (CWPR 194). Zuckerman's indignation is a way of handling his agony. And Appel, his voice losing its influence to Zuckerman's generation, his body weak with age, uses Israel's destruction as a metaphor for not only his own end but the brutalization of the real world upon what he deems essential. "This book," says Roth of *The Anatomy Lesson*, "is about physical pain and the havoc it wreaks on one's human credentials" (CWPR 194). This applies as much to Appel as to Nathan. Both fight the other as a substitute for battling the pain they cannot fight. Turning each other in their own Kaddish they hide their eyes from the Kaddish they cannot contend with.

Howe and Appel battle anarchy and Roth and Zuckerman battle structure. Howe fights not against Roth but against the dissipation of any tradition. Roth fights not Howe but the nets of tradition. Each responds to a totalizing force that seems to promise an end to their individual selves.

Howe sees in the nihilism of the modern times a disposal of the past, the advent of a world in which nothing has meaning, in which nothing is true, nothing is sacred, nothing is cherished, nothing is real, a world of absolute abandon. Roth sees in Howe's judgments the danger behind a call to tradition. Tradition is the order to which one must adhere, the absolutist ideology that deems one friend or foe, acolyte or blasphemer, the code that denies difference, denies choice and change.

Howe fears the antinomian impulse he reads in Roth, an impulse that can lead to a barbarian culture, while Roth fears what was once called The Beast, authority and tradition in all its corrupt overarching power. Howe fears one face of the Holocaust and Roth the other. Howe fears the orphan or Pipik world of emptiness and atheism and Roth fears the tradition-bound or Lonoffian world of ideology and meaning. These are the clear structures of power which reach beyond individuals and which disempower man, the distinct power that controls by its own malevolent and deceitful will, and the power of chaos that wreaks havoc without reason, without explanation. These are the powers that be, the powers which circumscribe Roth's imaginary worlds.

"Everywhere," argues Norman Manea, in his book of essays on the Holocaust and dictatorship, "there was the insidious, dilated presence of the monster called the Power....The power of darkness" (6). His description of his Romanian past serves well as a bold overview of Roth's fictional canvas. From Roth's early story, "The Final Delivery of Mr. Thorn," in which a postal worker is dragooned into retirement by a government that inspires only terror in is employees, to *Operation Shylock*, in which the Israeli government's presumes to cut a full chapter from "Philip Roth's" confessional book, a power is ever-present, an inheritance of the Holocaust, a hand hidden in the clouds but ready and able to reach down and pluck whatever it desires from its underlings, mere man.

The government is Roth's persistent representation of the repressive and deadening power that weakens the individual. Tricky Dixon is only the most absurd portrait of the irresponsible and banal authority figures Roth has scoured for decades. Eisenhower, Bush, and Quayle have all been satirized by Roth's acerbic pen, but beneath the wry jocularity is a deep bitterness at the damage the leaders impart, their disproportionate power, and their ability to keep their citizens quieted and bedazzled by rhetoric and spectacle.[14] They are the American purveyors of the lie, the poor cousin to the manipulators of Eastern Europe.

The government's perniciousness is reaffirmed and reified by the recurring setting of Czechoslovakia behind the Iron Curtain, a world of "suffering resulting from a life deprived of freedom," as Roth describes Klíma's novelistic setting in *Love and Garbage* (CIP 14). Roth uses Prague as a partial backdrop in three novels, and returns again and again, by means of literary allusion, to the Prague of Kafka, and later of Klíma, Kundera, and Havel. The Praguian world is Roth's metaphor for the concentrationary-world itself, a world of deceit, of powers subjugating and disarming and dehumanizing men and women. The "Russification" mentioned in *The Prague Orgy* is an able trope for the dangers all powers possess potentially, the power to make thought homogeneous, to restrict movement, to disallow and marginalize art and intellectual curiosity, to turn writers and thinkers into virtual slaves (426). What Roth's protagonists witness in Prague is no less than the colonization of minds, an effort they battle, too, in their daily lives, striving to hold fast to a personal set of values amidst an unceasing assault to sap originality to maintain order. "The good colonial life," Kepesh calls it: the life handed over for the sake of comfort, for easy answers (POD 55). "It isn't for nothing," Kepesh adds, "they hate giving up those empires" (55). The striving for Empire, for total control of one's subjects, is the common compulsion of all powers, the systematic annihilation of individuality, of uniqueness. It is a striving brought to its pernicious zenith by the Nazis. That imperialistic longing is not only prevalent in man's relation to a government, but is echoed daily in the personal relationships amongst men and women. The degradation at the top trickles down and infects each strata of society. Colonization begins at some ephemeral top and works its unseemly way into the unseen nadir.

The call for absolutes is a call for authority. It is this call that Roth understands is behind Howe's reverent worship of tradition. Art should adhere to a pattern, the critic says; art should inspire, praise, allow for celebration, not disparagement, of Jews. Art should offer confirmation of one's prejudices, the logic follows. "It is not the function of art to wallow in dirt for dirt's sake, never its task to paint men only in states of decay," Manea quotes Hitler's Nuremberg speech of September 1935 (87). "Art must be the handmaiden of sublimity and beauty," it goes on, "and thus promote whatever is natural and healthy" (87). These words, ostensibly harmless, banal, inaugurate a manner of criticism that devalues art and demeans the artist, making him into a petitioner for some interest. It is these words which show so many critical remarks made against Roth to be so very wrong-headed and counter-productive. The legitimate fear of losing a tradition, of sullying Judaism's name, of marring the past, leads critics towards a reactionary and historically failed and deadly thought-pattern.

Manea speaks of the way in which the censorious words of authority impact on every second of his writing life, focusing him on a "single obsession:" "that my book should not be co-opted by the system" (69). Praise becomes read as a revelation of failure, and enmity inspires. The authoritarian world, then, has is subtle advantages; it creates an environment in which real literature gains value, in which its very existence is called for to battle repression, to hold onto truth amidst the "Jerkish" of the likes of Roth's Dixon and Manea's Ceausescu (CIP 16). Roth mentions the "muse of censorship" (CIP 16), and Manea quotes Borges's comment, "Censorship is the mother of metaphor," suggesting the benefits (albeit they are few) of living under siege (30). The power becomes the legitimization of the writer's efforts, the clear enemy that gives meaning to one's words. "I wonder," Roth asks Klima, "what will happen to your writing" minus an "objective sort of evil" (19). Roth's question can be reformed to fit his own writing life: what would you're writing be without the Holocaust, what would your subject be with no evil, no horrible memory, no debacle? Repression breeds strength, makes dissent more valued, literature more cherished. The samizdat edition of a book is read with more intensity than any easily available text.

Life takes meaning from what challenges it, from what it must battle. The power that controls offers a defined enemy, a purpose. It is this impulse for purpose that attracts man to authority. "Authority," Manea writes, "fulfills the need for security and order," and as such it maintains its hold (87). Totalitarianism and authoritarianism work not only by threats and by violence but because they respond to a distinct need for surety, the need that explains Portnoy's headlines, Kepesh's roles, Tarnopol's literary manhood, and Zuckerman's application to medical school. The childish craving to be controlled, which Cynthia, the eleven-year-old daughter of Martha, admits to in *Letting Go*, does not dissipate in childhood. It stays within and is awakened as life becomes more troubled and terrifying.

Lonoffian authority's danger and power, then, lay not only in its malevolence but in its attractiveness. Lucy Nelson, drawn to the seductions of authority, is Roth's most clear portrait of the totalitarian impulse and the totalitarian threat. She is, at first, the innocent subject pulled and controlled by an ideological-myth, and then, later, the employer of that ideology. Lucy finds in totalitarian certainty her means of surviving. Hers is a world where the American tradition becomes law, where adherence is more important than independence.

Her counterpart, as discussed, Willard, epitomizes the opposite worldview. He embraces formlessness and democratic changeability. Roth, discussing the disparity between the American world and the Eastern European world under Soviet domination, states that for Americans "Everything goes and nothing matters," while for Eastern Europeans "Nothing goes and everything matters" (CIP 16). Daddy Will acts out the American model and Lucy the Eastern European model, and in their respective failures the failures of each system are made evident. For Lucy nothing is allowed and no one can speak without repercussions, while for Daddy-Will everything is allowed, the trespassing of codes, the failure of responsibility, lies.

The empty world, where nothing is explained or can be forecasted, where truth hides forever, where atheism is the predominant mind-set, casts a similar dimness over Roth's characters as the black presence of absolute authority. That nothing can be verified, that no pattern emerges over time, that life seems more and more a product of chance, fosters an impotence not unlike that of living in a colonized country, under the rigid control of a dictator.

"What law? Whose law?" Portnoy asks of the world (34). No law seems self-evident. "Oh, they will get us for that," says Tarnopol, "but who will get us?" (327). Who is in control? Is anyone in control? The world offers no evidence to ultimate meaning. It seems a frightfully precarious place. The survivor, Barbatnik, tells of his wife's death, and adds, "And it happened out of nowhere....How else?" (POD 258) Loss just appears, change happens, time moves, luck jumps about without giving any clue to its arrival or departure. There is no wisdom, no controlling voice, no meaning in the world.

Oblivion, eternity, death, call to man more vehemently in a world of unbelief. When Kepesh begins his story of his fantastical transformation he tells his readers, "Reflect upon eternity, consider, if you are up to it, oblivion, and everything becomes a wonder" (3). The terror of time bedevils the atheist because he sees no hope in life, no meaning in his time. This world of apparent complete freedom and pleasure-seeking is that deconstructed universe, that orphan world that Howe reads in Roth. The terror of tradition, he would appear to say in his three essays, is nothing against the terror of nihilism and disintegration.

The American reality, first discussed by Roth in "Writing American Fiction," while vastly preferable to the Eastern European reality, is pictured sliding towards chaos, becoming a place, indeed, where nothing matters. The picture Roth paints of democracy for Klima is an unflattering picture of meaninglessness run rampant, a world of "Total Entertainment," where "boring, cliched television" is watched "all the time replacing literature and thought (CIP 22). The danger of democracy, of freedom itself, is the danger of trivialization.

The orphan universe leads to a decline of seriousness. "I don't think," says Roth in an interview of March 1993, "there's a decline of the novel so much as the decline of the readership....there's been a drastic decline, even a disappearance, of a serious readership....We are down to a gulag archipelago of readers. Of the sort of readers I've described there are 176 of them in Nashville, 432 in Atlanta, 4011 in Chicago, 3,017 in Los Angeles, and 7,000 in New York. It adds up to 60,000 people. I assure you there are no more (PRD C13). In Pipik's time literacy is only a burden.

Literature cannot thrive in anarchy or in totalitarianism. Both systems diminish individual thought. In a world of absolute meaning literature serves no purpose other than to confirm the already believed truth. In a world of no meaning literature has no place, for it can add nothing, explain nothing, suggest nothing.

Roth delineates the dangers of both worlds and then looks to write in the tension between them. The goal for Roth's characters is to find that precious middle-ground, to not give into the bottomlessness of the orphan nor to become the mindless proponent of a predetermined myth of meaning. What Roth locates as the dichotomy between the "Jewboy" and "The Nice Jewish Boy" is nothing less than the dichotomy between the orphan and the acolyte (RMAO 35). Roth talks about the importance of emancipation in his life and work (CWPR 280). He speaks in 1991 of a recurring "need to be emancipated" from even those things which "liberated" him (CWPR 280). His works, consequently, particularly in their discussion of authority figures, take their form from the quest for emancipation. Emancipation, though, must not be confused with pure freedom, for emancipation is dependent upon an authority from which one deviates or escapes. Emancipation suggests not the undermining and disestablishment of all authority but the need for that authority if only to set the rules from which one dissents. Roth accepts Howe's complaint, even as he holds onto his own visions. As he must learn to live with the Lonoffian and the Pipikian father, and the ambigious mother, so, too, the writer must learn to accept the praise and the dismay of authority, without giving in, and without bowing down to it.

In "The Box of Truths," another Bucknellian story, the young writer feels his rejection by a publisher of "Goliath-like proportions" (12) as "prison bars" (10). But rather than constrict him further the unsettling words "Rejected," and "not accepted" awaken him, forcing him to question his assumptions: "Had he ever considered so searchingly, so sympathetically real people," he asks himself (12). To blindly turn away and turn a deaf ear to all authority is to lose one's own autonomy, as surely as one would lose it by adhering tenaciously to that authority. The difficult, but necessary, job is to adhere and rebel at the same time, to distinguish what one should admit and what one should reject, to form a "box of truths," an individuality, from the self and from the world, from the interior and the exterior, from acquiescence and rebellion, from the Jewboy and The Nice Jewish boy.

Doubt shows itself as the only viable perspective for both writer and man, neither an adherence to authority nor a disavowal of everything. Neither traditional world nor orphan world provides the means toward enlightenment. Tradition cannot be derided completely, nor must it be followed in lock step. In "The Final Delivery of Mr. Thorn," the mail-carrier refuses to deliver a letter to the Tomiseks which might tell of their son's death. "This letter," he thinks, "would end everything, all hope, all faith" (24). The letter would erase all doubt and doubt is hope, for doubt allows the imagination to construe possibilities still undenied. To remain within the suspended world of doubt is to hold on to hope, to neither give in to Lonoffism or Pipikism, to become neither Lucy or Willard, to neither cleave to power or deny all power.

Roth's is a world of powerlessness. Even if there is meaning to be found it is not self-made but created by some other. If there is meaning there is meaning, if not, not; there is nothing man can do. Into this his characters are born and their suffering begins with this knowledge. But doubt keeps them moving, creating, fighting on. And writing itself is evidence of the fight. That the writing continues, that someone takes pen to paper and writes day after day is testament to the inability to give into bleakness.

And that bleakness, in Roth's work, is a direct descendant of the Holocaust. When Milton Abravanel cries out, in "The Sex Fiend," "Thirty years old and I feel like I'm dead! And none of you know - you don't know.

You can't imagine. The world. What fury! What rage! What savagery!" we know his pain is a correlative of his job securing reparations for the Jews in Germany (2). His pain comes from knowledge of the Shoah, and Roth's bleak vision, too, springs from that knowledge. It is the Holocaust that warns against both absolute authority, an "external power," as Klima puts it, "which can at any moment come in and beat or kill him," and nihilism, a world without "why" (CIP 20). The Holocaust, Howe argues, was a "peculiar blend of ideology and nihilism" which released "the satanic energies of Nazism" (SW 426). The camp world is the ultimate expression of the con-centrationary universe Roth writes of and into, a world where authority rules by absolute decree, where men and women are killed by a malicious power structure, and where those same men and women feel that the world has lost all meaning, that nothing can be true ever again.

In response, Roth embraces a literary form of Jewish religiosity. According to Aharon Appelfeld, "All religious belief is based on two great feeling: the feeling that one is but dust and ashes, and the feeling that man is created in God's image. The equilibrium between these two feelings is what formerly gave the Jew his pride and his humility" (23). Roth's work develops from the tension between the fact that man is mortal and the incli-nation that there is some meaning in the world. To maintain the balance, to hold onto the fence, is to find a way of living in the concentrationary uni-verse.

Roth's literary strategy, then, is not far from that of the tradition Howe could not uncover in his works. His has been a deceptive manner of fiction-making, neither a complete rebellion nor a complete acceptance of any-thing. Roth has been able to both challenge and celebrate the powers that be, to challenge the parents and to express reverence for them, to malign authority and suggest the dangers of a world without authority, to criticize democratic chaos while singing of its freedoms. In Roth Kafka's words - "Dear Parents, I have always loved you, all the same" - explode with ambi-guity, respect joined with rebellion, fear with awe, love with hate (18).

And so in 1993 Philip Roth is presented with the Literary Arts Award by The National Foundation for Jewish Culture. The tradition personified, years after Howe's articles, accepts him and celebrates his contribution. His voice, that evening, is sincere, his speech concise, mixing humility and pride. But having been accepted Roth must have had a moment of doubt. After all, as he said in 1984, "the opposition has allowed me to become the strongest writer I could possibly have been" (CWPR 189). As the opposition sits now politely applauding him, the speaker must wonder if he has lost something now that the authority, the mothers and fathers who shouted epithets, finds him suitable for their honor. His voice, though, betrays none of this questioning, and yet one could not but sympathize with Roth if he felt, for a moment, the award to be as much a curse as a blessing.

Notes

1.   His absolutism is paralleled In Libby's father who sends her a letter rejecting her request for money. It begins, "Dear Mrs. Herz," words which immediately accentuate the distance of the writer from his daughter (133). "My obligations," he continues, "are to sons and daughters, family and Church, Christ and country" (133). She has broken the rules, married the enemy, betrayed her roots; to these crimes there is no forgiveness in his stodgy heart. "You have defied your father, your faith, and every law of decency, from the most sacred to the most ordinary," he writes, haranguing in the tone of a possessed preacher (133). "The obligation of the sinner is to rectify his sins....For it is privation," he concludes, "that shall lead you to the Shining Light" (133). The voice is that of the fundamentalist, of one who turns his ears and eyes from what goes against his unswerving and unquestioned laws. How different, contrary, in fact, from the timid voice of Mordecai Wallach crying out, weeping only for love. Libby's father's tone is the tone of the Lonoffian father and is not limited to the voice of evangelical Christianity but has its Jewish echo in Leonard Herz's irrevocable condemnation of his son and his son's new goyish wife.

2.   But hers is a strange rebellion, for as she adopts the opposite linguistic sphere of her grandfather she embraces with great vehemence his superficial worldview. The pose that he presents to his neighbors, and the cliches he spouts to his family and friends, become, to her, rule of law. Where he feels no allegiance to the banalities that fly haphazardly from his mouth she attempts to make those banalities true. Her rebellion is mixed; it supports the myths and conventions of Daddy-Will and of his community but it adds to them a militancy that points an accusing finger at all those who say the words only to act with disregard to them. Even in rebellion against the Pipikian father, even in the fulsome rapture of Lonoffian surety, the child returns to the father's words. The father's influence works powerfully upon even the most fervent progeny. That Lucy takes on a diametrically opposed vision of language to her grandfather only highlights the influence this weak father exerts. To rebel is to recognize the power of the object of the rebellion.

3.   Roth argues of Whitey that he is "equally loved, hated and feared" by Lucy (RMAO 26). And, indeed, for all the diatribes and assaults she points at him there is a moment in the text where love shows through. The father who played the "yump" game, who clowned and coaxed and held his beloved daughter, who calls her "Goosie" with affection, though he has failed her, and though he has awakened fear and distrust within her, retains a sympathetic hold upon her through the first half of the novel (179). Though he is pathetic he remains recoverable. Part of her impulsive grasping to conventional codes is an attempt to repair her father, bring him into line,

save him. Lying in bed, pregnant and afraid, her father comes into her bedroom to offer consolation and advice. Lucy thinks, "She was going to cry: they were talking" (179). For her it is a magical, transcendent moment, a turning point. "At long last," she asks herself, "those terrible days of hatred and solitude, over?" (180). To be reconciled with her father brings new hope. But her ideology is so firmly fixed by this point that she can only accept him if he has fully changed, if he has become her idea of a father. And he will not, he can not.

4.   Portnoy's naming of his women is driven by this same desire for categorization, closure. "Legs Dembosky, Bubbles Girardi, The Pumpkin, The Pilgrim, and The Monkey, exist less as women than as representations, types. "Legs is an "icon," a "dumb, blond, goyische beauty" (54). Bubbles is an anti-Semitic "shikse" (180). The Pumpkin's name is followed by, "New Canaan, Foxcraft, and Vassar," as though she can be defined in four words (262). The Monkey is Portnoy's dream of "Thereal McCoy," the sexual adventurer incarnate (131). If she, more than any other, is allowed to escape her categorization it is only for a pastoral moment. For a weekend in the country Portnoy sees The Monkey as Mary Jane, someone beyond the "Betty-Boop-dumb-Cunt" (221), someone for whom he can ask himself, "Could I love her?" (223). But soon thereafter Portnoy manipulates her back into her slated position, warning her, on the way to Gracie Mansion, "When we get there don't start talking about your wet pussy to whoever opens the door," and finally finagling her into a menage a trois in Rome, an act which confirms his stereotype of her and enables him to leave her (237). If The Monkey is allowed to escape his tightened definition of her then his entire lexical effort is put at risk. He begins to feel himself sink back into his father's indeterminacy, the language of indefinitiveness, the language of impotence.

5.   Milan Kundera suggests the women are "derived from literature: Birgitta is the heroine of a pornographic tale; Helen, a Femme Fatale out of some exotic/erotic detective fiction; Claire is a fairy out of the purest kitsch" ("Some Notes on Roth's *My Life as a Man* and *The Professor of Desire*" 166).

6.   Critics have interpreted the title of the novel in various ways, affixing a multifarious collection of definitions for 'Professor." Bernard Rodgers summarizes "the many connotations of the the the novel's title" (161). Rodgers argues that Kepesh "professes - lays claim to, frankly admits, affirms allegiance to, at times claims proficiency in, and seems to have dedicated himself as to a religious order to - desire. He is a professor of - a university teacher of, an instructor in the skilled art of, and one who professes his sentiments and beliefs about - desire....he is a man who in the words of the Random House Dictionary of English Language, 'makes a business of an occupation or hobby in which amateurs often engage" (161). The varieties of meaning put forth suggests that Rodgers is more open to the ambiguity of language than the character he investigates.

7.   As Beverly Edwards calculates, *The Ghost Writer* is penned "chronologically after *The Prague Orgy* by at least eleven months," suggesting, as she states, "that the trip to Czechoslovakia...enables Zuckerman to write again after his years-long writer's block" (195). When *The Prague Orgy* ends Nathan is ready to revisit the past, revisit the father without adopting a Pipikian stance of denial or a Lonoffian stance

of emulation. He gains the balance of insight to allow him, in *The Counterlife*, to finally become a father

8.   It asks not just for words but for deeds, for reformation. Portnoy yells to his doctor, transferring Spielvogel to Sophie, "Because to be bad, Mother, that is the real struggle, to be bad - and to enjoy it" (124). But Portnoy, like all of Roth's protagonists, cannot enjoy their badness, cannot enjoy what they perceive as a strike at their mother's heart. They compensate and compensate, trying desperately to win their mother's full approbation, to win a restored innocence. Portnoy remembers each of his transgressions like a rap sheet and he sentences himself to a hard labor of anxiety, impotence, and unending guilt. Even his job, Commissioner for Human Rights for the City of New York, can be seen as compensation for all his crimes against humanity, his self-directed sentence of community service.

9.   As to how Roth found his way to Josie, given Zuckerman's argument that "Josie isn't something that merely happened to you, she is something that you made happen" (169), a more tenable explanation than that she embodied "everything the Jewish haven was not" - that she was, in effect, meant as a shot to his mother and her middle-class house - is that she, for all her hysteria, her madness, appeared to Roth as definable, clear, fitting a developed. stereotyped role; she was, to a young man in need of clarity, a composed and discernible, if exotic, woman, an answer to the mother's ambiguity (174). Josie, like her fictional stand-in, Maureen Johnson, is a devilish and tragic figure but as such she can be quantified and understood. Her history makes sense, her actions make her despicable to Roth, simply an enemy who dies without a trace of remorse grazing his psyche. "Maureen Johnson," argues Shechner, "is a fearsome woman," who Peter "fears and despises" (126). He is drawn to her not from masochism and not as Schener suggests, in order to destroy her," but to banish for a time the disjunctive mother, to tie himself to something he can feel sure of, something surfeit with absolute meaning (126).

10.   Henry's intellectual and emotional siblings include Brenda Patimkin, Paul Herz, and Lucy Nelson; children unwilling to accept an unclear matriarch. Brenda cedes to her mother's wisdom, disregarding her fits of anger and her cruelty. Paul Herz forgets his mother's betrayal, and imagines her as a weak and knowing victim striped of self, left "clinging to her son" (583). Lucy Nelson, too, sees the mother as victim and victim only, but not a victim to be pitied, in Lucy's cold ideology, but to be chastised and despised. Her mother stands as an emblem to rebel against, an emblem of female subservience and cowardice. As The Darling dissolves into her men the mothers dissolve into their children's image. Seen in this cartooned way, the child establishes a clear relationship to her mother, a deadening and deadly vision.

Nathan's epiphany, his intellectual and emotional merging with his mother's ambiguity, is echoed to a greater or lesser extent by Portnoy, Kepesh, and Gabe Wallach. Alex ends his impotence-expunging narrative still without a clear or consistent idea of the mother. He does not accept this condition, as Zuckerman does, but he does not impose a false clarity to ease his pain. He remains within his conundrum, within his questions.He is still "whimpering on the floor with MY MEMORIES! My endless childhood!" (271). And yet he shows signs of not relinquishing the friction, the endless debate. He will not simply give up one side of the mother for the other. He retains enough intellectual and moral integrity to keep himself from simple closure. Of his childhood he bellows, "Which I won't relinquish - or which won't relinquish me! Which is it!" (271). He wants a solution but won't fashion an erroneous one. He is torn by ambiguity but won't bury his mind to achieve peace. David Kepesh becomes a breast, and, in many ways, that transformation into a part of the body associated initially with the mother, brings him closer to an acceptance of his mother's ineffability. Becoming a gendered object, as he does, he learns to reject simple quantifications of people or of events. As his mother must strive to escape the boundaries of sex he must try to escape the boundaries of the tragic joke played upon him. And he must do it without recourse to definitive interpretation for interpretation leaves him an object, 'The Breast,' to be studied and labeled, dehumanized, circumscribed only by his predicament. He learns to recognize that his is, in Roth's words, "an ambiguous struggle shot through with contradiction and bewilderment" (RMAO 73). He is more than his circumstance, more than his body. Gabe Wallach, left with a letter that contradicts everything he once believed of his mother, begins *Letting Go* a dissected man, unable now to unite the mother of the letter - her hands weak and uncontrolled - with the mother he had grown up with - seemingly perfect, in control of her hands and everything she touched. Choosing not to accept that bifurcation Gabe makes the conscious choice to emulate and believe in the mother's remembered power and surety. But that attempt fails when Gabe acts out his "one decisive moment," risking the Herzs' child by bringing her to Bigoness to persuade him to make the adoption legal (591). In the midst of the confrontation Gabe losses complete control for the first time. He surrenders his hands, collapsing from terror, and is left in a posture of total submission: "He did not take his arms from his ears" (588-589). Gabe gives up sovereignty over his hands, lets his emotions rule him and is left enervated but liberated. He realizes, later, that he has experienced a "dissolution of character," and is ready to begin again, to attempt to create a new Gabe, one not burdened by a code of behavior, and unafraid of ambiguity (589). Gabe learns over time what the short letter might have taught him much earlier; that the mother's ambiguity is her humanity and her power.

11.   Certainly Roth encouraged this view with several titillating comments made early in his career. "I am not a Jewish writer," he said at a conference in 1963 in Jerusalem, "I am a writer who is a Jew. The biggest concern and passion in my life is to write fiction, not to be a Jew" (SDII 35). Roth seems to be concurring with Howe's observation, fueling his fire. He goes on to say, "I do not write Jewish books, French books, or American books" (SDII 60). Roth does not reject tradition, then, but refuses to be a slave to it. He rejects the appellation Jewish Writer not to close himself off from the past but to recuse himself from simple categorization. He challenges Yuakov Malkin's definition of a Jewish writer as one who "seeks to celebrate the virtues of the Jewish people" (SDII 60). To do so is to be no more than a propagandist, a slave to readers, a slave to polemic. A writer writes to challenge, both himself and his readers. "The Jew," Roth says, "is to the Gentile world what the writer is to the world itself" (SDII 61). The Jew denies the Gentile's their certainty, their surety,

questions their religion, their morality, and it is the writer's job to act similarly, to question conceptions and verities, to force a reader to look anew upon his world.

What Roth admits here is that his writing philosophy is heavily indebted to a Jewish vision, that history and tradition have not passed him by. That his interpretation of Jewish history is not the same as some others is evident. His idea of the Jewish sensibility is inclusive to non-Jewish writers like "Gogol and Dostoevsky" (SDII 75). "What seemed essential to Jewishness," Roth states, "was dissent" (28). The Jew celebrates dissent because his history is plagued by the repression and disallowance of dissent, the stifling of the questioning voice. For Roth, to be simply included in the Jewish tradition would be to be thrown into a neat pile, one's force etiolated by approval.

12.   Howe exhibits an almost vindictive blindness in his two subsequent essays on Roth, both of which make some cogent comments only to follow them with a reassertion of Roth's lack of Jewish tradition. One can point to Roth's disingenuous and incendiary comments, made in 1963, as the trigger for Howe's anger. The young writer maintains, "It seems to me that the largest burden a Jew has is, not having the courage to accept one's Jewishness, but having the courage to deny it" (SDII 75). Surely those words tell of a misreading of history. For certainly only twenty years earlier the courage of Jews was not to deny but to hold on to their identities. To hold on to the oppressed label, Jew, regardless of one's religious convictions, was to assert solidarity to the disenfranchised many and to risk one's own place in the world. In the same session Roth remarks, "But I still find it hard to figure out what in my work is Jewish" (SDII 74). Can these two irresponsible statements made by a youthful writer trying with adolescent bravado to separate himself from the Jewish writers who surround him be enough for Howe to see in Roth a direct challenge to all he cherishes, to convince him that his initial fears are well founded? It is unlikely and yet there is little else to account for his interpretation. As Roth has said, speaking of Howe predominantly, it was "one of the oddest misreadings that any contemporary writer has run into" (CWPR 188). Directed at a writer who has been criticized for being too Jewish, for restricting himself to the same small world over and over again in what seems an obsessional and solipsistic manner, Howe's accusation is indeed difficult to fathom.

13.   In Roth, Howe has chosen not some distant entity whose assault is plain and clear to all but someone who is tied closely with Howe himself. For, in fact, it is Howe's own ideas that Roth employs almost as a blueprint for what Howe takes to be Roth's most vulgar, ugly, abusive, and weakest work, *Portnoy's Complaint*.

In 1946 Howe wrote a short essay, titled "The Lost Young Intellectual," which outlines an early version of what Portnoy will rail about. It is an essay which tells of the "alienation" of the "young American Jew" who "teeters between an origin he can no longer accept and a desired status he cannot attain" (361). "His problem," Howe writes, "usually finds its central focus in his relationship to his family" (362). Portnoy is the lost young intellectual, Howe's "marginal man, twice Alienated" (362). As in Portnoy's family the father, in Howe's conception, "is not really the power in the family, the mother is often much more 'practical' and decisive" (363). "The father," Howe continues, "desires in his son the fulfillment of his own underdeveloped and frustrated ambitions" (363). "In my liberation,' thinks Portnoy, of Jack, "would be his" (8).

"In relation to the mother," Howe's piece goes on, "the problem involves emotion more status" (365). Portnoy's tenuous and tenacious attachment to his mother is here presaged. The mother, Howe suggests, controls through "food" (365). There is even a similar anecdote found in Howe's serious essay and in Roth's raucous novel. Howe describes an incident at school in which he is asked to identify a fork and he calls it "by its Yiddish name; a goopel" (364). Portnoy describes an incident in which the teacher holds up a "spatula" and Portnoy, accustomed to hearing his mother call it a spatula, thinks the word Yiddish and so "could not think of the word in English" (96). The action is inverted; Howe thinks the Yiddish to be English while Portnoy thinks the English to be Yiddish (an inversion which suggests which direction each is looking) but the substance is the same: The identity found at home is in conflict with the identity forming in the new American world.

"The dilemma" Howe investigates takes various forms (366). It can cause a "split in personality" (366). It can produce mental and physical "sterility" (366). It can cause difficulties in "his relationships to women" (367). "Of course," Howe concludes, "fortunately - few individuals suffer from all the characteristics listed here" (367). What Roth has done is to create an individual, Alexander Portnoy, who does suffer from all the traumas Howe lists - and a few more. Roth takes Howe's essay and infuses it with a new vivacity, a new language, one which both announces the dilemmas and which, in its unique utterance, attempts to escape them. His is a language that mixes the sententiousness of Howe's article and Howe's tradition with the language of the vaudevillian and of the decidedly real, absurd world.

And Roth reaches a similar conclusion as Howe. Howe maintains that "it is difficult to be a Jew and just as difficult not to be one," a simple and incomplete idea that Portnoy must accept as well (362). Both Howe and Roth celebrate their "rootless" condition as a means of holding on to their "complexity" in a world of burdens (367). Roth's man in the middle is akin to Howe's lost intellectual. Is it, then, Roth's appropriation that so enrages Howe? Does he see Roth's use of his own words, in what Howe considers an obscene and impertinent manner, as a personal attack?

14.   Eisenhower is mocked for his absurd and self-serving evening's prayers in "Positive Thinking on Pennsylvania Avenue." Bush's pro-life stance is parodied in "Pro-Life Pro," in which the President calls for a cessation of both menstruation - "murder of a human egg" - and masturbation - "murderin sperms by the millions, and every one of them a potential life" (5), and Quayle is lambasted for his explanations as to why he joined the National Guard, in "Oh, Ma, Let Me Join the National Guard"

CHAPTER THREE

Portnovian Dilemmas

Ven der putz shtcht, ligt der sechel
in drerd.
                        - Philip Roth
                        - Portnoy's Complaint

Descartes formulated a world torn in two, a world where the individual feels
a chasm within, a clear separation between the thinking mind and the
extending body. "This 'I' by which I am what I am," Descartes writes, "is
entirely distinct from the body and could exist without it" (10). The body is
a machine which belongs to the world of matter, while the mind resides in
a higher dimension, defiled by the body's urgings. Descartes's arguments
are designed ultimately to prove the incorporeality of the soul, its non-
reliance on the body's existence.

Roth, too, writes of a world newly dissected, but Roth begins not in
Descartes's metaphysical realm but within the quotidian world. He begins
by positing the question of the mind/body dualism as it fashions itself on
earth, in life, within the day to day dalliances and conflicts of man's existence. For the metaphysical world is now responsive to the world of atrocity. The individual who makes the decision to believe himself either a corpo-
real machine, a servant to Dionysus, or a rational mind, a slave of Apollo,
makes a choice not unlike that of the Nazi puppet. And so Roth inherits
Cartesian dualism and repositions it in his fiction, making Descartes's
abstractions real, and moving gradually towards a consideration of
Descartes's questions of soul and body, matter and mind, rethinking and re-
enlivening Descartes's metaphysics for the concentrationary universe.

The historic dualism Descartes first uncovers is transformed in Roth into two versions of letting go: one which finds solace in the moral and intellectual sphere of the brain, letting go of the Dionysian body, and the other in the guiltless hedonism of the corpus, letting go of the Apollonian mind. But, as David Hirsch writes, "both the 'Apollonian' and the 'Dionysian' present a troubled reality in the context of the Holocaust" (12). Both are suspect. For, as Hirsch continues, "We know that Hitler exploited Dionysian tendencies in the German Volk" (12). To exist as only a body is to allow all excess. "At the same time," Hirsch argues, "Reason was put to use in organizing a brilliant bureaucratic structure designed to exterminate human beings. The death camp itself is the ultimate example of Rationalism gone mad" (12). Man, in Roth, must choose whether to isolate one side of his self and conform to one version of letting go - to relapse into a Nazi-like emptiness - or allow the two sides to exist simultaneously within, to allow the traumas and the pain of their confrontation to continue unabated in order to hold fast to an integrated self, to exist - without letting go - as a divided being, never at rest.

The Portnovian dilemma replaces Cartesian dualism: The body and the conscience war with one another, two disparate entities fighting over the same personage. "Portnoy's Complaint" (port'-noiz kem - plant') is defined as "A disorder in which strongly-felt ethical and altruistic impulses are perpetually warring with extreme sexual longing, often of a perverse nature" (7). The ethical and altruistic impulses are societally generated and responsive to the mind, while the extreme sexual longings are a product of the body's organic pulsations.

The body exerts its influence: Portnoy admits, "Ven der putz shtcht, ligt der sechel in drerd" ("When the prick stands up, the brains get buried in the ground") (128). It complains of repression and promises extraordinary delights. It searches for instances of release without fear of punishment. The mind promises its own rewards, rewards of honor, pride, respect, but it can diminish one, fill one so surfeit with prohibitions that the body becomes impotent, unable to even act on the most harmless of instincts. "But," yells Portnoy, "What my conscience, so-called, has done to my sexuality, my spontaneity, my courage" (124). The mind protects but protection taken too far is imprisonment. "I am marked like a road map from head to toe with my repressions," Portnoy exclaims (124). Both mind and body practice a form of totalitarianism, and it is that totalitarian strength that both tempts one and pushes one away.

Both the mind and body provide pleasures and aches and in their interaction they seem to make pain a prerequisite of life, or so imagines Portnoy. Portnoy's session is an attempt to subdue the id or the super-ego. But the solution he imagines stands not as a victorious end but as a final defeat, a severing. By seeking a certain letting go, a closing down of either mind or body, characters fall into a preset trap Roth mentions in an interview with Joyce Carol Oates. Speaking specifically of *My Life as a Man* Roth says,

"I have always been drawn to a passage that comes near the end of The Trial, the chapter where K, in the chapel looks up toward the priest with a sudden infusion of hope.... 'If the man would only quit his pulpit, it was not impossible that K. could obtain decisive and acceptable council from him which might, for instance, point the way, not toward some influential manipulation of the case, but toward a circumvention of it, a breaking away from it altogether, a mode of living completely outside the jurisdiction of the Court. This possibility must exist, K. had of late given much thought to it'" "Enter Irony when the man in the pulpit turns out to be oneself" (RMAO 108).

One's pulpit is not so much what Rodgers calls one's "useless fictions" (49). Rodgers places too much emphasis on the one fiction discarded or retained. What permeates the novels, and what animates the characters, is not so much a fiction from youth but rather the idea of fictions, of structured patterns and codes of behavior and thought. When Roth speaks about one's pulpit he means both the individual fictions a person grasps to and a mind-set adaptable to any unalterable system. To be trapped is to be made a subject of a system, to conform to it without question, as the victims were forced to do, and as the victimizers chose for themselves.

Securing themselves to a pulpit, to a half-life of the mind or of the body, the men and women flay a layer of their selves. The pulpit is the means of repressing the Portnovian dilemma, but ultimately it becomes a means for repressing individuality. To watch as this repression is enacted is to witness the ways in which man has been tempted to a self-severing, how he, even now, is drawn to a Nazification of self.

In Letting Go Roth provides sketches of many characters who willfully subscribe to a pulpit, who slay their duality with a fascistic faith in either rationality or in corporeality. Only Gabe refuses this easy fixity. As Donald Kartiganer argues, "Gabe yet remains at the centre of the novel's transformational power" (93). He is ever transforming himself, letting need and purpose battle on still.

Gabe Wallach's complexity allows for a frequent misreading of his character. Gabe is often read as the antihero of the text, the failed man, the villain whose coldness displaces all human characteristics. Rodgers claims that every action Gabe takes "can be viewed as the result of ulterior or selfish motives" (51). Everything about Gabe, according to this perspective, is calculated, the result of a solipsistic plan to keep others from interfering or colliding with his minutely constructed personal world. Gabe's story is less clear. It is more revealing to see him as a man wanting only to be good, and torn apart by his disparate drives.

Gabe is burdened by a particular guilt. His is a post-Holocaust sensibility which makes him feel responsible for the world, as if his every action had the potential for causing disaster, as if his ostensibly easeful life inversely creates another's hard life. When he sees an ambulance on the road, he pulls his car over and rushes toward the stretcher. He looks down at the victim and admits, "What I saw surprised me. The face sticking up above the blanket belonged to nobody I knew" (54). His conscience tells him to remain uninvolved, for involvement leads to damage. Both Gabe and Paul subdue their hearts, trying to "do no violence to human life" (3). Gabe's adeptness surpasses his double's and thus his heart seems absent to those around him, but it is most assuredly there, "pulsing" with life (359). Alone with Martha that pulsing beats fervidly as Gabe grasps Martha's breast. His conscience never reigns supreme, the hands as though willful spring into action.

Gabe and Paul share a basic dilemma, the dilemma of dualism. Though they come from different backgrounds, have different relationships with their families, and are, in essence, vastly different men, they both are decimated by the interplay of heart and head within, and by their desire to enact a vivisection of themselves. Dualism for the children of the Holocaust generation is a frightening prospect, more evidence of an uncontrollable, precarious civilization, while for the victim generation, for those like Charlotte Delbo, duality must be forced into being.

Towards the middle of the novel Paul and Gabe shake hands. Gabe comments, "I don't think it would have shocked either of us then if we had embraced" (227). And later, grasping each other's hand again, they finish speaking and yet "continued to grip each other's hand" (441). In those moments they express an inexpressible, wordless, bond between them, a bond of both heart and mind. The hands, the embodiment of both mind's rationality and the heart's chaos, join together finding comfort in one another, comfort in the emotional connection, a connection of skin, and in the connection that seemingly suspends action for a moment, a grip that keeps the hands under control, surrounded, encased. The difficulty they find in releasing one another is the difficulty of re-entering their conditions. For a moment they have equanimity.

But that moment, which might act as a opening, an elucidation, instead is a parting for Gabe and Paul. As they release each other it is as though they have touched for the last time. Paul anesthetizes his divisions, performing surgery upon himself, while Gabe finds no panacea for his own. After his dissolution - brought on by a brief but compelling complete surrender to the heart he had battled for so long - Gabe ends unafraid, receptive even, of his own dualism. Kartiganer recognizes that Gabe is about to enter into "a full engagement of the opposing sides of self" by refusing to accept "accommodation" (93).

Only Gabe survives, like Ishmael. Gabe survives the wreckage of his age by grasping to the same awakening as the victims. In Roth's idiom Gabe quits his pulpit, finds a way to live outside the jurisdiction of the court. In an interview Roth states that he views "Gabe Wallach, Alexander Portnoy, and David Kepesh - as three stages of a single explosive projectile that is fired into the barrier that forms one boundary of the individual's identity and experience" (RMAO 85). Roth goes on to say, "Gabe Wallach crashes up against the wall and collapses" (RMAO 85). Though he collapses, Gabe's story has not ended, for that collapse signals a beginning, the first advance of an ever-moving projectile. Everyone else lay dormant on land while Gabe tests the tumultuous waters, the deceptive and changeable sea, a reflection of a self's variety. His is finally an acceptance of the dual presence of mind and body, an acceptance of the concentrationary universe's ambiguity as it is expressed inside himself, an acceptance of two forces struggling within, attacking and responding to one another.

Descartes allows for this interaction by creating an organ he labeled the "pineal gland," the link chain between mind and body (15). Roth's protagonists feel doubled, cut in two, one part a "stimulus response device" and one part a "thinking thing" (236). It is how they respond to this split that tests their character: Do they become, like Martha, Paul, and Libby, one thing devoid of instinct or of rationality, or do they, like Gabe, allow the pineal gland to exist, allow two selves to occupy them, to navigate and torment them with their contradictory messages? Do they adopt a pulpit or do they forswear pulpits, preferring tension to simplicity? These philosophical and internal questions take on a new imperative in the new world. The legacy of the Holocaust is fear, fear of the carnal, fear of the rational, and fear of meaninglessness; yet it is that same legacy, the terror it inspires, which moves one to look for a pulpit of the carnal or of the rational to restore a lost and imagined order. To let go of a side of self is to fail, to let go of a pulpit is to invite pain but to remain an individual, halved but more whole for a riven self.

In his review of "Goodbye, Columbus" Saul Bellow suggests that the question of "worldly goods versus the goods of the spirit" is the central conflict of the novella (78). Bellow points at the same conflict the characters in *Letting Go* must either minimize and alleviate, or accept, the conflict of need (worldly goods) and purpose (the spirit). The terms are different but Bellow notices what is the first indication of the Portnovian complaint that finds full expression in Roth's fourth book.[1]

Neil is suspicious of his heart, suspicious of its motives, of its uncanny ability to trick his mind and conscience. For Neil the true self depends on the mind's persistence, its evaluation and its dogged challenging of the heart. He is like Leo Patimkin, Brenda's father's half-brother, burdened by a bitter conscience. "Even the pleasures I can't enjoy," says Leo (116). Leo, like Neil, is beset with integrity. It is after Leo and Neil have their conversation that Neil looks down on a sleeping Brenda and wonders, "How would I ever come to know her...for as she slept I felt I knew no more of her than what I could see in a photograph" (118). He thought that in time he would see a deeper vision of Brenda, a Brenda beneath the pretty exterior.

Neil is "split between the disapproving moralist and the acquisitive self," as Rodgers points out (45). The acquisitive self, he believes, is what draws Neil closer to Brenda, allowing her to take command of him. In his prayer

Neil locates this self: "If we meet You at all God, it's that we're carnal and acquisitive, and thereby partake of You. I am carnal, and I know you approve, I just know it. But how carnal can I get" (100). He fears he will become all carnality, a virtual lust machine, his conscience unplugged. Bellow feels that "Neil's meditation is curious...why should it please God that we are carnal or acquisitive? I don't see that at all" (78). Neil sees carnality as self-evident, a part of you given by God and therefore pleasing to God. What Neil objects to, and what he supposes God to object to, is the notion that carnality is its own power.

But what Neil reveals in his passionate prayer is more than respect and trepidation towards his carnal side. What he reveals is a hidden pulpit, the underlying urge that compels him towards the culmination of his story. Linking the carnal to the Godly ("damn it, God that is You," says Neil) is what his dream has always been (100). His romanticizing of Brenda has been a means to assert a singular self, to ascribe longing to rational goals. Neil distrusts lust and instinct and trusts finally his conscience and mind. He wants to surround his instincts with nobility, his felt urges with meaning; he wants to turn what is felt as superficial desire into a slave to the mind's ethical plan. To ascribe the body's temptation to the mind's master plan is to deny carnality its difference, its separation. It becomes the hand of God, the hand of rationality; it loses its mysteriousness, its own unique properties. Instead of accepting his lust as a separate part of his whole self, Neil wants to make it a property of his head, a messenger for the mind.

Neil's denial leads him to Boston, to a decision to marry Brenda. He must make a commitment, he feels, for he has been driven by a rational mind conscious of its actions. In order to prove to himself that it has been his head all along that has ruled him, that his body's pulsations were only the means to the intended end his head had decided upon, he resolves himself to marriage, not doubting any longer Brenda's character. He can trust his body for his body was lead by a clear mind. He need no longer question himself; his pulpit has clarified all. His purpose is apparent to him; his purpose defines him.

With Brenda's unforeseen rejection Neil is shocked into a new awareness. Set up for defeat he is shaken alive. "Losing" Brenda is transformed into "winning" his doubled self back (135). After Brenda's rejection Neil wonders, "What was it inside me that had turned pursuit and clutching into love" (135). Neil had turned need (pursuit and clutching) into purpose (love) because he could not abide the idea of two contradictory parts of himself residing within, pulling him this way and that. He needed order, needed to believe that if there was no order in the desolated world outside himself, at least there was order within him, needed to see himself as one thing working methodically towards some final goal. Neil adds to his query, asking what was it inside him that had "then turned it inside out again" (135). What has turned it inside out is his reborn duality born of Brenda's submersion into the Patimkin world of need. "Whatever spawned my love for her," Neil wonders, "had that spawned such lust too?" (136). The love flourished to give credence to the unmindful lust. Neil's craving for a rational self had turned an object of pure desire into an object of pure love.

Love and lust, Neil now realizes, drive each other, confuse and undermine each other. One cannot allow either to take absolute control. To allow both to exist as separate islands within is to put limits on each. The divided self offers a test to itself, while the singular self swallows whole all questions. Neil gives up the comfort of a pulpit for the freedom of the dual-self. He ends unsure of who he is and where he will go, but more leery of the urge to unite his contrary impulses, leery of subsuming one in the other. He is still that diffusive self searching for some definition of his being, some picture of his worth, ever trying to answer the question, "What is it to be what I am?" (I-GC I)).

Neil's eye is the key to his "I." He learns to distinguish shadings where others see blacks and whites. The deeper eye melds the aesthetic with the intellectual eye, the way two eyes meld together to see one thing. The deeper eye sees impressionistically, knowing that what it sees cannot be trusted. "I am certain that I am, but what am I? What is there that can be esteemed true?" Descartes asks at the beginning of the "Meditations," a question Roth introduces and remarks upon when speaking of David Kepesh and his transformation into a 150 pound breast (RMAO 71). Does the "I" that the eye reveals define a self, or is there more, and what constitutes that more, that full self? This is the question that links Neil to Kepesh, Kepesh to Tarnopol, Tarnopol to Portnoy, Portnoy to Zuckerman, and Zuckerman to Roth. Descartes's preliminary query is the query Roth and his protagonists enmesh themselves in. Am I this body or this mind, both, neither, something else entirely? Am I what I feel or what I know, what I see or what I am blind to? Neil's eyes tell him a more profound story than the paper-deep Patimkin's eyes tell them, but how far, he wonders, will those eyes take him, what are their limits, what myopia lay undiagnosed, unseen, and untreated? How much blindness is implicit in one's character, how much can be overcome? Like Descartes's doubts, there is only so far one can take oneself out of one's own limits, out of the manner one sees or thinks. There are limits impossible to traverse, knowledge that study will not pull to the surface, presuppositions that hold back clarity. Descartes's "blank slate" is an impossible goal for the mature human, conditioned already by so much.

Neil throws his pulpit aside, cognizant of his own haziness, his own murkiness, but more aware that that very haze is not only a facet of being lost but of the possibility of discovery. Roth's character's lostness is a condition more to cherish than that of Patimkin-like satisfaction. Loss, like exile, is predicated on possibility, on a future, on a constant renewal and reinterpretation of vision, lost but to be found.

Like Neil, "Kepesh is lost," explains Roth, lost "somewhat the way Descartes claims to be lost" (RMAO 71). He is alive, of that he is sure, but to what end, to what purpose? It is a question which, in his convalescence,

Kepesh considers and agonizes over, but it is not a question born of this unlikely metamorphosis, rather it is a question which suffuses David's life from his earliest days, a question which occupies David throughout not only his narrative of disaster, *The Breast*, but throughout his narrative of temptation, *The Professor of Desire*.

David Alan Kepesh wrestles with the Cartesian dilemma long before he is torn from any empirical sense of himself as human, as a man. His "overarching desire," as Roth says, is to "somehow achieve |his| own true purpose" (RMAO 70). The desire Kepesh discusses, then, is not simply the manifestation of sexual longing but a deeper, more penetrating, instinct towards self-knowledge, towards some kind of graspable truth. "I am one thing or I am the other," Kepesh declares (12). "Than, at twenty, do I set out to undo the contradictions and overleap the uncertainties" (12). His interior battle between need and purpose is complimentary with his battle with the world's opaqueness. The concentrationary world is rife with indecipherability, with unanswered questions. Kepesh acts out his interior battle in hopes of finding a clarity of vision not only of himself but of the world as well.

Instead of viewing himself as an amalgam of roles, with an amalgam of influences, he maintains an either/or perspective on identity, hoping to fit into the role of "scholar" or "rake" (17). Literature becomes not an avenue for awakening and selection but an avenue to find a true self. Kepesh turns to "archetypes" for self-revelation (37). To be a literary man is to depart from the body, silence its caterwauling, sweep everything under the rug of scholarship. His description of himself as a "Stellian man" points out not only that he is "a man never at home, never at rest, never satisfied, always a stranger," as Rodgers claims, but that he is desperate for fulfilling a pulpit, a definition in which to encase his disordered self (162). Literary models are embedded within Kepesh and it is from them that he interprets the world. To be a literary man, then, is to let the well-defined role Professor - someone who stands aside and observes dispassionately - overtake one's individuality, to become a title, to become whole through a negation of a part of oneself.

In his introduction to his comparative literature class Kepesh outlines the goal for his narrative: "Above all," he imagines telling his class, "I hope by reading these books you will come to learn something of value about life in one of its most puzzling and maddening aspects. I hope to learn something myself (184). Through literature he is to learn who he is. "What a church is to the true believer, a classroom is to me," he admits (185). He seeks through works of the imagination a churchly truth, a pulpit.

His preface to his unseen students provides the clues to the two antipathetic directions he will look for that truth. He states: "As you may have already surmised...the conventions traditionally governing the relationship between student and teacher are more or less those by which I have always operated" (182). Conventions underlie his teaching style. He teaches according to a code of conduct. He wears "a jacket and a tie" and removes his watch at the start of class placing it in its traditional spot on the table top, a sign of professionalism, of seriousness and continuity (183). And yet he asks his students to refrain from talking about "'structure,' 'form' and 'symbols'...to try living without any classroom terminology at all, to relinquish 'plot' and 'character' right along with...'epiphany,' 'persona,' and, of course, 'existential' as a modifier of everything existing under the sun" (183). He both embraces conventions and wishes to undo conventions, recognizing them first as ties to a solid past and then as an impediment to free thought, a hazard and a cause of lazy-thinking. In his lecture, and nowhere else, Kepesh unites his two selves, holding them together. "I am devoted to fiction," he concludes, "but in truth nothing lives in me like my life" (185). The realms are distinct but they are both present, both part of him. Kepesh asks for a "referential relationship" between life and art, a conjoining of the world of language and the world of action, the world of form and formlessness (185).

That conjoining is only possible in the classroom. "To my mind there is nothing quite like the classroom in all of life" (184). Contradictory elements can only exist side by side in an unreal enclosure, not in the concentrationary world of "unrelenting forces" and "debilitating experience" (185). The role of professor fits seamlessly over him but it is a role that offers little sustenance outside the "bright and barren little room" (184). "I want to cry out," Kepesh writes, "Dear friends, cherish this!" as if the classroom were the last Eden, the last gasp of innocence before reality remakes everything (184). What Kepesh fails to grasp is the reason for the placidity of the classroom, namely its retention of his own duality, the duality he fights against so hard in his life away from students. There is a tension alive in the classroom that feels to Kepesh like wholeness, a balance created which promises not closure but changeability. Kepesh enunciates this tension without holding fast to it.

In his dream of Kafka's whore this same lesson is spoken quite directly and again it disappears with its utterance, What Kepesh learns in the schoolhouse and in his sleep eludes him in his life. In that dream David is invited to "inspect her pussy" (191). After deliberating he tells himself, "But why not? Why come to the battered heart of Europe if not to examine just this? Why come into the world at all? Students of literature, you must conquer your squeamishness once and for all! You must face the unseemly thing itself!" (191). In that moment, in the safety of his dreams, he has touched the heart of the shadow that has terrorized him, the darkness that demands he not allow the body or the mind full possession of him, that demands he accept his duality, his fragile self, his weak body and his merciless mind. But what he enacts in his dreams he cannot enact in life, unwilling to look at the nakedness of his world.[2]

David's sleeping realizations fail to reach his waking self, for that self is surrounded by a pulpit so strong that it pushes awareness deeper inside the body's shell. Kepesh is labeled Professor of Desire, but what does that label signify? he wonders. Should he subvert "Desire" with professorial control or subvert "Professor" with raw passions? One or the other he insists, till the end, till the change, must be his true self. One role, his pulpit tells him, will ease the uncertainty and heal the anguish. In his essay, "Man in a Shell," Kepesh writes about Chekhov's characters, who are held back by their learned conventions and their natural drives, ever imprisoned, trying "in vain to achieve that sense of personal freedom" (158). The essay tells of "longings fulfilled, pleasures denied, and the pain occasioned by both" (157). Pain is a product of both need and purpose, and of their interaction, but pain is existence, blood, survival, and Kepesh's search to deny pain is finally a search to deny life, to deny experience. He wants essences, wants, in Kant's words, to turn "phenomena" into "noumena," to turn appearance into solid truth, to make life as interpretable as fairy tale books. "Literature got me into this and literature is gonna have to get me out," he might say, echoing another Rothian man, Peter Tarnopol, who is no less intent on uncovering a literary identity, an identity reified by language (MLAM 194).

Both Kepesh and Tarnopol are unable to find the error inherent in their search for what Roth calls "a description" of themselves, without the aid of a disaster (CWPR 80). Kepesh's transformation is his avenue to growth and Tarnopol's many years spent with Maureen Johnson Tarnopol is his own horrible path towards enlightenment, away from the pulpit of certain literary truth. Kepesh is transformed in *The Breast* but transformed not from animate, productive teacher to fleshy, inhuman beast but from victim to autonomous individual. His physical metamorphosis is imposed upon him while his more elaborate and more important metamorphosis he achieves for himself.

Though both men's narratives are recollections, each is written with a different intention. Tarnopol uses writing to understand and reinvent himself, to locate the cause of his misfortune, and Kepesh uses his narrative to impart wisdom, to replay his experience from the vantage point of awareness. Kepesh, in effect, gives a lecture, self-implicating and self-aware, calling for a throwing down of the pulpits of understanding. Kepesh, as a breast, forgoes the pulpit of interpretation. Opening his mind to doubt, Kepesh finds himself anew. He is not only a body part, or, as he imagined himself, all brain, but both intermingled within the 150 pound thing that lies docile in its huge harness. His vision opens, his invisible eyes see.

The language of doubt, of revision, is David's new language. The language he spoke of in his introductory lecture has come to life. And it is not a language of defeat but of revitalization. Kepesh escapes what few others are able to escape, the paradigms that rule life and constrict freedom. And freedom is this century's most persistent dilemma; the need to be free implodes from within, from an inheritance of freedom's antithesis.

Kepesh holds fast to desire as it is defined by Rodgers, "perpetual and undiminished longing" (101). As a breast satiation and culmination are out of the question. As a breast "there is no orgasmic conclusion to my excitement," Kepesh explains, "but only this sustained sense of imminent ejaculation" (45). No closure, no epiphany. What Kepesh is left with is promise. He reaches a point of friction, a taught hold between need and purpose. He is both a Professor and an unquenchable quivering organism of desire. He moves, now, with hardly a transition, from "contemplation of the higher things" to "contemplation of the lower" (84), from "delusions of grandeur" to those of "abasement" (82), from a belief in that which is "simple and clear" to an acknowledgement, even a welcoming, of arbitrariness and mutability (82).

A language beyond the pulpit of interpretation, beyond the confines of literary criticism allows both drives and conscience to interact simultaneously, to battle and to engage each other, for language need not be in league with any overwhelming truth. Kepesh's realization is a restatement of Tarnopol's claim that words can only approximate reality. Words need not be allied to a pulpit, need not reverberate with absolute meaning or with absolute meaninglessness. A pulpit clouds the mind, throws a shadow over thought.

When Tarnopol decides to marry his nemesis, Maureen, he is in the throes of a pulpit-enhanced delirium. Recounting the maguffin of his story, the turning point of his life, the moment of self-surrender to the duplicitous enemy, he calls a halt to his narrative to reflect upon the factors which have led him to enact this act of self-destruction, this act so inimical to his best interests. "It seemed," he writes, "then that I was making one of those moral decisions that I had heard so much about in college literature courses" (193). Literature surrounds his every action. For Peter literary models serve as exemplars for his own life. He looks upon the great books and the great masters with awe, viewing their words reverentially. "Perhaps," he wonders, "if I had not fallen so in love with these complicated fictions and moral anguish, I never would have taken that long anguished walk to the Upper West Side and back, and arrived at what seemed to me the only 'honorable' decision for a young man as morally 'serious' as myself" (194). These quoted words work messianically upon Tarnopol's actions, moving him in a direction anathema to his desires.

His intellect works against his instincts, his sense of purpose undermines his needs. Transforming his life into a fiction of Nathan Zuckerman, Peter writes of Nathan's attraction for Lydia Ketterer. Zuckerman admits that regarding Lydia he was "utterly without lust" (69). But lust has come, to Nathan, to signify nothing less than frivolity, childishness, moral-pubescence. His own quest, he feels, has taken him beyond simple visceral lust. His insistence on putting, as he says, "my tongue where she had been brutalized," is an act of literary grandiosity, not of desire, performed as if that act "could redeem" him, an act which parallels the writer's willingness, his need, in fact, to touch the horror that he was spared, to look for redemption where there is none (72).

To look at the first words of each section of My Life as as Man is to watch Tarnopol's progression towards a quitting of his pulpit. "Salad Days" begins with the words, "First, foremost," words of surety and definition (3). They introduce a writer and a character who believes wholeheartedly in language, who believes in word's perfectibility. "Courting Disaster," contrarily, begins with a negation, "No" (33). It introduces Tarnopol's other half, the half that Susan attracts, the side drawn to meaninglessness, which distrusts all words. These first two fictions describe a numbed self, numbed not by actual menace, as it was for Delbo, but by the memory of that menace, by its inheritance. "My True Story," however, begins with a question, "Has anything changed?" (101). Tarnopol moves through the two extremes of need and purpose, the two ends of his pulpit, to reach a median, a position of questioning and not of surrender.

There is pain in balance, the pain Zuckerman felt in The Ghost Writer. The burden of duality is a human burden, a burden of the times carried by so many of Roth's men and women. The Portnovian dilemma is introduced in his early story "Defender of the Faith." "Sergeant Marx," Roth tells Jerre Mangione, in a 1966 television interview, "doesn't know how far to go to stop [Grossbart]. He's very hesitant to be savage, very hesitant to be openly cruel. He really can't deal with his cruelty" (CWPR 5). Marx is stymied by an inability to act against his morality, to trust his blood; he is made impotent by all he knows from his time in Europe. Like Helen, in The Professor of Desire, "moral repugnance" intervenes (218). "How far do you go?" asks Roth (CWPR 6). When does morality inhibit action, when does the moral code act against self-interest, he asks himself? And, then again, when does need inhibit morality, when does an instinctual response damn and debase a man?

To ignore these questions is to dehumanize oneself. No character, then, is more human than Alexander Portnoy, who lends his name to these questions, who pronounces them with every word in his long session with Dr. Speilvogel. Portnoy is "torn by desires repugnant to my conscience and a conscience repugnant to my desires," as he says (132). Is he, he asks, the "Assistant Commissioner of Human Opportunity," the public servant to morality, or "Commissioner of Cunt," a slave to desire and immorality? (204). He must be one or the other, an eater or a talker, "base and brainless" (204) or "A hundred and fifty-eight points of I.Q." (204), an 'ignoramus' (204) or "Albert Einstein the Second" (4). His "spellbound" reading of Freud's "Contributions to the Psychology of Love" has convinced him that one current of feeling - need or purpose - must be subsumed in the other for a Freudian illumination to take place (185). Portnoy's pulpit begins with Freud. Freud's words are truth to Alex. He comes to Speilvogel not as a naive and problemed layman but as a sophisticated reader of psychoanalysis.

He narrates his own story as a Freudian case study, imposing Freud's theories and semantics on his actions, looking to Freud to solve the problem of living in the post-Holocaust world. And yet his reading of Freud is faulty.

Portnoy puts great emphasis on Freud's suggestion that for catharsis to take place it is necessary that "two currents of feeling be united: tender, affectionate feelings, and the sensuous feelings" (PC 185-86). Portnoy reads union to imply stasis. He reads Freud's essay as making the case for the dissolving of disharmony rather than for fostering its continuation. Portnoy seeks a blending, a melding of his duality, blaming his impotence on division and dissonance. With Freud as guide, Portnoy waits for one current to fall to the other.

Freud's essay does state the need for a "confluence of the two currents," but confluence, even more than union, suggests not a subduing of either but an intermixing, a continuing flux between the two (56). The currents remain separate, individual, distinctive, but rise together like waves, pushing and pulling at one another. Later Freud writes, "In times during which no obstacle to sexual satisfaction existed...love became worthless" (57). When needs are unrestrained love loses its value. Love, Freud goes on, "developed greatest significance in lives of the ascetic monks, which were entirely occupied with the struggles against libidinous temptation" (57). Where conscience intervenes with desire sexuality and love become more valued, more intensified. "Instinctual desire is mentally increased by frustration of it," Freud argues (57). Instinct comes alive when its is challenged by conscience, conscience finds its meaning in its collision with desire. Both are enlivened by the presence of the other, not by one's subjugation of the other. What Freud asks for is not a victory of need over purpose, or purpose over need, but their constant belittling interaction.

But Portnoy, heedful of *his* Freud, rejects interaction and continues searching on for the Freudian gem that will lead him to his own Palestine. Freud's insistence on language, on talking, further animates Portnoy's journey. For Alex there are two types of language, civilized discourse and animal howling, and they are synecdoches referring to his internal contradictions. Need is joined with ungrammatical declarations, noise, the screams of pain or pleasure, while purpose is joined with eloquence, pure argot, perfect syntax. He is drawn to both the "pitiful and pathetic" (206) writing of the Monkey and the "cutesy-wootsy" innocent language of the Pilgrim's speech (233).

Portnoy believes that in one linguistic sphere he will find his tone, his meaning. He derogates one and then the other, alternating in his distaste for sophisticated words - "babble-babble" - and for the nonsensical mouthings of his "slimy...Dionysian side" (79).

Portnoy's search for a woman is consistent with his search for a language, with his search for wholeness. "This one has a nice ass," he says, "but she talks too much" (103). One woman's language undermines her physical attributes. "On the other hand," Portnoy continues, "this one here doesn't talk at all, at least not so that she makes any sense - but, boy, can she suck" (103). Her sexual prowess seems to spring from a faulty vocabulary. Portnoy divides the world as he divides women; linguistic agility is linked with sexual limitation and linguistic coarseness linked with sexual know-how. One precludes the other, and Portnoy must choose which sphere he must anchor himself in.

The dichotomy in *Portnoy's Complaint* matures into the modern philosophical battle of speech and writing, the pulpits of Plato and Derrida. Speech is allied with purpose, with language in its purest form, while writing comes into an inheritance of anarchy, noise, the primeval voice of chaos. Plato's privileges speech, verbal communication in which words and their meaning are locked together, in which words spring from the mouth fully formed, perfect. "Plato," argues Jasper Neel, "undeniably condemns writing," while Derrida condemns Platonic speech (1). Derrida celebrates writing for is gaps, its non-referrentiality, its free-floating, always alternating formlessness, its incompleteness, its rejection of truth. For Derrida there is no transcendental meaning, no signified, only play, traces, difference.

Derrida and Plato occupy the far perimeters of the dialectic of language, comparable to Portnoy's division of the Monkey's impure writing and the Pilgrim's pure speech. And Plato and Derrida are both indicted by the Holocaust. Plato's privileging of absolute truths anticipates Hitler's sure pronouncements, and Derrida's slipperiness makes guilt impossible; the truth of the horror becomes deconstructed.[3] To which, finally, will Portnoy and the text show allegiance? What Roth has created is a novel about speech (the spoken narrative of a patient to his analyst) and infused it with the properties of writing (irony, tropological uniformity, depth, plot). As Hermione Lee argues, "Roth is turning an oral tradition into a written one" (PR 33). Roth unites Derrida and Plato, allowing the two to mesh. The arguments against writing are made in writing, the arguments against speech made in the voice of an eloquent speaker. There is a search for closure but that closure is always deferred. Roth presents a narration that doubles Portnoy's dilemma and offers a way out of that dilemma.

When Alex states, "Words aren't only bombs and bullets - no they're little gifts, containing meanings," he touches upon the union which he has resisted (222). Words are both the provinces of the heart and of the head, of aggression and of love, of sense and of senselessness. Words are both Platonic gifts and Derridian bombs. The dissonance of Portnoy's monologue is the dissonance of these two discourses dueling. Language leads to the catharsis of screaming, screaming informs the considered prose. The tension produced, both in the speaker and in the text, is the tension that animates both, that creates the agony expressed and the comedy which offers a bridge from despair.

Neel defines "successful rhetoricians" as those who "keep Plato and Derrida at work at all times...but never subordinates them...so that neither the Platonic search for truth nor the Derridian strategy of deconstruction overwhelms the process" (205). Roth, always heedful of the philosophical implications of the Holocaust, is the quintessential writer of this middle ground, the ground between need and purpose. Neel views this kind of rhetoric to be an attempt "to liberate ourselves from philosophy" (211). What Neel means by philosophy can be understood as the pulpit. To liberate our pulpits is to neither be a slave to any one theory or to the idea of theory at all.

To liberate ourselves from all philosophical systems, though, would be to turn from knowledge, from questioning, and from the past. In Roth, philosophy and fiction are present in each other. Roth's novels are dialogues across time and history, across disciplines. Descartes defines the split that Roth rewrites. The Cartesian split between mind and body is transferred into the felt division in Roth's characters. Roth seizes on Descartes's doubt and his iconoclasm as central principles for his own work. But Descartes's final supposition - that the body and soul are distinct and that the soul can exist beyond the body's disintegration, that God has decreed this and so it is inherently so - falls to convince Roth. Where Descartes's doubt leads him to a pulpit of religious certainty, Roth's leads him to further doubt.

Descartes maintains that he is a being "which does not require any place, or depend on any material thing in order to exist" (236). The soul is incorporeal and lives on after death. Roth takes up these further Cartesian questions briefly in *The Anatomy Lesson* and in *The Counterlife*. What is the body's purpose? Zuckerman asks. Is it merely a mechanism outside the mind, or is the mind part of the body? Is the body a means to salvation or an appendage to be forsaken? Zuckerman feels he must choose between the Lawrencian esthetic of the body or the Sadian esthetic, one which preaches that the physical is the means towards the spiritual and the other which embraces pleasure for its own sake.

In *The Anatomy Lesson* Zuckerman is consumed by his body, by his materiality, hobbled by pain, unable to forget his corporeality, even for a moment. His pain is located "in his neck, arms, and shoulders" (3). He has a "spasm in the upper trapezius," an "aching soreness to either side of the dorsal spine" (6), his "rib cage was askew," his "clavicle was crooked, his left scapula winged out at its lower angle like a chicken's," his "humories was too tightly packed into the shoulder capsule and inserted in the point on the bias" (8). He is "laden with an upper-torso," "saddled with fifteen pounds of head" (10). He has a "denuded scalp, fleshy hips, hone, softening belly" (32). He is burdened with himself, with his body, and wants only escape. No one can be more longful to believe Descartes's dictum then Nathan. To exist without the body would seem an answer to his anguish.

But his body is also the avenue of illicit, unfathomable pleasure, the joy provided by the many women who surround him, satisfying him endlessly. And though he wishes for a "release from self" he is unsure of what that release entails (274). The body, he understands is both distress and nirvana. What is life without the body? Zuckerman's rambles teach him that he is his body. "Your tongue lives in your mouth and your tongue is you" (278). There is no existence outside the body. "Illness is a message from the grave," Zuckerman contends, "Greetings: You and your body are one - it goes, you follow" (254). If he must still decide which definition of the body to live with, he must at least admit that his corpus is him, from that fact there is no escape.

"The body and the mind are one," claims Shuskin in *The Counterlife*, and Zuckerman admits, "No disputing that" (52). And yet the structure of *The Counterlife*, the dream-like quality of its story, suggests a moment of wistful doubt. For though Henry dies in chapter one he comes alive again in chapter two, and though Nathan dies in chapter four his ghost visits Maria in the same chapter, and he is alive again in chapter five. The novel denies logic, denies a final ascension to any pronouncement. Doubt follows even to this point. Roth is neither a Descartian nor a materialist. He moves back and forth between belief and disbelief, as his characters move back and forth between need and purpose, always transforming, always in tumult.

Descartes's ability to heal the mind/body dilemma is a product of his time. In Roth's post-Holocaust world to assert the soul's non-physicallity is to too simply heal the pain of the Holocaust's losses. For if the victims of the slaughter still exist beyond their bodies, their tragedy loses some its force. To accept Descartes's thesis, for Roth, would be to turn from the facts that call not for simple idealistic solutions but for examination.

Descartes's separation of the mind and the body becomes an important facet of the Nazi attack. Rationalism - the organized, logical, fastidious, organ of the death-camps - is deprived of its salubriousness. And irrationalism - the illogical, instinctual actions of the murderers - too becomes bereft of its attractiveness. Separated, as Descartes would have them, and as the Nazi would employ them, they leave each other to reek their own havoc, unharnessed by their opposite. What transpires inside the individual has its analogue outside. To simply throw a pulpit over the battle between need and purpose is to excuse oneself from the hard facts of the concentrationary universe. For Roth this is not only a personal but a societal failure.

Like Henry, who "was somehow not quite course enough to bow to his desires, and yet not quite fine enough to transcend them," Roth is not quite believing enough to accept the soul as immortal and separate and yet not quite nihilistic enough to give up all hope (CL 54). Caught between the two currents of feeling Roth hangs his very human hat on no pulpit.

Notes

1.   Marilyn Fowler calls Neil the quintessential "Rothian protagonist," and sets her definition in a Portnoy-like dichotomy. Klugman is " a blend of the ethical Jew and the more conventional male" (107). What Fowler means by conventional male can only be surmised but ethical Jew is a less slippery appellation first found in Roth's 1974 essay, "Imagining Jews." The young and confident Roth takes to task no less than Bellow and Malamud for presenting Jews only as "actors in dramas of conscience where matters of principle of virtue are at issue" (RMAO 280). Roth complains that Malamud and Bellow employ their own pulpit when writing about Jews, making their Jews into caricatures, men without flesh, without desire, men defined only by questions of mind. Their Jews are drained of blood in an effort to protect the Jewish image after the Holocaust, to posit Jews as moral and intellectual paragons undaunted and untempted by drives beneath the shoulders and waist. Fowler's conventional man, then, must be the ethical Jew's antithesis, the man cut off from conscience, grounded only in desire, in the need for accumulation and pleasure.

2.   The dream exposes Kepesh's dilemma. Read as an attempt to demythologize Kafka and as "a desecration of Kafka's image" which "subverts the lectures attempt to reconcile the conscientious dedicated life of the mind with the shameful secret life of the body," it is more accurately seen as Kepesh's subconscious realization of his need to resist paradigms of either need or purpose (Quart 70). It is an attempt to redirect Kafka from the realm of the imaginary and replace him in the real, to view Kafka in the light of the Holocaust, to rescue him from hagiography and return him as flesh and blood, as dual, halved, human. In the dream Kepesh states simply, "Franz Kafka was real" (188). If Kafka is real, containing both body and mind, then, as David admits, "so am I real" (188).

3.   The case of Paul de Man is intructive here. de Mann's Nazi past was denied by his deconstuctionist followers, by declaring his pro-Nazi writings to be not what they most assuredly were. de Mann was freed of guilt by a belief in language's ambiguity. If nothing is true, if the authour is not responsible for his words, no guilt follows the anti-Semite. The attractions, then, of deconstruction are self-evident for a man with de Mann's history.

CHAPTER FOUR

Holocaust Writing

Why come to the battered heart of
Europe if not to examine just this?
Why come into the world at all?
'Students of literature, you must
conquer your squeamishness once
and for all! You must face the
unseemly thing itself! You must
come off your high horse! There,
there is your final exam.'

- Philip Roth
- The Professor of Desire

"Black milk" enters our consciousness as one of the most remarked upon
and treasured metaphors of the Holocaust, encapsulating of the reversal of
normalcy and the metamorphosis of what once nourished into that which
sickens. Milk, the breast's incorruptible source of life, is transformed into
the poison the prisoners drink as they dig their own graves in Paul Celan's
"Fugue of Death." A poem about retaining autonomy while under the command of an avaricious destroyer and about the disintegration of values and
of civilizing concepts that once sustained the speakers, it is also a poem
about poetry and music, about the rhymes and verses that are sustained
even after catastrophe.

Its music, its beauty, the cadence of its striking repetition, make prob-
lematic our relationship to it. As we read we are enveloped not so much by

its sadness as by the pleasure it gives to us. The poem acts as a catharsis for our sorrow, evidence, as Lawrence Langer suggests, that "what dims the light of creation need not extinguish the lamps of language" (H&L 15). It is, then, transformed from a poem of destruction to a poem of promise and revitalization. Pleasure and hope sing from the ashes and we recognize why Theodore Adorno and George Steiner warned so vehemently against, as Steiner put it, "an art of atrocity," explaining that "The world of Auschwitz lies outside speech as it lies outside reason" (123).

The immediate, clear, danger of speech is the danger of making horror palatable, making a fetish of extermination. The reader, as well as the writer, is not immune to this danger, for as he reads Levi and Kosinski he experiences an aesthetic joy in language and story. One is reading about horror, confronting disaster, and yet one is protected and distanced, a part of and apart from at once. "You're of the little pocket of Jews," Philip is told, in *Deception*, "born in this century who miraculously escaped the horror, who somehow have lived unharmed in an amazing moment of affluence and security. So those who didn't escape, Jewish or not, have this fascination for you" (D 140). Fascination connotes not merely curiosity or morbid wonder but excitement, the thrill of investigating an event beyond the realm of understanding, an inexhaustible and unique subject. It is the fascination that both moves Roth and his protagonists and which cements a sense of shame, a twentieth-century original sin.

Philip's lover asks him, "Are you that in love with suffering" (D 139). Suffering becomes eroticized, a love object to be explored and exploited. It becomes something to search out, not only for beneficence but for self-ennobling. "Enter Zuckerman, a serious person" (TPO 462), writes Nathan in his diary, as he makes his way through, what Roth calls, "the shrine of suffering, Kafka's occupied Prague," questing after Sisovsky's father's Holocaust tales (CWPR 251). Zuckerman looks to Anne Frank and to war-ravaged Prague, to "ten little stories about Nazis and Jews," stories "about the worst life has to offer" (TPO 435), to feed "his insatiable desire to be a serious man taken seriously by all the other serious men like his father and his brother and Milton Appel" (CWPR 251). But the price of that seriousness is the guilt of knowing that it must be built upon a ghastly reality, that if it can be attained it is only because of a prior devastation, the suffering of others, like the music of Celan's "Fugue."

To speak, then, to address the horror in any shape or form, is to be susceptible to this accusation, is, in fact, to invite it. And Roth does invite the arrows of calumny upon himself and his surrogate selves. His is an art not of self-love but of self-challenge, self-rebuttal, and self-questioning. What is often characterized as solipsism is less a fascination with his own image than a fascination with his own culpability, a culpability that begins with a fascination with the Holocaust. Holocaust writing entails a self-immolation. "I portray myself as implicated," says Philip, "because it is not enough just to be present" (D 184). Roth's characters are not like Narcissus, in love with their own perfect image, but rather they are disappointed, remorseful, almost sickened at their uncreased features, features they envision alongside the mirror-image of the others, the victims. The pettiness, the "thinness" of their own dilemmas confronts them in the face of the omnipresent survivor (GW 151). "In the aftermath of that testimony," "Philip Roth" remarks of the words of the camp-prisoner, Rosenberg, "in the aftermath of Demjanjuk's laughter and Rosenberg's rage, how could the asinine clowning of that nonsensical Pipik continue to make a claim on my life?" (OS 303).

How much is one to disregard of one's own troubles? How much must one sacrifice? These questions attack the writer as he picks up his pen. How can he speak at all, about anything? When the questions begin, the writer becomes hedged in by doubt, restricted by his own superciliousness, the knowledge that his own pain "pales" before the truth of the destruction (OS 77). And if he does deign to take up the Holocaust, the questions become even more difficult. Beyond beautifying it, making it into a story of uplift, there is the knowledge that in the search for seriousness, in the brave attempt to escape triviality and look squarely at the faces of slaughter one will inevitably fail, one will offend, one will besmirch memory in some way, because one is seen by others and imagined by oneself as unauthentic, and so not entitled entry to that history.

The "real" Jews, many feel, are the survivors, those who have tasted the black milk: In Roth they are Tzuref, his eighteen children, and the greenie in the black hat ("Eli, the Fanatic"), Solly, the diner owner (Letting Go), Barbatnik (The professor of Desire), the imagined Amy Bellette (The Ghost Writer), Dr. Kotler (The Anatomy Lesson), Sisovsky (The Prague Orgy), Aharon Appelfeld (Deception & Operation Shylock), the imagined Kafka ("Looking at Kafka"), Werner ("The Contest for Aaron Gold"), Primo Levi (Patrimony), Cousin Apter, Rosenberg, and Smilesburger (Operation Shylock).

Solly's "concentration camp number on his forearm" gives him stature beyond his position; "the Herzes respected him fiercely" (LG 112). When Mr. Kepesh introduces his friend Barbatnik to David and Claire he says "Dramatically, and yes with pride - 'He's a victim of the Nazis'" (POD 236). As "Philip Roth" watches the trial of John Demjanjuk, the man accused of being Ivan the Terrible, he glances at several elderly spectators whom he first dismisses as "retired" men and women "who had the time to attend the sessions regularly" (OS 67). "Then," he remarks, "I realized that they must be camp survivors" (OS 67). They change before his eyes, rise upward. He now wonders, "what was it like for them to find standing only a few feet away...Demjanjuk's twenty-two-year-old son?" (OS 67). Their thoughts, their feelings are no longer dismissed; their very bearing speaks to him with new energy and depth. They are made eminent by their history, a history that concurrently degrades the pain Roth's post-war characters suffer.

The "authentic" pain of the survivors belittles the "unauthentic" pain of the spared (OS 125). "My father survived Auschwitz," the Israeli lieutenant, Gal Metzler, tells "Philip Roth," "when he was ten years younger than I am now. I am humiliated that I can't survive this" (OS 169). Compared to the Barbatniks and the Apters, the Zuckermans and the Roths feel themselves as false, their lives a "nothing" (AL 67). "Philip Roth" describes the "antithetical twentieth-century Jewish biographies" (OS 201) of Aharon Appelfeld and himself, and it is the unforgotten distance "between the shetl-born and the Newark born" that haunts his narrative (OS 312).

Appelfeld and the others are imprisoned and starved, murdered and incinerated, orphaned from family and exiled from home, while "Roth" is "disgracefully being held prisoner by no one but myself," as he must acknowledge (OS 315). Tarnopol is incapacitated by Maureen, Kepesh is crippled by desire, Klugman made childlike by silly Brenda, Epstein made ill by lust, Novotny is hobbled by back pain, Zuckerman is disabled by fame, and Portnoy, impotent in Israel, wonders, "How can I be floundering like this over something so simple, so silly, as pussy!" (248). Their weakness speaks louder because it is paired with the strength of the remembered others.[1]

Eli makes the distance between the survivor and the American Jew clear when he sits in Tzuref's chair and finds himself unaccustomed to the "sharp bones of his seat" (E 249). The comfort Eli takes for granted is an impossibility for the school-master. It is felt by Eli and by the protagonists who follow in his path as an elemental distance that must be respected and remembered. "I was not a Jewish survivor of a Nazi death camp in search of a safe and welcoming refuge," Zuckerman explains (CL 58). The "American-born grandson of simple Galacian tradesmen" cannot know what the survivor knows, cannot feel the scars he feels (CL 59). The American Jew and the camp Jew must know each other, as Nathan explains brothers know each other, "as a kind of deformation of themselves" (CL 89). They are counterparts, living counterlives, separated by time and luck.

"What have the Holocaust survivors done and in what ways were they ineluctably changed?" Roth asks Aharon Appelfeld (OS 214). The question exposes Roth's longing to conjoin with his counter-self, to know the other as oneself, to cleave to their "distinctly radical twoness" (OS 200). To become another, see as the other sees, depart oneself and enter one's compliment, one's double, is an idea that repeats throughout Roth's works, beginning with Eli and the greenie. Henry, having become Hanoch, wants to say, his brother argues, "I am not just a Jew, I'm not also a Jew - I am a Jew as deep as those Jews," as deep as the victims (68). To see through their eyes, to think with their memories, he feels, will give him a wholeness his own life will not provide. Roth's question asks for the same knowledge that Hanoch searches for at Agor. How are they different from me? his words ask. How can I understand them? Inscribed in that question is an espousal of guilt, the guilt that anyone who approaches the Holocaust must be prepared to admit; the guilt of being less than their counter-selves, the guilt of gaining a subterranean intellectual pleasure in probing the survivor, in asking the question, the guilt, finally, of having escaped the pit.

In *Operation Shylock* "Roth" imagines John Demjanjuk's thoughts about his own guilt: "Well, they might as well charge him with owing $128 million on the water bill. Even if they had his signature on the water bill, even if they had his photograph on the water bill, how could it possibly be his water bill? How could anyone use that much water....There has been a mistake....and I should not be on trial for this gigantic bill" (261-2). The Demjanjuk of "Roth's" imagination complains of disproportionate guilt, the same complaint Portnoy voices, and if for Demjanjuk it is not a valid question, for Portnoy and "Roth" it is a recurring and insistent query which explains much about their traumas and their resentments. For it is not Demjanjuk, after all, who speaks those words; it is "Roth." And it is "Roth" who admits, "I had dreamed that I owed $128 million on my water bill" (260). Here the metaphor is applied directly to "Roth," the writer and not Demjanjuk, the supposed Nazi.

Guilt devours "Roth" as it devours Portnoy and Zuckerman, guilt for trying to touch the concentrationary world and for failing. "All these voices, " Zuckerman states, "this insistent chorus, reminding me, as though I could forget, how unreasonable I am, how idle and helpless and overprivileged, how fortunate even in my misfortune" (AL 155). All the problems Roth's characters face, problems with parents, with their bodies, with their fears and desires are as nothing when placed next to the "true" victims, the victims whose absence has precipitated and enlarged those problems.

Anger follows guilt, the anger of not being allowed one's own misery, not being allowed one's own pain, of always having that other standing above calling one's tragedy comedy. Zuckerman's attack on Freytag, the "Forbidder," is also an attack on the Jewish dead who deny him his suffering, deny him legitimate complaint (AL 263).

Characters want to reestablish their selves, to become autonomous beings, at the same time as they want to remember the others and enter their consciousness. The self-fascination of Roth's characters is a narrative attempt to make themselves as real as the too-real victims, to overcome the guilt of their shadowed lives, a project which can only lead them deeper into the waters of self. Portnoy complains of being "locked up in me" (248). Zuckerman speaks of his "dwarf drama" (AL 145). And "Roth" hears the accusation, "You! You! Nothing in your world but you!" (OS 100).

Roth's solipsism is a means of exploring the way an individual, so cognizant of the Holocaust, moves back and forth on the seesaw of guilt, how he tries to both remember and to retain selfhood, and how those two activities undermine each other. Roth is not like Sylvia Plath, for whom the Holocaust becomes a metaphor for her own personal plight. Roth could never write the line, from "Mary's Song," "This holocaust I walk in," to explain his own misery (45). For Roth it is the impossibility of attaching the Holocaust to self that so anguishes him, the futility of the comparison. Roth's characters look inside because of their awareness of what came before, what they missed.

Crying with his sister, Portnoy thinks, "how monstrous I feel, for she sheds her tears for six million, or so I think, while I shed mine only for myself. Or so I think" (78). Portnoy's complaint is bound up with the six million; it is not a complaint born only of a particular childhood in a particular home but born of a particular history. His tears are never for himself, alone, his guilt not only for his own solitary actions. His sister's words are the words Portnoy silently and continually speaks to himself: "Do you know...where you would be now if you had been born in Europe instead of America....Dead. Gassed, or shot, or incinerated, or butchered, or buried alive" (77).

Roth's solipsism, like Portnoy's, begins outside himself. His characters are fascinated with their selves because they are tormented by the Holocaust. Zuckerman, a notoriously self-obsessed man, explains, "Though people were weeping in every corner of the earth from torture and ruin and cruelty and loss, that didn't mean that he could make their stories his, no matter how passionate and powerful they seemed beside his trivialities" (AL 138). It is this impossibility which gnaws at Zuckerman, which antagonizes him, and which spawns his writing. Roth's knowledge of the Holocaust tells him that to ignore the self is to let the victimizer win, to depersonalize all Jews. And still the worries of self cannot compete with the importance of the Holocaust. What Roth has done is to join the self and history, to watch one work in, with, and against the other, to focus on the individual while placing that individual in the historical continuum.

Neither Roth, Zuckerman, Tarnopol, Kepesh, nor Portnoy can make a claim on the Holocaust. Roth's Holocaust fiction is at variance with so much other Holocaust writing because he must always acknowledge its distance from its source, its insufficiency, the potential unseemliness of its conception. Naomi calls Portnoy a "self-hating" Jew, and he responds, "Ah, but Naomi, maybe that's the best kind" (265). Self-hating means self-indicting, a key term for Roth's fiction. If he is to look at the Holocaust from his secure perch he must admit his own dual-motivations, the pure motivation to grapple with the seminal event of the century and the impure motivation to make himself hallowed by making art of atrocity. Is that not a more interesting definition of "Portnoy's Complaint" than the battle between need and purpose, body and mind? "Portnoy's Complaint" defines Roth's art; the pull between a moral super-ego fearlessly investigating the unspeakable and the immoral id making use of the Holocaust, creating a career in its wake. It is that war which the "I" must be the battleground for, the place of combat where the sparks fly.[2]

"How were you to live from now on?" Appelfeld asks of the survivor (X). His question is at the root of Roth's creations, his reclamation of the "I" and his indictment of the "I." For Steiner trying to answer that question is itself an error; trying to look inside the survivor's heart is an assault upon the survivor. Steiner recognizes the same dilemmas Roth sews into his fictions but asks not for Roth's garrulousness, his games and puzzles, his doubts and accusations, his expressions of terror and impotence, but for wordlessness. Perhaps it would be more appropriate, Steiner argues, to leave the Holocaust in silence, to respect its uniqueness by not invoking it, like the name of God. Steiner argues that "history collaborates with invention to produce - silence," (123). For Steiner, then, Roth's meticulous intermixing is still inadequate, is still a blemish, a miscue, a noble attempt better left undone. As Adorno states, in agreement with Steiner, "How should art - how can art? - represent the inexpressibly inhuman suffering of the victims, without doing an injustice to that suffering?" (H&L 1).

Entering the Holocaust world, creating characters who wear numbers and who recount suffering, inventing fictions of survivors or possible survivors, somehow anesthetizes the actual Holocaust world, the real survivors and victims, stripping them of their true, unartistic stories. "There is no response great enough," argues Isaac Rosenfeld, "to equal the facts that provoke it" (BWA 197). That, certainly, no one, Roth included, could refute. But does that statement's power, then, command all to cessation? Does the doubt of writing about the Holocaust, or even after the Holocaust, grow so great that it imprisons the writer, blockades him from his interests, his moral obsessions? Should Roth stop in his tracks, *let the cold wash over him* ?

Countering Steiner and Adorno are such philosophers and poets as A. Alvarez, Sartre, Camus, and Anna Akhmatora, who reject silence as a response to catastrophe, who know that only description of misery, as Akhmatora's "Instead of a Preface" makes clear, can salvage humanity from that misery. Alvarez sees art as having a restorative function which would "make further totalitarian atrocities impossible," Sidra Ezrahi explains (BWA7). Sartre proselytized for a new literature of "extreme situations" (BWA 7). And Camus stated succinctly, "To talk of despair is to conquer it" (BWA 7).

For Roth neither position is fully acceptable. Silence is the initial impulse for the writer. The hurdles which stand in the way of an imaginative treatment of the Holocaust - especially by one physically untouched by it - grow larger and larger as pen is set to paper. Even for a writer, like Roth, who lets his doubt, wariness, and guilt show with every word, silence seems the more respectful and unselfish stance.

But, then, the poet must view silence as less a reaction than a surrender, less a remedy than an avoidance. To be silent is to announce loudly that not only have the victims been made mute, but even the poet has been beaten down, his voice burned out in the ovens.[3] Speech is essential, an answer to death, a pronouncement of the Nazi's failure to subdue everything. To hold back speech is to respond sheepishly to a persecution of memory. "All the tolerance," Roth argues, "of persecution that has seeped into the Jewish character...must be squeezed out, until the only response to any restriction of liberties is 'No, I refuse'" (RMAO 220). This is what the Holocaust, "the death of all those Jews," has taught Roth; not "to be discreet," not "to remain a victim," but to risk indiscretion, to wade into the dangerous sea of history (RMAO 221). To fail to write, to fail to raise his voice, is "to act as though it already is 1933 - or as though it always is," writes Roth (RMAO 221). The difficulties the Holocaust present are only an impetus for more words. For the writer the impenetrable problem calls for study, the locked door calls for an unfathomable key.

Still, there are self-imposed boundaries that the writer puts in place. There is an accommodation to silence but it is a willed accommodation, a sign not of defeat but of forbearance, of intellectual restraint, which expresses both self-control and an acknowledgement of the Holocaust's sanctity. Adorno makes an addendum, saying that no artist can allow the "artistic representation of the naked bodily pain of those who have been knocked down by rifle butts" (BWA 11). For Roth this becomes a personal guideline.

Roth does not recreate the camps, he does not write texts with a survivor as the narrator. His works have no Sammler or Herman Broder, like Bellow and Singer, authors who, though they were spared the camps, are less reticent about creating a central voice who was not spared. Only in the early unpublished play, A *Coffin in Egypt*, and in the early short stories, "The Contest for Aaron Gold" (in which his camp experiences in Germany are barely mentioned), and "Eli, the Fanatic" (a story more about Eli than about the survivors he connects with) does Roth deviate, suggesting that his ideas about the Holocaust had been in their infancy in those years, still developing, and so in those works the Holocaust is more obviously present, his fascination less shaded from view. After 1959 there is always a distinct intermediary, a voice which either hears or creates the other voice of the camps. "It was a world," Howe intones, "for which, finally, we have no words" (SW 432). Howe's position is actually akin to Roth's, and his statement takes us to the heart of the multiple definitions of the concentrationary universe.

The concentrationary universe is both the universe of the camps and the universe in which the next generation is imprisoned. Roth shelters the camp universe with the words of the post-war universe; it is the play of the two that draws the tensions of his fiction. The camp world is barely visible, barely understood, barely mentioned, and its shrouded distance, its intermittent effusions, give it more potency in Roth's work than in much obviously mimetic dramas of the anus-mundi. The galvanic presence of the Holocaust is only enlarged by Roth's type of silence. Appelfeld relates a "proverb from the Mishna, 'Silence is a fence for wisdom,'" which he applies to his own sparse use of adjectives and which can also apply to Roth's careful excisions, the absence suggested by hints and allusions (72). Roth needs a readership ready to follow silence, to supply history, to look beneath the water to the Hemingway-like iceberg that supports the seen tip. In a world of trivial and lackadaisical reading or a world of amnesia, Roth's work will seem to contain a lack - and so readers and critics will turn to questions of autobiography, to superficial talk about obscenity and sex, to theories that explain all. Readings reveal, often, more about what the reader doesn't know than about what the writer hasn't provided.

It is not Roth's job to educate. Kitsch, like the television movie, *Holocaust*, is designed to tell a story as though the audience has no information. That is its danger. Alfred Kazin points out that "an amazing number of Germans confessed that the film |*Holocaust* | had awakened them to the full extent of Hitler's destruction of European Jewry" (ix). What can be expected, then, for those ignorant viewers (and their brethren everywhere) to make of Roth's diffuse discussion of the Holocaust? How reasonable is Roth's silent speech in a world where the Holocaust disappears from memory, or a world where only direct and harrowing images and descriptions are able to grasp read-ers? If kitschifying television movies and cinematic-extravaganzas are need-ed to tell the forgotten story, to jar shamelessly at emotions, then Roth's novels are counterparts to them, fixatives to their stark banalities, their dan-gerous simplifications. Roth's novels use knowledge and expand definitions to contradict the melodramatic pictures brought by readers to them.

Roth's silences must be turned to speech by the critic's hand. Silence is not absence. Howe reminds us that "In ancient mythologies and religion there are things and beings that are not to be named....Perseus would turn to stone if he were to look directly at the serpent-headed Medusa, though he would be safe if he looked at her only through a reflection in a mirror or a shield" (SW 429). Roth pursues a Medusa-method in his writing about the Holocaust. The giant beast is always there in reflection, in gaps and associ-ations. "I think," says Roth, "for a Jewish American writer there's not the same impetus, or, oddly, even the necessity, that there is for a Christian American, like Styron, to take the Holocaust up so nakedly as a subject, to unleash upon it so much moral and philosophical speculation, so much harrowing, furious invention" (RMAO 136). For the Jewish writer the Holocaust's grizzly reality need not be invented anew. "For most reflective American Jews," Roth continues, "I would think, it is simply there, hidden, submerged, emerging, disappearing, unforgotten. You don't make use of it - it makes use of you" (RMAO 130). In that last sentence Roth's philosophy is stated emphatically: The writer lets the Holocaust seep into his words, between his paragraphs.

In *The Anatomy Lesson* there is a fine example of how the Holocaust juts its way into narrative. Mr. Freytag and Zuckerman are driving to Mrs. Freytag's grave and Nathan sees "miles and miles of treeless cemetery, ending at the far horizon in a large boxlike structure that was probably nothing but a fac-tory, but that smoking foully away through the gray of the storm looked like something far worse" (257-258). Nathan's mind is surfeit with Holocaustal imaginings; they bulge at his senses so that a factory is immediately trans-formed into a crematorium. In one moment we are traveling through Chicago, in the next we are watching the ashes of Jews drift over the sky. One sentence takes the reader into one concentrationary universe and then leaves him back in the other. Now Nathan's rage at the Jewish dead in the cemetery becomes clear. His is the anger of the man who cannot forget, whose every ache is balanced against the howling pain of millions. A short metaphor and then we are returned to America. Silence and speech come together. There is no Camus-like descent into the intricacies of the massacre nor is there an Adorno-like turning away from the image.[4]

"I no longer believe in the magic of the spoken word," writes Elie Wiesel, in seeming agreement with those who call for a muting of speech (Berger 9). But Wiesel, clearly, has not heeded the advice of silence. Wiesel's use of the word "magic" differentiates him from the more restrictive philosophers of Holocaust writing. Wiesel is here disparaging the Platonic wholeness of words, their ability to grant transcendence. He mistrusts words but that mistrust only makes his need to write more vehement. When Steiner claims that the Holocaust is "outside reason" he is stating this same idea. If speech cannot be dispensed with it must be chastened. If the Holocaust is not beyond speech, if silence is defeat, then it is, at least, beyond explanation, beyond meaning. Anyone writing about the Holocaust must refrain from the suggestion that their stories "could 'make up for' or 'transcend' the horror," as Howe notes (SW 431).

There is a tradition, in both American and European philosophy and literature, of viewing periods of terrible victimization and trauma through the language of heroism and transcendentalism, to view horrific suffering as ultimately liberating, to see in catastrophe evidence of man's unquenchable will to live, man's unbreakable determination, man's ability to rise from terror and humiliation stronger and more intact than ever before. "Suffering," argues Terrence Des Pres, "has come to be equated with moral stature, with spiritual depth, with refinement of perception and sensibility" (45). In devastation one discovers meaning. Tragedy is released from its original perspective and metamorphosed into promise, into truth. In this manner we regain control over that which is beyond our control.

It is a natural human response to employ interpretation as a means of healing, of holding onto some solid ground. And it is a response not alien to Holocaust-memoirists and poets. Langer calls the language of this response "the grammar of heroism and martyrdom" (HT 1). He recounts a "newspaper editorial" which calls a "film about opposition to the Nazis in the Vilna ghetto 'a tribute to the redeeming power of resistance'" (HT 1). Later, Langer turns to Martin Gilbert's book, *The Holocaust*, a text written, Langer explains, "with a ruthless and unsettling resolve not to masquerade the worst" (HT 163). And yet even Gilbert's brutal forthrightness ends claiming survival as "a victory of the human spirit" (HT 163). Gilbert's last paragraph, Langer argues, is an effort "to rescue some shred of meaning from a hopeless situation" (HT 165). To force meaning where meaning is distinctly not present is to partake in a hopeful misreading, a misreading filled with "accolades" which "do not honor the painful complexities of the victims' narratives," as Langer argues (HT 2).

Roth's characters attempt a similar interpretive effort to gain control over their own convoluted lives, an effort which mimics the efforts of those writers who seem to need to pin their texts on meaning in order to withstand the crush of unexplainable facts. Portnoy calls for "Dignified suffering! Meaningful suffering!" (251). Zuckerman, who sees "virtue in suffering," wants only to find the virtue, the explanation, of his own physical and psychological torment (TPO 456). "You don't want to represent her Warsaw," Zuckerman tells himself, "it's what her Warsaw represents that you want: suffering that isn't semi-comical, the world of massive historical pain instead of this pain in the neck" (AL 144). If, the logic goes, his suffering were more like that of Poland's victims it would be more bearable, more worthy; it would harbor a possibility of depth, of eventual growth.

"What did it mean?" asks Zuckerman (ZU 4). To find meaning for Nathan, or for Tarnopol, or Novotny, or Kepesh is to subdue anguish, to categorize and therefore ameliorate pain. They seek a convergence of anguish and meaning, a convergence which degrades the memory of real suffering, suffering without epiphany, without interpretation. By sheltering themselves behind cliches of survival they avoid any honest evaluation of sorrow and catastrophe. Everything is wrapped neatly in a package of hopefulness and all that is lost are the victims' voices and the difficult unvarnished truth.

There is an "impulse to seek a moral" which confronts anyone who looks towards the Holocaust, Appelfeld explains (13). But that impulse must be forsaken for it is the impulse of one "with an ideological bent," one who must "offer explanations" even when none are available (Appelfeld 14). To turn to ideology when the disaster one is studying is a legacy of ideology is to begin one's exploration in ignorance, to effectively cut oneself off from understanding. Still, argues Appelfeld, "We quickly fled towards the historical lesson, to seek the lowest common denominator of that horror" (14).

Paul Johnson elucidates the historical explanation for the Holocaust: "The creation of Israel was the consequence of Jewish sufferings" (519). The Holocaust was, Johnson claims, the last "necessary piece" of the "jigsaw puzzle" which "helped to make the Zionist state" (519-520). History validates Auschwitz, in this view, makes six million deaths "necessary," indeed it "helped" the Jews, finally. In *The Counterlife* Nathan recounts his father's vision of Israel in similar terms: "Militant, triumphant Israel was to his aging circle of Jewish friends their avenger for the centuries and centuries of humiliating oppression; the state created by Jews in the aftermath of the Holocaust had become for them the belated answer to the Holocaust" (62). The father's Lonoffian belief system allows the Holocaust to be redeemed in history. The victims are necessary losses towards a greater strength. History is molded to grant form to that which has no form; endless murders are encased into a vocabulary of purpose. Each death is a bridge towards Zion and the individual death is washed away. The continuum is never put at risk. "There at least," the rationalization goes, according to Appelfeld, "is apparently a cause and, seemingly, an effect" (14).

"A theological moral was immediately added to the historical one," Appelfeld continues (14). "Wise men arose and labored to erect a new theology" (14). The theological explanations are uniformly linked with the idea of sacrifice and punishment, to the ancient belief that every bereavement suffered has a purpose towards some predetermined goal, and that all victims are either needed for the sacrifice or serving a just sentence for some sin. The Prophet Amos's statement, "You only have I known of all the families of the earth, therefore I will punish you for all your iniquities," is called on to assert the religious meaning for the Holocaust (Berger 1). "The sufferings of Auschwitz," Johnson explains, "were not mere happenings. They were moral enactments. They were part of a plan. They confirmed the glory to come" (519). The Nazis become God's messengers, God's soldiers. The ovens are machines not of barbarity but of cleansing, of purification. The theological paradigm is designed to maintain the covenant, to heal the felt rift expressed by the caller to "Philip Roth," in *Operation Shylock*, "Philip Roth, where was God between 1939 and 1945....That was a dereliction of duty for which even He, especially He, cannot ever be forgiven" (206). That question is eliminated by absolute faith, as are all questions. "And was it for their sins," "Appelfeld" asks Smilesburger, "that God sent Hitler?" (OS 110). To answer yes to that question is to condemn the six million again, to turn them from victims into sacrificial lambs and sinners.

In addition to Appelfeld's two examples of moral-creation, a third must be added, that of personal ideology, the private ideology that men gather to their breasts to ease the burden of memory, to keep anomie at bay. The survivor devices his own schema, his own explanation for his good fortune. Like Bruno Bettelheim, who asserted that his own intellectual and moral strength were the major factors in his living through Auschwitz, these survivors look for a distinct formula within which to place their experience. Bettelheim takes an element of chance and luck away and in so doing uplifts himself and his fellow survivors and provides a blueprint for resistance. In his essays there is expressed the notion that survival can be learned, that what happened to him can never happen again if only each potential victim becomes like himself. Those who died become failures, not strong enough, not prepared and autonomous enough to resist. Bettelheim's mythology is a, perhaps, well-intentioned effort at protecting the self's power, but like any all-encompassing myth of the Holocaust it does more damage than good; it evades the essence of the unique destruction.

What the Holocaust teaches Appelfeld is quite different: "you are not your own person, will is an illusion" (15). The Holocaust is "conceived....as an episode, as madness, as an eclipse that does not belong to the normal flow of time, a volcanic eruption of which one must be aware, but which indicates nothing about the rest of life" (37). There is no "spiritual vision" to attach to the Holocaust (Appelfeld 55). "It can be explained," argues Wiesel, "neither with God nor without him" (Berger 3). Survival was luck, victimization was chance. The Holocaust belongs to the "incomprehensible, the mysterious, the insane, and the meaningless," argues Appelfeld (39). All categories fail. By denying this we make our own concentrationary universe easier to bear but we falsify the past. "Murder that was committed with evil intention," Appelfeld insists, "must not be interpreted in mystical terms" (39). To do so is to assume that the Holocaust changed nothing. It becomes mitigated by reason.

"There is no meaning here at all," "Philip Roth" realizes in *Operation Shylock* (202). No meaning, just facts. An explanation for Roth's insistence on the simple truth of his confessional novel shows through this statement. Roth is restoring facts as facts to their rightful place in this odd novel. Events can be ambiguous, farcical, unbelievable, and still be true. "But Hitler did exist," the author notes, "those twelve years cannot be expunged from history any more than they can be obliterated from memory, however mercifully forgetful one might prefer to be" (43). Nothing can be doubted only because of strangeness or illogic in Roth's story, certainly not the Holocaust: And it does not have to contain a succinct meaning on which we can hold ourselves afloat. "The meaning of the destruction," "Roth" continues, "of European Jewry cannot be measured or interpreted by the brevity with which it was attained" (43). Nor can it be measured or interpreted based on any criteria. It denies our conception-hungry minds. The Holocaust, as Steiner held, is beyond reason; it simply is.

In *The Breast* Roth delineates the path of one man through a trauma which defies interpretation and which denies the healing lexicon that Kepesh initially tries to impose upon it. In that short novel Roth explores and criticizes the urge toward meaning, toward redemptive language which incapacitates so many of those who explore the concentrationary universe and who live in its shadow. In his final rejection of that noble vocabulary of reason Kepesh finds an honest voice, a self torn and battered but a self who lives in truth.

In a conversation with Alan Lelchuk, about *The Breast*, Roth says, "I've frequently written about what Bruno Bettelheim calls 'behavior in extreme situations'" (RMAO 55). Bettelheim's extreme situation is, of course, the camps. *The Breast*, then, can be seen as an oblique concentration-camp commentary, the words of a man experiencing a very real, unanticipated, and unreal change, and trying to understand that experience. Kepesh follows the patterns of Holocaust writers, shifting through meanings until, at last, the whole idea of meaning becomes anathema. In *The Breast*, Roth argues, there is "No crapola about Deep Meaning" (CWPR 57). To give into meaning, for Kepesh as it is for Roth, is to deny experience, to cowardly retreat into ideology (CWPR 57).

The voice which narrates *The Breast* is a voice recollecting itself after a change has already occurred. The questioning, insightful voice is not an accurate picture of Kepesh prior to his transformation but rather reflects the new Kepesh born of his descent into the real world. The language of meaning is the language Kepesh, as a Professor, has long been initiated into. It is therefore not surprising that when he finds "the flesh at the base of my penis had turned a shade of pale red" he interprets it "at once" as a sign of "cancer" (5). Though it is a painful interpretation it is, nonetheless, something he can understand and latch onto. Kepesh's first theory, upon finding himself blind and immobile, is that he has become "a quadruple amputee" (19). He turns to a recognizable category to find a classification to situate his ordeal, albeit a tortuous category. To find explanatory words is to remain tethered to the world. He looks for "something...anything...some clue, some lead" (71). If logic leads to a discernible cause then a cure can perhaps be found.

"It's a dream," he explains to himself (54). When this scenario fails to convince him Kepesh decides, "I at last realized that I had gone mad. I was not dreaming. I was crazy" (55). Madness, at least, fits into a pattern, suggests curative possibilities. Madness suggests, to David, a reversal of reality, a turning around of perspective and language. "My illness," he explains, "was such that I was taking his [Klinger's] words, simple and clear as they were when he spoke them, and giving them precisely their opposite meaning" (57). It is not reality that has come undone but David's eyes and ears. "I got it from fiction. The books I've been teaching - they put the idea in my head" (60). He converts himself from a breast into a text, a form he can work with so much more easily, a form more amenable to excavating meaning.

With each interpretation Kepesh expects release, epiphany, insight leading to a miraculous return of sanity. As each interpretation fails to bring forth the needed escape he turns to another. "That is what I couldn't take," he tells Klinger, "a happy life" (71). He has gone mad to depose his own contentedness, to pull the rug out from under his own feet. But that, too, offers him no answer. He turns, reluctantly, to an acknowledgement of his condition, of the facts: "I AM A BREAST" (18). It is with that simple declaration that Kepesh loosens himself from an endless and ultimately unsatisfactory search intended to impose meaning on meaninglessness. "Things have been worse and will be again," Kepesh tells his audience (75). It is not a paean to nihilism but a concrete statement of fact. Accepting uninterpretability is not defeat. Kepesh exists in a world of linguistic boldness; his honesty brings him an autonomy that no constructed myth could confer.

Rilke's poem, which Kepesh recites as an epilogue to his tale, offers no redemption, just reality, no moral, just facts, no deep and transforming message, just truth in all its uncertainty, like the story it follows. Rilke's "You must change your life" is not, as Kepesh explains, "an elevated statement," clear and impervious (88). Merely it states the obvious. Life must change, change is inherent, and change does not always promise meaning or growth. To extract meaning from that line is to impose meaning upon it.

Kepesh discards a falsely optimistic dogma in favor of a more forthright stance. Change is possible, hope is possible, but they must exist within the world of facts and actions. To find comfort in the language of redemption, the Apollonian dialect, is to deny horror, and to fall into the slough of silence, defeated nihilism, the Dionysian dialect, is to deny reality. Neither is a sufficient response. In *The Breast* Kepesh explores, in his microcosm of the world, the various ways thinkers have tried to understand the horror in their past; and he finds, after many false starts, what Elie Wiesel might call a "fresh vocabulary," not an antidote but an inversion of Hitler's distorted language (Berger 3). Kepesh grows into Roth's tongue.

In 1960 Roth had already suggested the insufficiency of the language of redemption. What many critics, Bernard Rodgers prominently, take as an essay calling for the writer to find, in his writing, an "ideal balance" between society and the individual, "Writing American Fiction" is, in fact, a more bold tract (Rodgers 18). Roth notes the "nervous muscular prose," the practitioners of which are mostly Jewish, and wonders if this prose does not suit the age "because it rejects it" (RMAO 186-187). The strong prose, the "bounciness" which suggests "pleasure," seems a substitute for what the writer cannot face, the destructiveness, the powerlessness of life (RMAO 187). "Why is it," Roth asks, "that so many of them wind up affirming life?" (RMAO 188). The affirmation feels forced, false, a balm that obscures but does not heal. "The moral is bouncy," Roth notes (RMAO 188). The intent of the celebratory prose seems much the same as Kepesh's intent on words of reclamation, and its effect as impotent. Roth looks to Ellison's Invisible Man and away from Styron's Kinsloving, Bellow's Henderson, Herbert Gold, and Curtis Harnuck and their joyful exclamations, their neat conclusions of solace. Ellison's hero explores the world and investigates the cloistered self and his ending, like Kepesh's, "does not seem to him a cause for celebration either" (RMAO 191).

"Writing American Fiction" recognizes in post-Holocaust writers what Langer calls, "The mind in search of sedatives and antidotes," a normal response to "mediate atrocity" (HT 9). "The air is thick these days with affirmation," states Roth, but it is affirmation in the midst of nothingness, in the midst of fictional vistas, like Henderson's Arctic (RMAO 188). Defeated by the concentrationary universe the writer looks to language and away from his world to grasp desperately at hope. But, as Des Pres writes, "the world is not what it was;" it no longer makes "sense to speak of death's dignity or of its communal blessing;" there is no sense in attaching words of heroism onto the Holocaust landscape (4).

The oft quoted excerpt from "Writing American Fiction" - "The American writer in the middle of the twentieth century has his hands full in trying to understand, describe, and then make credible much of American reality. It stupefies, it sickens, it infuriates, and finally it is even a kind of embarrassment to one's own meager imagination" - strikes the observant reader of Roth as similar to remarks made by various Holocaust-writers about the impossibility of capturing the Shoah on paper, of describing what is indescribable, of the imagination's weakness against such an uninventable reality (RMAO 176). Saul Friedlander comments, "reality itself became so extreme as to outstrip language's capacity to represent it altogether" (Young 16). The Holocaust world is like Roth's America, an "impossible real," to borrow Maurice Blanchet's phrase (HT 39). Roth's essay describes the danger of attaching erroneous meaning on a post-Holocaust world, as it describes the writer's angst in coming after an event that defies the writer's capacity to understand or to create. Roth uses America as a more amenable arena to work out what will later in his work express itself as a concentrationary problem and not a local dilemma.

Claude Lanzmann writes, "The destruction of Europe's Jews cannot be logically deduced from any...system of presuppositions....there is a break in continuity, a hiatus, an abyss" (HT 427). It is that abyss that Roth must be referring to when he writes of the difficulties of the writer in the "middle of the twentieth century," sickened and stupefied, "horror-struck" and "awe-struck" (RMAO 178), withdrawn "from some of the grander social and political phenomena of our times" (RMAO 180). "Our subject resists the usual capacities of mind," writes Howe, in "Writing and the Holocaust," and a distinct echo of Roth's essay is heard (SW 424). The Grimes girls act as the ostensible trigger for Roth's essay, but behind them stands a more recalcitrant reality which the young writer seems unwilling to look at forthrightly. Roth's eyes, too, are cowed by the Holocaust. His belatedness to that event strikes the reader as more insistent and informative than the aggrandizement of the murder of twin teenagers from Chicago.

Michiko Kakutani points out that "Philip Roth made these observations back in 1961 - before the assassination of President John F. Kennedy, before the assassinations of Robert F. Kennedy and the Rev Dr. Martin Luther King Jr., before the social upheavals of the late 60's, before Vietnam and Watergate and Iran-contra" (C13). Roth's essay relies on an event that stealths itself in silence. "The chief obstacle to correct diagnosis in painful conditions," reads the epigraph to *The Anatomy Lesson*, "is the fact that the symptom is often felt at a distance from its source."

The painful condition of the American reality discussed in "Writing American Fiction" has its source in a more distant past than Roth's remembered Chicago. In *Zuckerman Unbound* it is that American reality which appears to be harassing the newly famous writer, tailing him like a spy, causing paranoia to grow like a tumor inside him. "Vietnam was a slaughterhouse," Zuckerman thinks, "and off the battlefield as well as on, many Americans had gone berserk" (7). The world has gone mad, thinks Zuckerman, everyone is a version of Oswald or Ruby. But is it Vietnam or assassinations, or even fame that locks Zuckerman inside his shell of self? Rather they are evidence of the disequilibrium of the concentrationary universe, evidence that the world has been knocked off-track and is drifting ever further into "anomie" (ZU 6). It is not Oswald's ghost or Ruby's ghost that returns and returns in the Zuckerman books but Anne Frank's, placing her world alongside the contemporary world that Zuckerman complains against. If Zuckerman represses that world, her face, it returns, over and over again, to remind him that his angst springs not from a history he observes day to day wandering manic Manhattan but from a history that overwhelms and is prologue to that chimerical city.

Zuckerman worries about a world where "only annihilation gave satisfaction that lasted," an allusion which peeks further backward than the 1960's (ZU 8). For Nathan, as for his father, the "two points of reference in all the vastness" are always "the family and Hitler," and from those mutually entangled webs Nathan's consciousness is born (ZU 199). The father's history is his history, the narrative of his life. Oswald and Ruby are covers for what truly frightens the Jewish son. As Nathan reflects upon his old neighborhood he is struck that "the Jews had all vanished" (ZU 223). Vanishing Jews walk beside the New York Jew, so ostentatiously present, fawned over, and stalked, a reminder of what he owes to time, to chance, and of how quickly even the most present of people can be made to disappear.

When Zuckerman's mother, in *The Anatomy Lesson*, is given a piece of paper to write her name upon, after developing a brain tumor, "she took the pen from his hand and instead of 'Selma' wrote 'Holocaust,' perfectly spelled" (41). Like her son, her deepest fear is encompassed in that word. "This was in Miami Beach in 1970, inscribed by a woman whose writings otherwise consisted of recipes on index cards, several thousand thank-you notes, and a voluminous file of knitting instructions. Zuckerman was pretty sure that before that morning she'd never even spoken the word aloud" (41). Other words shield that one word, bury it, as much for the mother as for the son. "It must have been there all the time without their even knowing," thinks Nathan, now seeing clearly what has resided in the mother, furtively, for so long. (42). The word defines the perspective, the way she sees the America of the 1970's and the way her son understands his own imprisoned life. It is passed from one to the other and though Zuckerman carries it around, "in his wallet," with him he need not, for it is deeply etched in him, and for Roth no less than for Zuckerman (RMAO 136).

When Roth is asked, of Zuckerman, "Why can't he throw it away?" he answers, "Who can? Who has? Zuckerman isn't the only one who can't throw this word away and is carrying it with him all the time, whether he knows it or not" (RMAO 136). Roth's America, in "Writing American Fiction," and in his own fictions, is understood as an echo, a remainder, a result, and a reminder of the Holocaust. Roth's individuals are stuck in history and that history conceives the current world. The world feels so estranged from them because of the wake that lay behind them, the world buried deep in their minds, carried along wherever they go. "Without this word," Roth continues, "there would be no Nathan Zuckerman, not in Zuckerman's fix. No chiropodist father and his deathbed curse, no dentist brother with his ferocious chastisement. There'd of course be no Amy Bellette, the young woman in *The Ghost Writer* who he likes to think could have been Anne Frank. There'd be no Milton Appel with his moral ordinances and literary imperatives. And Zuckerman wouldn't be in his cage" (RMAO 136).

Consciousness of the Holocaust redefines Roth's landscapes. To be Jewish, for Roth's characters, is to live in history. Roth returns again and again to Jewish demons, Jewish questions, because he must. Like Leslie Fielder, he must acknowledge that "in some ultimate sense" he is "a Jew; Hitler had decided that once and for all" (XVII). But by returning he need not be telling the same story again and again, and he does not. The critic sees Jews and assumes one story, one idea. He categorizes the Jewish tale in a way Roth seeks to disparage. That the stories are similar need not mean they are the same. Roth rewrites Appelfeld's insistence on referring to Jews as "we" to his own insistence on making each Jew an "I" (11). He moves into the same territory only to express the variety within that territory. A cursory reading leads one to see him as a writer retreading the same ground, when in fact each novel tries to find a new crevice in the road, a new direction, a new perspective. The one constant is the Holocaust, the obsession that must, albeit quietly and without sureness, return and return: Roth's characters, Jews and non-Jews alike, live in the concentrationary universe; from this there can be no divergence from text to text.

Notes

1.   "Jews are either authentic or unauthentic," argues Alan L. Berger, though he expands the definition of authenticity to those who show "A willingness to confront the Holocaust, to renew, in however modified a form, the covenantal framework of Judaism" (9). Though his reworking of the terms allows authenticity to the post-Holocaust generation it still maintains a strict differentiation, now not between survivor and progeny but between secular Jews and those who turn towards covenantal Judaism. "Secular doesn't know what they are living for," says a worshipful Jew to Zuckerman at the Wailing Wall, asserting Berger's logic, using it to classify and disparage the unbeliever (CL 100). The marking of authenticity is a means not of celebrating or cherishing but of dividing, dispersing Jew from Jew with the same intellectual construct which separated Jew from Gentile in Europe: One has status, the other none, one has worth while the other is but a false projection, a jew but not a Jew.

2.   But whose I is it, critics wonder, Roth's or his protagonists'? That question is, for the most part, a banal and uninteresting question, a question more to do with, as Roth says, "gossip" than with literature, yet it does open up an avenue for exploring Roth's autobiographical style, a style which has more to do with a Holocaust-consciousness than most would admit (CWPR 122). Roth picks up the autobio-

graphical style because it is the style which implores itself because of his subject matter. "The Holocaust," Howe writes, "was structured to destroy the very idea of private being" (433). Roth reasserts the private being, the self wrestling with its demons. "The interior," Appelfeld says, of the Holocaust-victim, "was locked away" (X). Roth unlocks the interior and exposes it compulsively. Of course, this could be accomplished in a purely fictional narrative. Had there been no correspondence between Roth's world and his characters' the subjective I is still the focal point of these fictions. This is true, too, of Roth's effort to impugn the I within the narrative; his effort to expose what maligns and makes guilty these protagonists. And yet a pure fiction does not account for the writer's malignity, or his own guilt. Roth's impure writing subjects not only the narrators to accusations of "loshon hora," of "evil speech," but Roth himself (OS 333). The wall that Roth opens between himself and his surrogates opens the floodgates of criticism upon himself; he invites the misreading.

3.   Here I invoke the "ovens," to do what? To make a simple point? To convey the depths of the error of silence? To point concretely to an image that will drive home the hazard of Holocaust-writing? To add zest to an academic study? To make the sentence dramatic? To give my work an aura of seriousness? To set myself up for criticism for using a metaphor I have no right to? These questions are demanded from within each time an image like the ovens is used. It is just these questions which keep the writer away, which warn him, harass him, judge him. How much is honest exposition and how much exploitation? How much is called for and how much is simply too much?

4.   Roth does not disparage Steiner or Adorno but reinterprets them. Their idea of silence is suspect from the start. For if no words are to be written how do they account for their own words. Howe suggests, of Adorno, "Perhaps his remarks are to be taken as a hopeless admonition, a plea for improvisation of limit that he knew would not and indeed could not be heeded, but which was necessary to make" (SE 430). For Howe, Adorno and Steiner make their manifestos not to discourage all speech but to instill a certain consciousness in those who would speak, to make them leery and thoughtful, to make the Holocaust a separate entity, a separate disaster from other subjects. "Through a dramatic outburst," Howe argues, "he [Adorno] meant to focus upon the sheer difficulty - the literary risk, the moral peril - of dealing with the Holocaust in literature" (428). Roth, it appears, reads Adorno in much the same way. Adorno's argument is used to warn against a Camus-like faith in speech's redemptive power.

CHAPTER FIVE

You Must Not Forget Anything

> I did not face the gas or the guns or
> the fences, but I am the son of the
> nightmare.
>
> - Joe Hirsch
> - Criticism after Auschwitz

The CAMP was hot. Two birds jabbered and in the distance Werner could hear a droning sound. As he trudged up the path the drone became louder until ahead of him he saw a half-dozen men milling around a squat, shivering, black machine (TCFAG 285).

Where are we? If we stop reading at this point in Roth's 1957 short story, "The Contest for Aaron Gold," we are left in a world we must be prepared for after following the concentrationary curve of Roth's later work.

The first paragraph gives way to the vernacular tone of the second; "'What the hell do you think I'm running here, Angelo,' one of the men was shouting. He wore a plaid, peaked cap, a white polo shirt that had CAMP LAKESIDE scrawled across the front, and rust trousers" (287). The attentive reader now has two tales to concern himself with, the tale of Aaron Gold and Werner Samuelson, and the tale of language that the first lines introduce.

The first paragraph suggests the dichotomies of this adolescent story. The "two birds" and the "grass" are placed against the "black machine" and the "asphalt road" it creates (285). The pastoral is to collide with the developed, to the pastoral's diminishment, the grass covered over, "flattened and finished" by asphalt, the sound of birds drowned out by an ominous

167

machine (287). To compliment that collision two world-views will fall against each other, that of Werner and Aaron, the craftsman and the artist, and that of Lefty Shulberg and Lionel Steinberg, the purveyors of the modern, of expediency.

Aaron's project in clay, his knight battling "a purple dragon with six heads and three tails" recasts the dichotomies of the camp in the realm of art (296). The knight on its spindle-legs is like the boy and his teacher, the grass and the sunflowers, the old world, alive with "beautiful objects of art" (288). The dragon, with its proposed mass of heads, is like Lionel and Lefty, the road-making machine, and the "scythe," which is used for "guillotining sunflowers" (294-295).

Werner is asked to choose between the old and the new, the past and the present, the pastoral and the modernized. In the end he cannot countenance a betrayal of Aaron; he will stand up for his own individuality and for the individuality of his student. But this is only the first story told, the simple tale of the "hero" fighting "the crass middle-class values of Camp Lakeside" (MacDaniel 8).

Werner's history compels his final action, his refusal to surrender his self to the camp world. "Not since 1940," Werner thinks, after settling himself into his shop, "when the Germans had chased him from his studio in southern Austria had he spent a summer in the country" (286). The language of the first sentence highlights this, seemingly, passing thought. Werner is a survivor, an exile from the Holocaust. Prepared by the ambiguous opening this detail now takes on a new resonance. Steinberg and Shulberg, the dragons, believe in order, routine, sameness, technology, strict morality, and they ridicule individual assertiveness. They are not Nazis by any means, or even an American facsimile, but for Werner they represent the forces that cannot be acceded to, that must be rejected. If in the past those forces could not be fought then in the non-threatening present to bow to them is impossible. If in the past the camp setting and the camp guardians would not allow dissension or escape then in the present both dissension and escape must be enacted. Werner must walk "out of the camp" simply because he can (290). To stay would be to blight his own history.

This, then, is the hidden tale Roth tells in "The Contest for Aaron Gold:" how the past affects the present, how history inserts itself into what seems a facile situation, how events in a man's own past transmute later into actions. This twin tale, which repeats itself throughout Roth's writings, introduces and defines the Holocaust- pattern, the past emerging like a ghost, corrupting the present, forcing men to act, to choose, and to remember.

Werner protects Aaron not only because he feels an affinity for the isolated, willful, and talented boy but because of his own memories of entrapment by authority. His recollection of Europe, his own forced exile from his art, makes his defense of the artist, even in summer camp, imperative. America is a polar opposite of besieged Austria, a world of summer idles and trivial wars, where neither life nor limb is threatened by a moral stand, but it does not exist alone, safe from history. The distance between Werner and Aaron is the distance of a story about Nazi ghosts oppressing one's consciousness and a story about the restrictive rules of an overly regimented, if effectively run, summer camp for children. Still that distance does not preclude contiguity. In Roth's works the story of the American children is both its own hilarious and pessimistic story and is intimately connected to the European story, the story alluded to in tropes and tones, indistinctly metamorphosing everything around it. As Werner walks out of the camp we are led deeper into the morass of his past. His is only the first shadow to stain the carpet that Roth's figure will emerge upon.

That Jamesian shadow grows with time, revealing itself to those who are willing to recognize it. The pieces come together, in fits and starts, hues hidden amidst whiteness overwhelm their background. The stories in *Goodbye, Columbus* join together, their sub-text linking them with what came before and what comes after.[1]

Neil Klugman escapes the nets of Patimkin bounty because he, like Werner, must remember the European past, the horror that the Patimkins have buried in the back rooms and sweetened with fruit. The associations Neil makes while listening to Ron's "Goodbye, Columbus" record are those of a man not only fated, but driven, to remember and act on memory. When Neil hears the disembodied voice he thinks, "Blitzkrieg," a word probably not even in Ron's vocabulary (103). Like Werner, Neil's thoughts turn back to a time that berates his current interests. His thoughts don't allow him the peace that Brenda and her siblings share. This is an idea that is repeated in all the stories in the collection; the individual acting out, asking questions, asserting himself to his own detriment. The heroes in *Goodbye, Columbus* refuse to surrender their bodies or their minds; they would rather act against what is deemed normal and appear fanatical to the subjugated others.

Sergeant Nathan Marx feels that his identity is threatened not by the army's authority but by Sheldon Grossbart, a fellow Jew who expects allegiance from Marx because of a common history. Marx, a "veteran of the European theater," has his memories played upon by Grossbart, who attempts to control and manipulate him through repeated allusions to those memories (162). "That's what happened in Germany....They didn't stick together," says Grossbart. "They let themselves get pushed around" (174). "Why are you persecuting me, Sergeant?" asks Grossbart, using the word that will elicit the most guilt. (188). "'I've run into this before,' he said, 'but never from my own'" (188). He both asserts commonality and then ties Marx to the victimizers. "They say Hitler himself was half a Jew. Seeing this, I wouldn't doubt it," he tells Marx (188). But it is the memory of Hitler, himself, and Hitler's destruction, that will not allow Marx to give in to Grossbart. Memory impels his conscience to act on its own precisely because Grossbart is a Jew. It will be better "For all of us," claims Marx, better for the

Jews if they are individuals first (200). The Holocaust must not paralyze him, force him to act against his judgment. He must be cruel, and he must accept his guilt, his "fate" if he is to live in the shadow of the Holocaust, a fate that is a product of both his past and of his actions, self-made from memory (200).

"Eli, the Fanatic" anchors *Goodbye,Columbus*, making prominent what sluiced between the pages in the other stories. The Holocaust story which ends the collection shines its light backward toward the other stories, making clear that the individual choices witnessed are made manifest by remembrance. There are those who forget the past (The Patimkins), those who misuse the past (Grossbart), those who act similarly to the oppressors (Russo, Rabbi Binder, Ozzie), and those who react against enslavement because of their attentiveness to history (Epstein, Neil, Marx). Those of the former categories are brought together with the Jews of Woodenton, and those of the later category are joined to Eli in this final confrontation.

Leo Tzuref arrives in Eli's life from the world of blackness. He leads Eli "beyond the dark, untrampled horse path" (249). Eli marvels at "the black circle on the back of his head" (250). Tzuref's home is bathed in "dimness" (250). "The lamps had no bulbs," Eli notices (250). Looking at the greenie "seated on a bench beneath a tree" Eli can only see "a deep hollow of blackness" (253). "A Bulb or two would have helped," thinks Eli, inside Tzuref's study (263). The "last gleamings" of the day barely reflect in Tzuref's window (263). Eli asks for "a little light, fearing that "In the dark...Tzuref might put him under a spell" (265). There is a power in that dark that frightens and calls to something within Eli.

Contrasting the blackness of the Yeshiva is the whiteness of Woodenton, with its "street light" shining over the streets and houses (249). Terrified after his first visit to Tzuref, Eli "hurried towards the lights" of his community (253). Woodenton is alive with electricity, suspended in "the yellow glow of the Gulf station" (269), brightened by "a burst of yellow" (249).

Roth transposes our normative assumptions about color's significance in "Eli, the Fanatic." White becomes associated with falsity, with impurity, with the lie, and black with honesty, resilience, and strength. Roth turns around, too, conceptions of normalcy and abnormality, with the conventional residents of the town, the ostensibly "Normal" men and women, seeming alien and unreal (254). Eli, the figure of ridicule, the man assumed to be having a "breakdown," transforming before his neighbors' eyes into "one of those goddamn fanatics," is the most human character in the story (258). "But if you chose to be crazy, then you weren't crazy," Eli tells himself (293). Eli chooses his fate, chooses to make his walk through town, chooses to risk his place in the normal flow of Woodenton. Moreover, his choice is made by accepting history, a world determined for him, beyond his control. The fanatics of the second order, in *Goodbye,Columbus*, find in their fate - their past, their time - an avenue for choice-making, for self-awakening. They make gestures towards their circumstances, find light in darkness, darkness in light.[2]

Eli takes on the blackness. "The shock at first was the shock at having daylight turned off all at once," Eli thinks, looking down at the box containing the greenie's black suit (285). His words lead back to Leo Patimkin, the light merchant, who understood the natural fear of darkness that terrorizes man. "Inside the box," Eli sees, "was an eclipse. But black soon sorted from black, and shortly there was the glassy black of lining, the coarse black of trousers, the dead black of fraying threads, and in the center the mountain of black: the hat" (285).

The hat holds a "terrible weight" and yet Eli puts it on and promises to wear it every year so that he might "never forget" (298). Eli shawls himself in blackness to find a bit of light. He sees what the easeful light has blinded everyone else to, how the whiteness has terrorized and numbed those around him. The men who come to sedate him "wear white shoes, white gowns, white skullcaps" but their whiteness "did not touch it down where the blackness had reached" (298). Blackness is not a disease to be erased, and whiteness is not a cure; the dark that cannot be touched by modern medicine is Eli's individuality, his strength. It is sad and weighty and terrible but finally more real than the sterility of Woodenton's bright lights.

Roth's story is not only about America's unwillingness to see the Holocaust but is about a basic human unwillingness to see the horror, to accept the Holocaust's non-redemptive truth, to risk discomfort, to escape the self-imposed boundaries of conventional happiness. This is the "characterological enslavement" that Roth speaks of in regard to his work (RMAO 108). The Holocaust past is put aside, denied in practice, to shield the individual, and in that shielding, that denial, the self is buried.

"A man's history is his fate," says the narrator of "You Can't Tell a Man by the Song He Sings" (246). Fated to the Holocaust man must choose how to react, how to act, whether to remember, and how, or to forget. *Goodbye,Columbus* repeats this problem in each of its stories, a problem *Letting Go* elaborates upon. Roth explains: "And in a way I see *Letting Go* coming out of - not directly, but in a hazy kind of way - 'Defender of the Faith' and 'Eli, the Fanatic'" (CWPR 6). He refers to the two most explicitly Holocaust-oriented stories to speak about his first novel, a novel with few references to the Holocaust. Roth sees the works connected by the idea of "moral fanaticism" (CWPR 9). "It seems to be a concern," Roth explains, "a kind of investigation of moral force, moral ambition" (CWPR 9). The moral imperative, the moral dilemma, faces Eli and Marx, and Paul and Gabe. "The central problem," Roth argues, "is really, 'How far do you go?'" (CWPR 6).

Paul and Gabe must decide how far they will go for happiness, how much they need give up, how detached they can remain, and how connected they are. The past hangs upon their shoulders. The world they live in is "fallen" (Rand 22). Gabe's mother's letter sits on his chest, the memory of his father's tears hound him. Paul's parents' denunciation cause his shoulders to drop, his hopes to fade. "The best thing for all of us is to let the past be," says Gabe (508). "I will make Paul forget the past," promises Libby (582). The past, though, is more than one's personal history. There is a legacy behind them, a legacy which Paul seems to flout by denying his parents' wishes, that Gabe seems to betray by turning from all heart-felt connections. That legacy is rarely uttered, but Roth's mention of the two precursor stories brings it into view. The camp survivor, Scully, and the elderly schemers Korngold and Levy, who refer to their landlord as "that Nazi" (105), speak for a different time, a time which flagellates Paul and Gabe, so miserable in their "abundance" (21). They are stand-ins for what isn't mentioned. Gabe walks in Iowa and thinks, "The November morning was dazzling, the dead were dead" (5). But for Roth's conscience-plagued men the dead are never dead, the past is as alive as this moment.

Gabe succeeds in advancing upon the past, learning something from its misery, while Paul escapes into ideology, responsibility, the now of life, oblivious, as are the secondary characters, that the ideological life has been morally deracinated by the Holocaust. Gabe refuses a solution, a meaning. "And that's in part," says Roth, "what the book is about...discovering that there are some things that are unresolvable" (CWPR 9). This is the answer to the Holocaust-thematic, defined as the battle between ideology and nihilism, inside one man or woman, or within the social or political world, the dual evils of the Holocaust world, the two models of thought discredited by it. The Holocaust- thematic, like the Holocaust-pattern, repeats through Roth's varied works, alerting the reader, like a secret code, to Roth's obsessional, albeit cloaked, return to the Holocaust and its imprint on the universe.

The lesson of the Holocaust-thematic, the answer inscribed within the play of debased absolutes, can only be learned if one is willing to go that far, to test one's moral commitments and moral motivations again and again. "For there are truths," writes Howe, "grim and blunt, which can make no claim to being 'redemptive'" (NB 253). They are the truths the Holocaust attests to, the truths the contemporary writer must admit. Howe adds, "And these are of a kind most writers pass by because they threaten to undermine both the reconciliations of comedy and the recognitions of tragedy" (NB 253-254). Comedy and tragedy provide a catharsis, a final easement that Roth's works disallow. There is always that questioning that lingers, a "more" that the reader must imagine.

It is that "more" that Lucy Nelson, Roth's next pro/antagonist will not accept. She wants closure, endings, justice, proper places for fathers and mothers, sons and daughters, husbands and wives, places never altered, roles never enlarged. It is her worship of order, of fated positions, that gives the novel what Rodgers calls, "the same gloomy aura of inevitability which marked Roth's first novel" (63). The idea of fate joins *Letting Go* to *When She Was Good* - the Jewish novel and the goyische novel - together, Rodgers argues. But fate is a thin umbilical cord between the two books. It is, rather,

Lucy's failure to see beyond fate, to see beyond the fixed ideology of the American myth, which joins her physical death with the emotional and moral deaths of Paul, Libby, and Martha, and which brings the two texts together. Fate is a pulpit; the inevitability of Lucy's decline is self-perpetuated by her faith in fate, not by fate itself.

Letting Go and *When She Was Good* are further linked by the replicating Holocaust-pattern. Each novel begins with a voice of the past. For Willard it is the past of "tyranny of cruel men and cruel nature," a past ruled by the brutality of his own father (6). For Lucy it is the past of her grandfather's innocuous and ineffectual goodness and her father's drunken irresponsibility and violence. Both are witness to a formative event; for Willard it is his sister Ginny's death and for Lucy it is the night she must call the police to save her mother from her father. Like Gabe and Paul, the face of the past - the letter for Gabe, the banishment for Paul - is the fate they must fight or become enslaved to. It is these events which erect a mind-set for each character, nihilism and silence for Willard, ideology and speech for Lucy.

The reactions of Willard and Lucy are exemplary of the two most readily available reactions to barbarity in general, and to the Holocaust in particular. Willard, in defeat, cannot believe in anything fervently again; meaning and language are forever tied to a world long destroyed. He finds silence a solace, avoiding memory itself. Lucy, in remonstrance of her grandfather's weakness, turns to ideological surety, the speech of the believer. By asserting meaning she defies the past, explains it, makes it a lesson, a means towards her own redemption; she can defeat and remake the past - like the poet of "Black Milk" - by the force of her own words. Willard and Lucy represent the bitter extremes of the Holocaust-thematic.

Sanford Pinsker gets close to Roth's center when he suggests that Lucy is a representation of "the American nightmare lurking just on the other side of the American Dream" (TCTH 43). But this is as far as Pinsker will go. Several pages later Pinsker notes, "the banality with which this type of subject infuses the book," and again he breaks off from the more weighty association (49). Donald Kartiganer notes the same presence of "an unbroken banality," suggesting that the book portrays "the triumph of banality" as it manifests itself, horribly, in the character of Lucy Nelson (94-95). Roth, too, recognizes the novel's "unrelenting concern with banality," without making clear why that concern predominates throughout the book (CWPR 40).

Aware of the Holocaust-pattern and the Holocaust-thematic the idea of banality is made more significant. Hannah Arendt's *Eichmann in Jerusalem: A Report on the Banality of Evil* offers a means of seeing Lucy's descent in a historical perspective. Eichmann is presented not as a madman but as the most ordinary of men. In fact it is his ordinariness, his willingness to believe in the hierarchical culture he finds himself within, that allows him to perform his evil without conscience's intervention. He suffers a "lack of imagination," like Lucy, an inability to become a self independent of the rules and mores of his community (287). "That such remoteness from reality and such thoughtlessness," argues Arendt, "can wreck more havoc than all the evil instincts taken together which, perhaps, are inherent in man - that was, in fact, the lesson one could learn in Jerusalem" (288). This is the lesson of Roth's novel as well. It is the inability to speak her own words, to see beyond convention and myth, that turns the plain young girl into a devil. She is not simply evil-incarnate but the result of ignorance, naivete, self-ishness, and, most portentously, the banal language implanted within her.

"It surely cannot be so common," writes Arendt, "that a man facing death, and, moreover, standing beneath the gallows, should be able to think of nothing to say but what he has heard at funerals all his life," and that these "lofty words should completely becloud the reality of his own death" (288). In *When She Was Good* Lucy Nelson, as close to death as Eichmann before the noose, can only say to herself cliched words; words learned and spoken throughout her life: "The good must triumph in the end! The good and the just and the true must" (304). Beclouded, like Eichmann, Lucy makes her impending death an impossibility. When Roth asserts the simi-larity of Americans to Lucy is he not pointing to the American, indeed the human, need to seek conformity and to avoid the precariousness of indi-viduality? Is there not a need to follow, to belong and believe, to stay with-in the set parameters, that makes us not unlike the masses who marched in lock-step with Hitler to their own debasement? In Lucy Roth has created a miniature Eichmann, an American cousin - less deadly and more sympa-thetic - of the ideologues, the fanatics of the first order, the regular men and women, who, in their rightness, destroyed themselves and their world.

Lucy would be the quintessential goy for many of Roth's Jews. She embodies the two most familiar visions of non-Jews, the sure, pure, American girl, she of the "golden hair" (42), as Portnoy puts it, and the vic-timizer, the fool, the enemy, the "little Eichmann" that Jimmy-Ben Joseph asserts is present in the "heart" of "every goy" (CL 189). In his interview with Aharon Appelfeld Roth argues, "I'd say that it's impossible to know anything really about the Jewish imagination without investigating the place that the goy has occupied in the folk mythology" (75).

The goy enters Roth's world, most prominently in *Portnoy's Complaint*, as the apotheosis of Alex's envy and of his hate and rage. Roth's third novel, his release from form, takes the Holocaust-pattern and the Holocaust-the-matic and fastens to them a new voice, the voice of the guilty, angst-ridden, young Jew searching for an identity as a Jew in a world of "goyim" (75). Portnoy wants to shed his past, his "suffering heritage" (75), and yet he is drawn back towards it, his instincts built upon the tribal "distinction" of "*goyische* and Jewish" (75).

"America is a *shikse* nestling under your arm whispering love love love love love!" cries Alex (146). But for Alex that dream is not enough to satisfy his cravings for a life all his own, without the specter of cattle-cars and fences always ready to flash across his mind. He wants the "self-confidence and the cunning, the imperiousness and the contacts" of "the blond and blue-eyed" (39). They are normal, free of taint, while even the good things in his life are tainted by memory, by responsibility, by rules and by fears. He must worry about "milchiks and flaishiks" while they eat wantonly, avariciously, in love, guiltlessly, with life (34). This is what all the "Shiksa-fancying," as Maria puts it in *The Counterlife*, is all about, this desperate urge to unhinge from the tribe (78).

Like Kepesh, looking to Claire for peace, like Henry Zuckerman, running away from his past to Israel, and like Nathan Zuckerman, creating a fantasy life with Maria in London, Portnoy longs for the imagined life of the goyim, the child's pastoral dream where no one was stamped with numbers, or silenced with gas, where the thoughts of gold teeth pulled and thrown on piles never enters his sleep, where the sight of chimneys alludes to nothing but a soft fire on a winter's night, where hair piled end to end, thirty feet high, serves only to remind him of the unlucky past of some other, the throttled history of a people not his own. That life can only be a fantasy; the past will not desist, not for Kepesh in his country home, or for Henry and Nathan in their adoptive lands, or for Portnoy, who finds his Jewish identity branded onto his soul. The tribe pulls from within.

"And you'll convert," he jokingly tells Kay Campbell (230). When she responds with incredulity Portnoy finds himself flabbergasted, bitter, defensive, hurt: "How could I be feeling a wound in a place where I was not even vulnerable?" he asks himself (231). The wound, lodged deep inside, hidden from himself, comes to the surface, reminding him of who he is, of what is conjoined to him.

With *Our Gang* Roth veers from the tightly bound world of the Jew to the satirical world of Richard Nixon and contemporary American life. The Holocaust and the goy/Jew dilemma seem light years away in this parody, which would appear to be a book only for its time, a relic of a newly famous author's rancor at the sitting President. But, the villain of *Our Gang*, Trick E. Dixon, is more than an exaggerated Nixon; he is also an example of a universal "authoritarian dignity," a typical, timeless representative of the deceptive and empty manipulator of language (RMAO 47).

Roth satirizes and exposes not merely Nixon's disingenuousness, his willingness to eschew morality for political power, but the historical resonance of Nixon's language and behavior, his linkage to a plethora of more and less diabolical predecessors. Roth maintains that H.L. Mencken was more "amused" by his own satirical subject than Roth is of his own (RMAO 45). The reason for his indignation "may be," he says, "that there's been a lot of terror packed into the short space of time that separates Mencken's 'gamalielese' from George Orwell's 'Newspeak' - related kinds of double-talk at which President Nixon is equally adept" (RMAO 45). Roth brings his observation on the contemporary scene into collision with his sense of the past, introducing the Holocaust-pattern as an impetus for the writer's attack. "It took Orwell," claims Roth, "and a second world war, and savage totalitarian dictatorships in Germany and Russia - to make us realize that this seemingly comical rhetoric could be turned into an instrument of political tyranny" (RMAO 45-6). What seems so amusingly absurd is actually absurdly deadly.[3]

The language of the lie, or "the fine art of government lying," as Roth calls it, reified by Hitler, is the subject of *Our Gang* (RMAO 57). Dixon's "totally meaningless words" (29) are not the "innocuous" blather he pretends, but a means of controlling those subordinate to him, a means of wrapping language in so many levels of contradiction and hypocrisy as to distract the public from any real thought, a means of hiding malice, and even atrocity, in babel (28). Dixon slowly melds into a more fearsome object.

Hitler's perverse categorizations creep over Dixon's tongue in the first chapter when Dixon refers to the civilian victims of Mai Lai as "the misfits, the bums, the tramps" (8). Slowly, with increasing clarity, the Hitlerian voice speaks in Dixon's and his advisors' mouths. Even fetuses are labeled "troublemakers" and "malcontents," by a government in search of a scapegoat, a victim to harness their power against (13). Of the boy scouts, Dixon's chosen enemy, the suggestion is made to "round 'em up, put 'em in the clink, and throw the key away" (43). The military coach adds, "Let's get it over with once and for all. Shoot 'em!" (43). Finally the inevitable suggestion is made by the spiritual coach, "Well...what about gas...poison gas...something like that?" (46). The possibility of "busing them there" is brought up (46). In close approximation to Hitler's words, Dixon calls his enemies a "contagion," comparing the need to murder them to the need to "excise a cancer from the living body" (120). There is even a hint of anti-Semitism in Dixon's relentless espousals: He points out that the enemy of America, the baseball player Curt Flood, is represented by "Arthur Goldberg, G-o-l-d-b-e-r-g" (100).

"I think what is then most disturbing to the reader is that he has found himself enjoying a fantasy that he has known in reality to be terrible" (RMAO 58). The laughs of today are sullied by the horrors of yesterday. The two stories collide in this still pertinent work of fiction, the story of America and Europe, the past and the present, memory and amnesia, clownishness and barbarism.

The oddness of Dixon's absurd comic-like world is not *sui generis* to a fantasy world, but is implicit in the quotidian, Roth's next novel, *The Breast*, claims in its first sentence. "Reflect upon eternity," Kepesh asks us, "consider, if you are up to it, oblivion, and everything becomes a wonder" (3). The unreal and the real are equally baffling, equally fantastic. That there is a "perfect rose" or an "imperfect rose," that the sun lights the earth, that death is forever, are daily reminders of a world more outrageous, more illogical than any of Roth's fictional worlds, even a world where a man can turn into a breast (3). But oddness is relative, and the oddness with which we are accustomed to from birth does not assault us as emphatically as the unaccounted for phenomena. It is the transition from this to that, from Kepesh to a breast, from body to gland, from professor to victim, that makes oddness felt as a dire threat. It is that change that attacks Kepesh, that alteration of all known oddness into an unknown oddness, outside the episte-mological categories he has lived within, that makes his incapacitation into a nightmare. And it is that alteration that brings to mind the alterations not only of Kafka and Gogol but of the Holocaust, as well. As the Holocaust vic-tim loses his sense of all reality, as he has all categories thrown loose and burned in a blaze of illogic, so, too, Kepesh feels his trauma as a loss of logic as much as of body, a loss of interpretation. For it is answers that Kepesh wants more then recovery, explanation before cure. That he learns to live without explanation, to see oddness as the only truth, is a tribute to his strength: His refusal to assert meaning where none is available, to find uplift in sadness, is a Holocaust revelation.

And it is a revelation that many could not find. Kepesh's initial failure parallels the ways in which much of America dealt with the Holocaust. *The Breast*, like "Eli, the Fanatic," tells the story of an America in denial of the European past. Like Kepesh, America turned from what was transpiring so many miles away, looked away for fear of seeing the truth, and then escaped the reality of the pointed facts with various modes of denial, explanation, theology, moral posturing, interpretation. Denial, like forgetting, became an American obsession.

In *The Great American Novel* Smitty complains of a similar effort at American denial. "Yes, I am speaking," he writes, "of the annihilation of the Patriot League. Not merely wiped out of business, but willfully erased from the national memory" (16). One may read this novel as one man's battle to have his memories validated against the mythology "a great power prefers to per-petuate that will not give an inch in behalf of that idealized mythology" (RMAO 90). Smitty wants to win back his past from official denial, and, in turn, redeem the facts from what he views as a massive effort at propagan-da. But, with Roth's consciousness in plain sight, we see Smitty as more than a singular voice; he comes to be understood as the voice of the past, the Jewish voice of exile wailing for remembrance. In *Operation Shylock* Smilesburger tells "Roth," "All your writing you owe to [the Jews], including even that book about baseball and the wandering team without a home" (388).

The Holocaust-pattern is clearly present in *The Great American Novel*, a past burrowing its way into the consciousness of the present. And the Holocaust- thematic is alive in the structure of the text. There are two truths, Smitty's and the "'real' American history" (RMAO 91). And both are somehow true and somehow false, facts rewritten to serve an agenda: Smitty's nihilistic agenda of deconstruction and the American government's agenda of ideologic myth-making. Roth mixes the "credible" with the "incredible," establishing what he calls, "a passageway from the imaginary that comes to seem real to the real that comes to seem imaginary" (RMAO 91).Neither is believed by the skeptical reader; even as he cheers Smitty's fabulation he knows himself to have had his own memories transcribed by the more mundane other conventional truth.

More specifically, *The Great American Novel* uses Gil Gamesh as a parodic Hitler to emphasize the end-point of myth-proselytising. The saga of the Rubbert Mundys takes place from 1933 to 1945, the years of Hitler's reign. It is in 1933 that Gamesh enters the league: "Adolf Hitler, Franklin Roosevelt, Gil Gamesh. "In the winter of '33 - '34, men women and even little children, worried for the future of America, were talking about one or another, if not all three," Smitty explains (79). It is Gamesh who, Hitler-like, intones, "I'm Gil Gamesh! I'm an Immortal!" (67). It is Gamesh who makes the fans roar "with arms upraised," as though they are yelling at "their Fuehrer" (73). When he gains control of the Mundys he screams, "The Revolution has begun! Henceforth, the Mundys are the master race" (355). He asks for "blood," "brawls," and "hate" (353). "It's hatin'," Roland Agni points out of his new manager's philosophy, "threatenin', cursin' - it's wantin' to kill the other guy, wantin' him dead - *and that ain't a game*" (354).

Where the slapstick of game-playing ends the reality begins; beneath the facade there is a world of persecution, of blood and hate. The American version of such persecution, the House Un-American Activities Committee, is introduced in the last part of the novel, another muffled echo of the more terrible forms persecution has taken. Smitty's "version of history," Roth contends, "has its origins in something that we all recognize as having taken place" (RMAO 91). Roth's comment moves beyond a reference to the communist witch-hunt to encompass much of Smitty's narrative, his outrageous, lunatical look at the world from 1933 to 1945 when a displaced minority was decimated and dispersed by a demented madman. If America would slide those events under the carpet of history Roth and Smitty will insist and insist upon their retrieval, on a permanent exposed stain. The "shelterless, shipwrecked, shucked, shunted, and shuttled," are Smitty's subjects (45). "The unfit, the failed, the floundering," he continues, "the forgotten," are his heroes (45). In Roth's three tall tales he uses America to tell a story about both itself and its European relations. That the books are satires, wild and often uproarious, makes clear the vast separation of the two continents; what plays as comedy in America has its origins in the deep tragedy of Europe.

"And in the end," argues Vaclav Havel, "is not the greyness and the emptiness of life in the post-totalitarian system only an inflated caricature of modern life in general? And do we not in fact stand as a kind of warning to the West, revealing to it its own latent tendencies?" (62). Roth expands the caricature to expose those latent tendencies not always dormant in forgetful America. Havel speaks of the "something in human begins which responds to this system" of the lie, the system that shrouds the present (53). In *My Life as a Man*, Roth's next novel, Peter Tarnopol is pulled toward the lie, toward victimization, toward the past, by a literary sensibility that wants life to be like art, a catharsis, a means of transcendence.

Tarnopol recognizes the post-modern wreckage of his age. "Why isn't there sin anymore?" he wonders (135). He looks to the Holocaust as the fault line of change, "the catastrophe of the century," he calls it (179). His attraction to Grete, "the student nurse in Frankfurt," is an attraction to her proximity to the horror (179). "I used to be fascinated by whatever she could tell me about her experience of the war," Peter explains (179). He is hypnotized by her experience because it is the antithesis of his own. "I happened to have been born a Jew not in twentieth-century Nuremberg," he has Zuckerman explain, "but in the state of New Jersey" (92). His own place and time is ill-defined against the monumental importance of Grete's time and place.

But Grete will not suffice for she does not satisfy that subsidiary craving of Tarnopol's, the craving not only to touch the victim but to become the victim, the craving Havel recognizes, to give himself to the lie, to become as defined and suffused with depth as the other victims of Gentile mendacity. "Human beings are compelled to live within the lie," Havel argues, both by their oppressors and by their own accedence, their own willfulness (54). Tarnopol is beguiled by Maureen's words because they give him meaning, albeit negative meaning, meaning as sufferer, as prisoner, as objectified slave. She makes him into what he most wants to be, like the others, like Grete's contemporaries, like the Jews amidst the "Polish peasantry," the stories of which, he says, "I used to hear as a child usually from my immigrant grandmothers" (91). There is a certain purity in victimization, the word-worshiper feels. He seeks to be not in control but "under control" (212). He had been programmed to believe her lies, programmed to fall under the sway of her tales of victimization and her power to victimize.

That Tarnopolian programming is described succinctly in Peter's story, "The Diary of Anne Frank's Contemporary" (245). In that story Peter's family has only the day before moved from one apartment to another. Peter, as he recalls, "couldn't seem to get myself to remember that we moved the day before and now lived elsewhere" (245). He arrives at his former home only to find it desolated. The story continues: "'It's Nazis!' I thought. The Nazis had parachuted into Yonkers, made their way to our street and taken everything away. Taken my mother away. So I suddenly perceived it" (245).

The Nazi threat, the Nazi memory, inscribes itself upon him, becomes the part of his consciousness that he cannot let go of. He longs to know the victims, to know the perpetrators, to understand what they understand. Fear and desire move the man of stories to look to the most fascinating and horrendous story to find himself. Maureen reels him in with her stories of a dilapidated past, a past associated with the suffering that so intrigues Peter. And she holds onto him with her sure lies, her authority, her willingness to give him a personal sense of enslavement.

Before David Kepesh turns into a breast he, like Tarnopol, finds within his heart the compulsion towards wholeness (MLAAM 330). He finds the victim role and the victimizer role equally provocative and tantalizing. He recognizes the pleasure of a "besiegiment of another," and the complementary wish to "be besieged and assaulted in turn" (42). The hidden dream, the dream that turned men into killing machines, is announced by the desirous professor and affirmed by his "collaborationist instincts," the atavistic impulse to take control, to destroy, to be one thing even if that one thing is a monster (42). And with it is born the masochistic, death-driven, dream, the dream to be controlled, manipulated, to be made into something definite even if that thing is a slave. It is, finally, the dream of vicariously entering the world of the camps, Barbatnik's domain, to feel fully tested, fully alive.

Kepesh will never be at rest, never at ease, for his time, he feels, offers none of the certainty, none of the significant pain of the other time. In Prague, Kepesh comes in contact with that which haunts and stimulates him: "Then," he announces, "for the first time I notice the plaques affixed to the length of cemetery wall, inscribed to the memory of Jewish citizens of Prague exterminated in Terezin, Auschwitz, Belsen, and Dachau. There are not pebbles enough to go around" (176). There are not enough pebbles for the victims, let alone a pebble for his own relatively minor pain. "Mr. Barbatnik," Kepesh says, "my father told us you survived the concentration camps. How did you do it? Do you mind my asking?" (254). It is the story which surpasses the other stories, the "survival story" Kepesh dreams of for himself, terrible, dramatic, real, unambiguous, fearsome, true (254-5). Barbatnik's story of living through the coal mines, being arrested by the Germans, escaping, being fed by German farmers, and finally being saved by the Americans, makes Kepesh's sorrow lose its sting, makes him feel that he has lost his own story.

The past will play havoc with his heart and with his head until he can acknowledge not only that the present cannot grant him the fullness he imagines others to possess, but that the past, the Holocaust past, does not grant that fullness either, not to Barbatnik, nor to the father who warns of a second Holocaust, nor to the millions and millions of others, victims and perpetrators alike. Their experiences of atavism and ideology provide no answer. *The Professor of Desire* ends in desperation, in hopelessness, with Kepesh a victim of his own imaginings, his own backward-looking brain.

Nathan Zuckerman, his heart looking back in the same direction as his literary brothers, carries with him "the white piece of paper with the word 'Holocaust' on it," a palpable sign of his obsession (AL 59). He carries it not only as a memento of his mother's life but as a reminder of the unspoken event that demarcates his movements. When Roth is asked, "But you're not saying that your subject in these books has been the Holocaust?" he responds, "No, no, of course not - certainly not in the way it's the subject at the center of Styron's novel *Sophie's Choice*" (RMAO 136). Roth first assures his interviewer that the Holocaust is not his subject in *Zuckerman Bound* and then he quickly modifies that denial with the words "not in the way." It is those words that betray Roth's position.

The Holocaust *is* his subject, but it is not as dramatically and unsubtly present as it is for Styron, who has little compunction about recreating

Mengele pointing Sophie's child to her death. "It works through Jewish lives less visibly," says Roth, "and in less spectacular ways. And that's the way I prefer to deal with it in fiction" (RMAO 136). It is like a word lost in a mother's memory, a scrap of paper in the wallet of her son, a curse streaming forth from a father's death-bed, a sight in the ashes of a factory, a ghostly old man walking in a cemetery, a pain stretching the length of a writer's body, an inconsolable memory plaguing the disturbed psyche of Alvin Pepler, a fascination with a missing manuscript, a ghost of a dead girl, an excoriation by a Jewish critic, a longing to suffer and to escape. It is there in the shadows, in the language of the characters; the tale of a world, as Doctor Kotler says, "decimated by Hitler," a world flushed "down the twentieth-century drain" (AL 116), " a vision," as Jaga says, "of all that went" (AL 137). "I just mean," says Roth, "that that little piece of paper in Zuckerman's wallet might not seem quite so small" (RMAO 137).

The Holocaust-pattern is made apparent in *Zuckerman Bound*, most obviously in the figure of Anne Frank, always reappearing, promising and ironizing the present. In *The Ghost Writer* she is the adolescent dream of suffering, and the reminder of inadequacy. In *Zuckerman Unbound* she returns in the figure of Caesara O'Shea, the Irish star, who spends a night with Nathan. Caesara, a living dream of escape and peace, tells Nathan, "Oh, I got into all this as innocently as any girl could. Playing Anne Frank at the Gate Theatre" (ZU 90). Even escape, for Nathan, returns him to where he began. "That Anne Frank should come to him in this guise. That he should meet her at his agent's house, in a dress of veils and beads and cockatoo feathers....Yes, he thought, life has its own flippant ideas about how to handle serious fellows like Zuckerman. All you have to do is wait and it teaches you all there is to know about the art of mockery" (90). Zuckerman's seriousness is made into a joke, his Anne Frank made into a plastic replica of the Anne Frank. Running from that ghost, from that mockery, Zuckerman will find in nothingness his imagined freedom, but that emptiness will always be weighted against the original Anne Frank, her concentrationary universe will always circle his, and his new freedom will only lead to a deeper confinement.

In *The Prague Orgy* the Czech actress Eva Kalinova is persecuted for playing "the role of the Jewess Anne Frank" (429). They, Zuckerman reveals, "the powers-that-be" (459), "have used Anne Frank as a whip to drive her from the stage" (457). Anne Frank has been expropriated by the anti-Semites who wish to universalize her plight, strip it of its Jewish essence, take her story and use it for their own ends. "No, there's nothing that can't be done to a book," thinks Zuckerman (457). Even Anne Frank cannot remain pure in interpretation. The ideologue will turn her story into one of redemption, "a declaration," as Sidra Ezrahi argues, "of ultimate faith in universal goodness" (202). And the nihilist, the manipulator, will turn her story into anything at all, into a useful tool, as the authorities do in Prague. The "Jewish saint" becomes a "demon" in their hands, "Anne Frank as a curse and a stigma!" (457).

That, finally, is what Prague teaches Zuckerman: that images are controlled and redefined by each storyteller, each reader and performer, by "you and me," as Zuckerman writes (458). The ghosts that have followed him are ghosts recreated in his own harassed mind. They are present, like his fate, but by rejecting an essentialist vision of them Zuckerman can create his own present, tied to the past but not bound by it. Back in "the little world around the corner" Zuckerman is free to revisit his past, to write his ambiguous story, to tell it over and over again (TPO 472).

Zuckerman receives two letters, one in *Zuckerman Unbound* and one in *The Counterlife*. Both impugn his writing for its dangerous consequences to Jews, using memory, as Wapter once did, and as Roth's critics have done, to bludgeon creativity. In *Zuckerman Unbound* a reader writes, "This is written in memory of those who suffered the horror of the Concentration Camps" (59). In *The Counterlife* Shuki reminds Nathan that he was once "condemned...for being unforgivably blind in your fiction to the horror of Hitler's slaughter," and then goes on to tell Nathan that his words are "potentially a weapon against us, a bomb in the arsenal of our enemies" (178). Both letters do, in their own, perhaps innocent, way what the powers in Prague did; they use interpretation to control. Their conclusions rest on the assumption that reading is a definitive and finite task, that a narrative's reception can be foretold and ordered. "This rebuke," thinks Nathan, "will follow me to my grave" (178).

It is a rebuke that *The Counterlife* undermines. No narrative can be responsible for its misreading. No narrative can be so controlled or so stable that it cannot be used by both enemies and friends. If Anne Frank can be misused how can we expect any other text to withstand interpretation? What Nathan asserts is that interpretation is never sure, that truth is never concrete, that every reading, whether of words or even of self, is a misreading, a version, a countertext, a response. This is an answer to the Holocaust-thematic, a response affirmed in the very semiotic and structural aspects of the novel which follows *Zuckerman Bound*. In this apparently post-modern novel Roth is allied to a version of deconstruction. It is Derrida's suspicion of ideology that Roth accepts as an antidote to the longings for the perfect one reading, for order, that his characters fall victim to.

Henry looks to Israel for spiritual rebirth, to Hebrew as a pure language, and to Lippman as the Moses leading the way to a reborn oneness, a truth. Nathan looks to Maria, to England, to his unborn child, the conventional family, as the means towards a physical and intellectual reincarnation. For both brothers impotency is their inheritance. "You are your brother," Nathan is told (347). Both begin with a patrimony, a spirit to wrestle with, a spirit which becomes part of their troubled, insecure, uprooted selves. They search for a new self, a self without contradiction, absent the spirit second-self. That spirit, or ghost, which took the form of Anne Frank in the previous novels, is here only outlined. It is the "inner preoccupation permeating nearly everything within the Jewish world" (351). It is the "unpredictable" element inside Nathan that makes him "furious" at perceived anti-Semitism (350). It is, moreover, heard in the voices of the Jews throughout the text: "You put Jewish babies into furnaces, you bashed their heads against the rocks, you threw them like shit into ditches" (204). "This didn't happen to one poor saint two thousand years ago - this happened to six million living people only the other day" (205). It is the ghost of Israel, the spirit that forges the "fantasy-life," as Roth calls it, of the country (RMAO 161).

"The construction of a counterlife," argues Nathan, of Zionism and Israel, "that is one's antimyth was at its very core" (167). Israel is a dream to "remake reality," to build upon the ghost and then to banish that ghost (167). The ghost is Zuckerman's muse and his censor: "I'd considered very deeply and felt vicariously the wounds that Jews have had to endure, and, contrary to the charges by my detractors of literary adventurism, my writing had hardly been born of recklessness or naiveté about the Jewish history of pain; I had written my fiction in knowledge of it, and even in consequence of it" (351).

Nathan's impotency is implicitly linked to this Holocaust ghost in a subtle but telling remark: "How many hundreds of hours of talk will it take to inure us to what's missing?" (209). What's missing is both his potency (his erection) and the six million. To answer impotency Nathan and his brother are plunged toward a false dream of potency, of meaning. And if impotency is hopelessness and fear, potency is death. Here Derrida's presence is felt. Derrida derides the metaphysical, the first principle, what in Roth is called Lonoffian surety, the potency of Lippman, of Henry, of Hitler. Derrida's project is initially a response to death, to all mortality. He creates his system to demean ideological constructs, to chastise those who would presume their one meaning as incontestable truth. Derrida finds the aporia and devolves the strict oppositions of a text, letting contradiction run free, granting ambiguity its place. The Counterlife is a manifestation of this theory, a swipe at ideology. Nathan celebrates the "and/and/and/and/and/" of language, and in so doing deconstructs the logic of the death camps (350). "Language and only language must provide the means for the release of everything," says Nathan (209). While his brother trusts in action, in the certainty of Agor's philosophy, Nathan finds in language an always renewing freedom, a continual metamorphosis from counterself to counterself.[4]

In Deception the flip-side of deconstruction is revealed, the side that does not fight the Holocaust mentality but gives in to it, hides it; this is the deconstruction that Paul de Man exemplifies, the deconstruction that Heidegger is father to, the deconstruction that Derrida looks away from. It is an answer to the ideologic impulse of the Holocaust-thematic which pushed so far embraces its antithesis, deconstructive nihilism.

What Roth has created, in Deception, is the portrait of the writer as carnivore, as vampire, dictator. His is the essential power in the novel, the power to ask, to choose, to order, to claim lies as truth and truth as lies. The modern author, in Deception, uses ambiguity, the Barthian fun-house aesthetic, to pardon himself, to avoid any responsibility. Nothing is true; everything is a game. It is a similar argument with which Zuckerman concludes *The Counterlife*, but here it is stretched, perverted.

Hermione Lee, in her perceptive review of *Deception*, remarks, "Roth is the authoritarian author, masquerading as one who gives permission" (41). However, it is not Roth who is the authoritarian but the character, Philip. Roth impugns the writer but the writer never impugns himself. Philip remains safe, hidden, invulnerable, using his tropes to excuse himself everything. For him, as for de Man and the Holocaust denier Ernst Nolte, deconstruction denies meaning and history, buries all in words. The past becomes a "supreme fiction," for Philip no less than for Nolte (Hirsch 76). Deconstruction is turned by de Man into a means to bury his own anti-Semitic past, to make his collusion with the Nazis a fiction. Deconstruction is suspect in a post-Holocaust world, a means not only of escaping ideology but of denying all facts. Deconstruction, argues David Hirsch, begins "recontextualizing Auschwitz," making it appear "much smaller and more trivial" (18).

The danger recognized after the Holocaust has its echoes during the Holocaust period. In its infant stages a kind of deconstructive logic was used to allow the imposition of a guiltless morality, a morality which freed its acolytes from looking back, from questioning what they had done, for what they had done was nothing, no-thing. The Holocaust condemns both essentialist ideology and deconstructionist nihilism: In *The Counterlife* and *Deception* Roth explores the folly and mind-numbing consequences of each.

The pastoral which is rejected in *The Counterlife* is the pastoral that Hitler calls for, the return to a "pre-biblical, pre-Christian past" (Hirsch 86). But in *Deception* it is the logic of that rejection that is now linked to Hitler, the Pipikian anti-pastoral portion of his crazed philosophy. If in *The Counterlife* Zuckerman learns to live without Lonoffian sureness then *Deception* answers with the contrary vision of ambiguity brought to the level of a totalized theory, ("Deconstruction itself now becomes the Logos," argues Hirsch (82)), of ambiguity as a means of avoidance and control.[5]

Vaclav Havel describes totalitarianism as having to "falsify everything" (45). Philip, too, must put everything through his fiction mixer, turning all intimacies into stories, all confessions into tales. Havel calls the oppressive system, "thoroughly permeated with hypocrisy and lies," and adds that it "pretends to pretend nothing" (44-45). Philip inverts this formula, he pretends to pretend all, but that inversion makes it no less destructive for the individuals who are its victims.

In the Holocaust universe ideology and nihilism are suspect; they are linked to Hitler and his genocidal program, ideological truths pursued by nihilistically brutal and guiltless slaves. And they are insufficient, too, in explaining the Holocaust; ideology denies victims their sorrow, dissolving them in platitude and affirmation, and nihilism is a surrendering to Hitler's hand, a permanent entrapment that makes Hitler the victor. The ideology of the settlers and the dreamers on the West Bank, seemingly responsive to the Holocaust, is pilloried in *The Counterlife*, and its negation, Philip's deconstructive malignity, with its suggestions of de Man, is similarly pilloried in *Deception*. The novels talk to each other, the later redefining the earlier tome, together finding a balance in the Holocaust-thematic.

Operation *Shylock* expands on, and moves beyond, *Deception's* criticism of *The Counterlife*, returning to *The Counterlife's* setting, Israel, and to its play of reality and fantasy. But here instead of claiming all as false the author insists, in interviews and in an essay in *The New York Times Book Review* that, in his words, "This happened" (C13) What is Roth's point in making this assertion again and again when his text offers both possibilities so clearly? Why does Roth go to the trouble of defending his position in countless interviews? Why in a BBC portrait of Roth does he create a black and white scene in which the supposed Pipik stands nervously ticking his head, seemingly unaware that he is being filmed? Why the games, if, indeed, they are games? Roth tells Dan Cryer, "It would be interesting if one critic or journalist would say, 'What if this guy's telling us the truth?'" (40). What changes if the story is considered as truth, as confession, the questions of verity dispensed with?

What changes is our way of reading. Symbol and metaphor are superceded by story. In an interview in 1981 Roth lambasted the disproportionate use of "structure, form, and symbol" to describe literary works (RMAO 120). He admitted, "I forbid my students to use those words, on pain of expulsion" (RMAO 120). By making us read *Operation Shylock* as truth Roth relegates those words to secondary status. What is important is not what reading we can give the book, what allegorical meanings we can discern, what interpretations we can forge, but rather the simple facts, the reality of the characters and their concerns. We are like Kepesh, thrown into an unbelievable world and told it is real, that it must be believed, that Pipik does not stand for anything, nor Smilesburger, nor George Ziad, nor "Roth" himself. We must give up our customary means of reading and delve, instead, into the muck of story as true story.

It is the point the text, itself, makes. "I don't think any of it is make believe," says "Roth" (200). The book is about mimesis, not invention. "Surrender yourself to what is real," "Philip" advises Pipik, "There's nothing in the world quite like it" (204). There are truths, there are facts, unexplainable and odd, but true nonetheless. The Holocaust is the ultimate proof of that, the fact that defies logic, that is "nonsensical and empty of meaning" (313). Aharon Appelfeld tells "Roth" that "Reality, as you know, is always stronger than the human imagination" (86). The reality he refers to is, of course, his youth as a Jew caught up in the Holocaust fires. "If I remain true to the facts," he insists of his Holocaust-ensnared youth, "no one would believe me" (86). Reality flies the nets of fiction. "The much-praised transfigurations concocted by Franz Kafka pale beside the unthinkable metamorphoses perpetuated by the Third Reich on the childhoods of my cousin and of my friend, to enumerate only two," writes "Roth" (29). The imagination stands gaping at the audaciousness, at the perverse genius of the real.

Mimesis denies both the simple interpretative urge to establish truth and the deconstructive urge to use aporia to deprive a story its legitimacy. The Holocaust-thematic warns against both urges, most pointedly in *Operation Shylock*. "The latest thing they've swallowed whole," opines "Roth," "is that it's impossible to report anything faithfully other then one's own temperature; everything is allegory" (215). This is the mantra of deconstruction, the infinite play of words that drown all fact, all authorship, in language. It is Pipik's mantra, and Demjanjuk's. "This is how Demjanjuk does it," thinks "Roth" (261). He is the demon side of deconstruction; his past metamorphosed into an emptiness, a nothing. "Everything putrid in the past just snaps off and falls away. Only America happened. Only the children and the friends and the church and the garden and the job have happened" (261). There is a disintegration, a dropping away of the past, of the self that one no longer wishes to face. "How could I be both that and this?" Demjanjuk asks with his every word (63). "Because you are," answers "Roth" (63). "You've really only lived sequentially the two seemingly antipodal mutually excluding lives that the Nazis, with no strain to speak of, managed to enjoy simultaneously," he adds (63). The Nazi lived and carried out his crimes through a disintegration of personality, an alternation of Apollonian certainty with Dionysian appetite. One self existed at a time, sheltering the other in forgetfulness, turning the truths of one moment into a mass of forgettable fictions. This deconstructive disintegration is a means of removing the stain of the Holocaust, removing the guilt, removing the very facts of atrocity. "The Germans have proved definitively," argues "Roth," "to all the world that to maintain two radically divergent personalities, one very nice and one not so nice, is no longer the prerogative of psychopaths only" (63).

Updike notes that in *Operation Shylock* "Roth's habitual polarities, goy/Jew and hedonism/altruism have been augmented by sick/well and disintegration/integration" (Recruiting Raw Nerves 110). To be sick is to be like Demjanjuk, or "Roth" during his Halcion days, separated from a self, one's duality negated, a victim of "self-abandonment" (22). To be well is to be integrated, not singular but dual, multiform, with selves interacting and interweaving within, all conversing and arguing, remembering and forgetting at the same time. "Amazing," says "Roth," "that something as tiny as a self should contain contending subselves" (152). The well integrates his subselves, the sick divides them absolutely. The Nazi lives two contrary lives, each exclusive of the other, as if acted by another man, while the integrated man must accept his contradictions, his niceness and his not-so-niceness, his conscience and his desires, and live with the consequences of each.

The integrated cannot leave one self behind, cannot use the deconstructive trope to make his past into a fiction. The truth of his story is his truth, mimesis is his curse and his cure. "The mystery isn't that you," "Roth" imagines saying to Demjanjuk, "who had the time of your life at Treblinka, went on to become an amiable, hardworking American nobody but that those who cleaned the corpses out for you, your accusers here, could ever pursue anything resembling the run-of-the mill after what was done to them by the likes of you" (63). They live with their second self attached to their shoulders, their second world always darkening their current life. Like the Israeli writer De-Nur, who writes under the name Ka-Tzetnik ("concentration-camp"), they are two men in one (Segev 11). The Holocaust is the second skin of the victims, and it is the second skin of the Jews and Gentiles in *Operation Shylock*. To deny that skin is to deny their selves, to come apart, become a half-man like Demjanjuk or Pipik.

Pipik's Diasporism plays on a desire to run from a part of one's self, to use disintegration as a means to close the door on the Holocaust. Pipik calls for "the reintegration of the Jew into Europe" (46). He tells "Roth," "Do not confuse our long European history with the twelve years of Hitler's reign" (42). Pipik imagines if Hitler's "twelve years of terror are erased from our past" (42), and his messianic project seeks to do just that, not to integrate past and present but to change the past, to begin the "conscience cleansing of Europe," to make memory disintegrate, to make history disappear (45). Diasporism is deconstruction by another name. Diasporism is, as Sidra Ezrahi explains, an escape into "textuality that doesn't kill," into language that is non-representational, language that is merely noise (Roth's Diasporism (RD) 41). Diasporism is escape, surrender, a means of excising a burdened psyche, just as deconstruction is an escape into charade, amnesia, and non-referentiality. Both are used to remove the second skin of the Holocaust from the victims and the victimizers alike, to deny the murderer his murderous past and the victim his nightmares. What gets lost, then, is the simple facts, the millions dead, the bones, the ash, the hair, and, finally even, the memory.

"Nazis didn't break hands," cries "Roth," "They engaged in industrial annihilation of human beings. They made a manufacturing process of death" (142). Language lies, words deceive: The facts must be stated, without garnish, without poetry, without exegesis. "Words generally only spoil things," Smilesburger tells "Roth" (333). Words spoil things both by turning events into meanings and by turning truth into lies. Words have become covers for facts, what Steiner and Adorno warned against. Pipik writes to "Roth," "I AM THE YOU THAT IS NOT WORDS" (87). But Pipik is all words, only words, words attached to no signified, words with no substance, no soul, words of play. And Diasporism is just play, too; "the privilege," as Ezrahi makes clear, "to try out any role, any character, without paying the consequences of identity" (42). Pipik's philosophy, and his self, has no "coherence," no "incoherence," "Roth" maintains (107). "He emanates the aura of something absolutely spurious" (107). He is a contemporary Demjanjuk, less deadly but no less vacant than his predecessor.

To have a self is to be doubled, to be two rather than one; that is the Holocaust's patrimony. For "Roth" and those more integrated men and women in *Operation Shylock* to be two is to be alive. The Holocaust is the double that demands this integration, the double that deforms the face of the women Apter meets on the street, that deforms Apter's face, that deforms the whole of Israeli life on whom "the grip of a horrible past was never relaxed" (263). And that double can never be minimized in words, forgotten in the assumption of a new identity or in the propulsion of a new philosophy.

The double of the Holocaust begins with Shylock, with the image created by Shakespeare and used ever since, the double, the "doppelganger," the "savage, repellent, and villainous Jew," the double, as Supposnik recounts, who is defined by three words, "Three thousand ducats" (274). "Yes," cries Supposnik, "for four hundred years now, Jewish people have lived in the shadow of this Shylock" (274). "This," he adds, "is Europe's Jew," the harbinger of the Holocaust (275). Words have effects: Shylock is born of anti-Semitism and gives rise to new anti-Semitism, is burnished in hatred and stereotype and is used by the Nazi to cement hatred.

"The fact," says Roth, of *Operation Shylock*, "is that its center is anti-Semitism" (Cryer 41). Anti-Semitism is the angel that must be wrestled with, the twin that will not depart. To turn from that twin is to turn from the facts, the words that tell the story of the "real horror" of the Holocaust (69). Shylock is the curse, for both European culture and for the Jew, the symbol of the guilt of a sophisticated culture's collaboration with the terror and the symbol that the Jew labors under, forcing memory, forcing a raw wound and a responsibility upon the self. The Holocaust-pattern is revealed in Shylock's gaze, the gaze of the distant past and the not-so-distant past, each circled around the other and circling the present. The self is divided, thrown forward, held back trying on and disavowing various costumes, various languages, various ways of seeing and of being seen. And it is all a way to live with the burden that the word "Shylock" and the word "Holocaust" connote. But behind the role-playing, behind the language that roars across the pages, that flows like a soliloquy on a make-believe stage, there is a fact, an event, that will bear no explanation and grant no reprieve.

In Roth's two works of non-fiction, *The Facts* and *Patrimony*, it is only memory that can restore a semblance of freedom, a slight reprieve. It is memory that brings the father back to life, that lets his voice live again, memory that brings Roth back to himself, that transforms the novelist into "the boy I had been when I went off to college, the boy surrounded on the playground by his neighborhood compatriots - back to ground zero" (TF 5). It is back to the facts that Roth always returns, back to his memories to give start to his imagination. "For me," he writes, "as for most novelists, every genuine imaginative event begins down there, with the facts, with the specific, and not with the philosophical, the ideological, or the abstract" (TF 3). He looks to reconnect "the structure of life without the fiction" in *Operation Shylock* as much as in his memoirs (TF 6). "If this manuscript conveys anything," he says of *The Facts*, "it's my exhaustion with masks, disguises, distortions, and lies" (6). He wants to see what was, to see memory as clearly as possible, to reenter the past without the novelist's tools or the critic's tools. "I must remember accurately," he tells himself (177). "You must not forget anything," he repeats (P 177). The patrimony, the shit he must clean up in his bathroom, is treasured because it is not "symbolic," because it "was nothing less or more than the lived reality it was" (P 176). It is real, and it is to the real that all memory eventually looks.

But memory is not without its own masks, its own lies and distortions. To remember is to create, to use imagination to structure the facts. The facts of the Holocaust are built on the precarious memories of everyone. Lawrence Langer has categorized various types of Holocaust memory, all of which are represented in Roth's works. To examine the progression from common memory to unheroic memory, in Roth, is to watch how memory has been accosted by the Holocaust, and how it has been realigned by those willing to face the facts, to see what others turn from.

Common memory is memory which can "mediate atrocity," which seeks to "reassure us" (HT 9). It is the memory that affixes interpretation to devastation, the memory Portnoy, Kepesh, and Tarnopol seek, the memory that uses language to make a nightmare into a redemptive interlude. It is memory that is unfaithful to the facts, memory devised in the hopeful imagination. It is Walter Hermann's memory, the memory of the Holocaust as an event not for remorse but for "exhibitionism" and hope (P 215).

Deep memory is the memory of the camps, the photographic dream-like recreation, the event seen as it was, with no mediation by time. It is subconscious memory, unspoken memory, memory of another self, the perfect memory that can never accurately be recorded. It is the memory held by Apter, by Barbatnik, by Appelfeld, by Dr. Kotler, by the Jews in Prague, by Sisovsky's father, by Jaga, and by Kepesh, too; the memory of his transformation into a breast which, though told, can never be seen as he sees it, felt as he felt it. It is private memory and is obscured by time, by new perception, and by the attempt to find words for it.

Deep memory becomes anguished memory, memory which forestalls action in the present. Langer quotes Nietzsche to describe how anguished memory incapacitates: "Without forgetting it is quite impossible to live at all" (HT 40). In Alvin Pepler, who tells Zuckerman, "I can't forget even if I wanted to," a concrete statement of anguished memory is enunciated (ZU 144). It is memory which straight-jackets the individual, imprisons him in a past he cannot put aside even for a moment. This, too, is part of Apter's soul, the part that keeps him an "unborn adult...a fifty-four-year-old who has evolved into manhood without evolving" (OS 18).

Humiliated memory is memory turned to nihilism, the memory of Pipik, of the orgy-goers in Czechoslovakia. It is memory that surrenders to the past, that disavows all meaning forever, that leaves man shattered, "left a victim to what Nietzsche called the 'blind power of fate...the tyranny of the actual" (80). It is a powerful pull, the pull of emptiness, of the abyss, as strong as the pull towards meaning is in common memory. This is another way to state the Holocaust-thematic: the movement between the heroism and ideology of common memory and the freedom and the meaninglessness of humiliated memory.

Tainted memory provides a means to balance the nefarious pull of those two absolutist modes of memory. Tainted memory offers a way to see the other world, to see that one's "internal system of belief" will not hold in every circumstance, that morality is relative (HT 123). It is the memory of Tzuref, of the greenie, the memory that tells them that "norms are not translatable to all cultures," that one's victimization and powerlessness are not forever, that one time does not define the next (Langer HT 123).

Langer does not mention lack of memory, but for Roth it is also an important concern. For all those who battle with the past, successfully and unsuccessfully, resourcefully and pusillanimously, there are those who battle nothing, who erase the past: the Jews of Woodenton, the counselors at Camp Lakeside, Sydney's mother, The Patimkins. For them there is no past, no memory, no Holocaust; they live desolated lives, deindividualized by their own amnesia.

Unheroic memory is the most sophisticated means of handling the Holocaust past. Unheroic memory is memory without answers and without surrender, memory of what transpired, and what it has done, and what it has cost, and what can be regained. When Kepesh finds his self in *The Breast* he does so by means of unheroic memory, the memory of an event that was real, that happened, that cannot be denied or explained, but which he has survived, which he can recount and can go on from. It is what Zuckerman finds in *The Counterlife*, and what Roth writes into life in *Operation Shylock*, the memory not of redemption or of obliteration, but of questioning and of imagining, of choice. "Unheroic memory is imbued with a spirit of irony, its defense against a reconciliation that it cannot embrace," writes Langer (HT 170). No reconciliation, no false hope, no fictitious certainty, and no absolute defeat, no stagnancy, no descent.

"Rejecting nihilism," Langer writes, "and heroism, the diminished self lapses into a bifocal vision, as its past invades its present and casts a long pervasive shadow over its future, obscuring traditional vocabulary and summoning us to invent a still more complex version of memory and self" (HT 172). Nihilism and heroism, the pull of humiliated and common memory, are balanced tensely against one another. Roth's ironic voice cuts between these two - the poles of the Holocaust-thematic - pulling back and forth until a diminished twentieth-century man, torn and battered, halved, guilty and afraid, can show himself with all his wounds, all his contradictions, all his terror, and see himself and still survive. Roth's prose uplifts the unheroic self, more real for his unsureness and for his willingness to confront memory and to still go on.

The problem of memory is the problem of writing in the post-Holocaust world. Memory precludes certain words, certain assumptions. And narrative inverts memory, how stories are told tells us how we will remember. Roth has used memory as his lantern. His writing begins and ends with a respect for and a fear of memory. Memory invades the present forcing silence where speech pounds against the mind. Memory prescribes parameters, issues warnings. And memory itself is the hope that keeps nihilism at bay. For memory denies that the past has swallowed up the present, that the Holocaust-pattern has worn down the next generation.

"Even if it's no more then one percent that you've edited out," Zuckerman writes to Roth, "that's the one percent that counts" (TF 172) Roth has stood between Adorno's silence and Celan's "Black Milk" throughout his career, holding back while telling an obsessional story of the Holocaust legacy in the American consciousness. He has left the Holocaust facts to the history books, subtly letting the Holocaust drift into his texts. Roth recasts the dichotomies of the concentration-camp world in the world of art, the world of fiction. That world is the imprimatura enveloping the foreground of his stories.

To look at *Operation Shylock* is to see a composite of Roth's oeuvre. What is the most important chapter in the book? What gives the book its title? Chapter Eleven, the unprinted chapter, the unspoken words. What is missing tells the story. What is unseen is what moves everything else. It is the Holocaust, like that chapter, barely visible, never directly related, that tells Roth's story. What is edited out, as Zuckerman says, is what counts.

Eli, looking for the greenie, looking for the Holocaust in Woodenton, is like the critic squaring his eyes to see between the words of Roth's works: "At first it seemed only a deep hollow of blackness - then the figure emerged!" (251).

Notes

1. Roth explains the gestation of his first, and, thus far, only, volume of short stories as both deliberately determined by his obsession with the difference between the European past he was fortunate enough to avoid and his own odd present life in America, and as forced upon him by factors outside himself. Roth, first, asserts, "The disparity between this tragic dimension of Jewish life in Europe and the actualities of our daily lives as Jews in New Jersey was something that I had to puzzle over myself, and indeed, it was in the vast discrepancy between the two Jewish conditions that I found the terrain for my first stories" (CWPR 128). He later comments that "George Starbuck...selected the stories, giving the book a Jewish focus which the random group of stories I'd submitted didn't quite have. George, in a way, determined my future, because I didn't think that was my subject. I didn't know what my subject was" (CWPR 282). Roth paints himself as both willful and as willless, the knowing writer drawing his fiction from a fascination with a disparity of worlds, and

the neophyte writer lead to his subject by his editor. This idea of chance and choice is reasserted later in the afterward of a twenty-fifth anniversary edition of *Portnoy's Complaint*, in which Roth presents himself as having found the first lines of all his books on a "81/2-by-11 sheet of typing paper" in the student's cafeteria (21). Roth uses this revelation to explain "just how little one has to do with calling the shots that determine the ways in which a life develops" (3). The "uncaniness" of the "pre-science" of several of the sentences must be attributed "to the workings of pure chance" (23). But chance does not explain all. It is Roth who must assume these lines as his own, as chronological, as meant for books that he must complete: "I saw," writes Roth, "that if ever a unifying principle were to be discernible in the para-graph, it would have to be imposed from without rather than unearthed from with-in" (22). Chance is molded by choice. Roth's subject is forced upon him and is cho-sen by him; both. The theory of Chaos, of determinism and free-will joined togeth-er, is given a human and aesthetic form. Roth writes his stories and Starbuck finds the organizing principle behind them, which, in turn, tells Roth what his subject is and will be. What Roth finds is chance, what he makes of it is choice. Roth is fated to his time, to his past, to the things he sees, the people he comes in contact with, but what he admits and what he ignores, what he draws himself to and what he pulls himself away from, are finally his to decide. The Holocaust is there in *Goodbye, Columbus*, as sub-text, not only because Starbuck has chosen but because Roth has written. He is chained to that memory, as are his characters, as he is chained to that mysterious 8/ 1/2 by -11 piece of paper, by a force of will.

2.   Echoes of Giorgio Bassani's Holocaust story, "A Plaque on Via Mazzini," are heard in "Eli, the Fanatic," and they help to explicate Roth's story, and, indeed, his whole volume of stories. In Bassani's story a camp survivor, Geo Josz, returns to his native town, Ferrara, only to find his neighbors unable and unwilling to acknowledge his past. Like Woodenton's residents they find this strange presence a reminder of a time better left sealed away, a disturbance to the dynamics of their business and social life. "What did he want, now?" they ask (Howe SE 443). As Irving Howe sum-marizes, "As if intent upon making everyone uncomfortable, Josz resumes 'wearing the same clothes he had been wearing when he came back from Germany.' His very presence is a reproach" (SE 443). Eli's presence, too, is a reproach to his fellow Jews who will sacrifice anything to hold fast to their normal lives, their safe homes.

3.   In "On The Air" Roth imagines a contest for the funniest thing in history: "Is it Hitler," he asks (17). The dictator, mixing his metaphors, obscuring the truth with euphemism, obscuring ambiguity with the language of truth, clownishly stomping his feet, throwing his hands stiffly into the air, is a model for both Manea's White Clown and Roth's American Clown. Roth points to Charlie Chaplin's *The Great Dictator* as a model for "the more outlandish sections of *Our Gang*" (RMAO 46). If Hitler is a White Clown, Manea asks, "is Chaplin, who has mined him with childlike irony, a tra-ditional Auguste the Fool?" (37). Roth, in *Our Gang*, attempts to carry the mantle of Chaplin and other Fools who use satire "to reveal just how serious" they are (RMAO 49).

4.   John Updike notes the preponderance of "Tirades, phillippics, self-exposi-tions," in Roth's novel (OJ 378). He argues that reading Roth is "like riding in an

overheated club car, jostled this way and that by the clamorous, importunate crowd of talkers while glimpses of the outside world tantalizingly whip past the steamed-up windows" (OJ 378). The outside world <u>is</u> the world of language, the real is as real as the latest impersonation. Roth's vibrant monologues of "deference, diplomacy, apprehension, self-pity, self-satire, self-mistrust, depression, clowning, bitterness, nervousness, inwardness, hypercriticalness, hypertouchiness, social anxiety, social assimilation" are expressions of life, of health, of the continuance of striving in the concentrationary universe (CL 134). The "ands" of *The Counterlife* offer no endings, no finality, no closure, no affirmation, no clean interpretation; they exist as Derrida's difference, to revivify language without falling prey to the trap of ideology and potency that language can be, and has been, lured into, from both fear and hate.

5.   In *Deception* Philip's lover plays "reality-shift," pretending to be the judge in a "feminist dystopia" (CWPR 257). "Can you explain to the court," she begins, "why you hate women?" (113). She convicts before a defense can be made, employing the code words of feminism, "sexism, misogyny, woman abuse, slander of women, denigration of women, defamation of women" (114). Presented as a game it serves only to titillate the writer, but in its relentless questioning it points a finger at Philip's own inquiring ways. He has created a writer's dystopia, shielding himself behind indeterminacy.

CHAPTER SIX

It's All One Book You Write, Anyway

I'd considered very deeply and felt
vicariously the wounds that Jews
have had to endure, and, contrary
to the charges by my detractors of
literary adventurism, my writing
had hardly been born of recklessness or naivete about the Jewish
history of pain; I had written my
fiction in the knowledge of it, and
even in consequence of it....

- Philip Roth
- The Counterlife

"It's all one book you write, anyway," says Roth. "At night you dream six
dreams. But are they six dreams? One dream prefigures or anticipates the
next, or somehow concludes what hasn't yet even been fully dreamed"
(RMAO 160). Writing, that guided dream, as Borges defined it, is, for Roth,
a restorative act, each book turning back towards that which presaged it.
Roth's work has been a continuation, a constant return to the same subjects, to the same milieu, the same bare obsessions. And yet each text
diverges in its own way, breaks down or sideways into a new layer of meaning and of questioning, looking in the same parcel of land for a new enlightenment, a new discovery, like an archeologist burrowing downward and
downward interminably unearthing new civilizations, new alternative interpretations of what lay atop.

As Zuckerman says, "Without fanaticism nothing great in fiction could ever be achieved" (AL 179). Fanaticism of the second order is Roth's blood, the pulsating current that drives him ever deeper into his subject, risking criticism, scorn, risking talk of unimaginativeness. But setting, tone, and style can be similar over and over again and still a new story is being told, a new direction taken, a new dream being given shape. Like Faulkner, turning back and back again to the South, to the legacy of the Civil War, Roth directs his scalpel to Judaism, to anti-Semitism, to the Holocaust over and over again. The obsession is the starting point, the first image, reformed and reformed, reaching out beyond its margins, grasping to it issues that transcend its seeming limits.

The "obsessional theme," says Roth, is the one the novelist "least understands - he knows it so well that he knows how little he knows" (CWPR 252). Roth is pursued by the doubt his subject provides. He writes into his obsession not because it is easy, or because it earns him praise but because there remain unanswered questions, unanswerable questions, because by returning he gnaws his way closer to a truth that will never show itself, because obsession is a way of remembrance.

Roth's Holocaust obsession is like Pynchon's obsession with entropy, Vonnegut's obsession with the anarchic pessimism born of the bombing of Dresden, Barth's obsession with the fun house, Gaddis's obsession with stylistic elision and with counterfeiting, and Styron's obsession with death and suicide. Obsession is not a point of summation or of closure; it is not the code word that defines a writer. Rather it offers a center from which a writer can turn in any one of a thousand directions. It is the form amidst the formlessness of the post-modern aesthetic.

And for Roth the Holocaust tells more than its own story, though its story is paramount. It tells the story of power and history, of slavery and freedom. Its themes survive outside their original context. The Zeks of the Soviet Union, the dissidents in China, the Kurds in Iraq can be found in Roth's world. And, too, the individual, the man with only a memory of family or of country, can find his story in these stories, the story of anger and betrayal, of love and lies, of power and sexuality, of language's encasement and its possibilities for release, of preconceptions and pulpits that order and stymie a life, of the first home, the first family, lost and recovered, and lost again, of the barbarism of words and the deceptions of authority, of a world which feels beyond one's control and that is, that was, and that can be again, and, finally, of the past and the memory that transforms, belittles, and which stirs the blood.

The individual is not lost amidst Roth's grand concerns, for it is the individual with whom Roth begins and to whom he returns, the individual gestures and idiosyncrasies, the one man's suffering, the one woman's healing, chased by the past and integrating the past. Personal struggle exists both in the world of history and outside it. Roth's work extends the democratic impulses of the novel as a form, not only offering a voice for the voiceless but now expressing how the voice of power infringes upon even those who are marginal figures. It reveals how the discourse of an age drips downward to insinuate itself everywhere. The characters strive within their familial settings and those strivings echo the larger strivings with history, with the Holocaust. The father calls the son toward the past, the mother's ambiguity is a metonymy for the concentrationary universe, authority's threat is more fearsome with the terrible abuses of authority still alive in consciousness, the internal struggles of need and purpose parallel the disparate points of the Holocaust-thematic; failure within points at the greater failure, the one's loss multiplied becomes the world's degradation.

Roth writes into the heart of not only the American and European darkness but into the darkness of the human condition. He wonders how man can make his day to day gestures after so much information has been taken in, after the sickness borne into the soul of twentieth-century man has been located but left uncured. The world is concentrationary now; any writer after 1945 must see this or see nothing: It is the fact which returns to the surface no matter how far one looks hopefully towards a future. Because of his status as a Jew and as an American Roth has been aware of this from the outset. His men and women exist in their time and outside it; they embody a specific American malaise, the malaise of knowing terror and power from a distance, and a universal malaise, the malaise of a civilization drawn closer together than ever before, where one people's horror is felt, like the tremors from a distant earthquake, by all others.

Literature is reaching towards that point of connection, a connection sprung from barbarity and from the desire for emancipation and for poetry in life. Roth's specific American literature speaks past its time, past its confines. His is a human voice born of an obsession which, in various forms, haunts the nightmares of a world living inside the memory of the disease of self-destruction. To limit Roth to his obsessions (to limit the idea of obsession) is to miss the gradations that he has woven into his texts, that knit each text upon the others, constructing an elaborate, miasmic text, a fantastic and ultimately unified dream.

Roth follows in the wake of another great Newark writer, Stephen Crane, who brought to his writing a suspicion of the verities traditional discourse encourages. Roth, like Crane, finds in literary impressionism a malleable prose style to explore the self in society. For Crane, as for Roth, "the apprehension of reality is limited to empirical data interpreted by a single human intelligence" (Nagel 19). Impressionism is allied to subjectivity, to the knowledge that there is no single impression that one may fasten onto, that life is the play of one man's myopia against another's.

Roth's impressionism looks back to James's The Ambassadors, but where James's impressionism remains located in Strether's developing consciousness Roth uses a parallax impressionism to move from mind to mind, from eye to eye. There is no true story, no clear picture. Facts are at the mercy of narration. Roth tells his father's story, in *Patrimony*, but the story is more his own. All stories return to the teller, inevitably.

Roth's work denies pure interpretation. Fiction and fact bounce off one another, leaving the reader in a grey area of imbalance. The novels that are ostensibly Roth's most autobiographical - *Zuckerman Bound, The Counterlife, Deception* - reveal themselves as fictions at every turn, while his most absurd fantasy, *The Breast*, seems wedded to autobiographical concerns (Roth tells Sara Davidson: "*The Breast* wasn't just about entrapment in the flesh...it was also inspired by some thinking I'd had to do about fame, notoriety and scandal. When the idea for the book first came to me, I had myself only recently become an object of curiosity, believed by some to be very much the sexual freak and grotesque" (CWPR 101-102)). The novel which appears the work of an unbound imagination, *The Great American Novel*, owes more to sources of fact (Roth gives special acknowledgement to the recordings in The Library of The Hall of Fame and to true-tales of ballplayers quoted in *The Glory of Their Times*, by Lawrence Ritter) than most of Roth's more realistic novels. To try to define Roth's texts is to be defeated. Interpretation reveals more about the prejudices and desires of the reader than it reveals about the texts themselves. Roth is ever aware of his own prejudices, his own ordering needs. In his novelist's autobiography, *The Facts*, he gives Zuckerman the last chapter to offer a contradictory portrait of the writer's observations and conclusions. For Roth, doubt is the first muse.

But Roth's impressionism cannot deny all truth. His is a mode of understanding and interpreting the flux of life without surrendering to meaning but without, also, turning all facts into subjective artifice. The balance between meaning and emptiness, between objectivity and subjectivity, is what Roth's impressionism searches for, pulling itself back and forth, skirting the extremes only to be hoisted back to the center. Between those who trust their impressions as truth and those who distrust even what they see with absolute clarity is a world of doubt and questioning, of searching and grasping, of tension and life, a world of both history and self, of the real and the imagination.

The impressionistic "I" is not one thing; it grows and shrinks, it develops and falters, it imprisons itself and frees itself, and often in imprisonment it finds new freedom, in freedom new imprisonment. Roth's oeuvre locates the furtive interchange within the "I" in the concentrationary universe, the universe that declares the "I" as at risk, in danger from outside and from within, from a past that unravels the present and a present that seeks to disown the past. The bookends of Roth's impressionistic style and philosophy are the two sides of the Holocaust, warning at one side against nihilism and warning against ideology at the other, denying at one end absolute truth and denying absolute meaninglessness at the other, calling at one end for memory and warning against the danger of memory at the other. The neologism, Rothian, is defined between these bookends.

Characters confront their precarious lives in the concentrationary universe by choosing between the antitheses of the Holocaust-thematic. They are like Kepesh, in *The Professor of Desire*, who feels he must choose a *role* to play, a role which parallels one of the two contradictory personae presented in Chekhov's *The Duel*: that of the morally questionable intellectual, Laevsky, or that of the morally irreproachable zoologist, Von Koren. When characters make a definitive choice they devolve their autonomy and devastate their selves. They become like Lucy, in *When She Was Good*, an ideologue whose *words* are never her own, like Trick E. Dixon, in *Our Gang*, for whom *lies* are the means of life, like Zuckerman, in *Zuckerman Unbound*, whose relentless *movement* pushes him into a world of meaninglessness, like Zuckerman, again, in *The Anatomy Lesson*, who falls to a cold faith in the stolidity of the *body*, and like Philip, in *Deception*, who uses the ambiguity of *truth* and *lies* to avariciously control his world.

Contrarily, when characters remain untethered they form multiform selves. They become like Neil, in "Goodbye, Columbus," who finds a new *vision* which rejects the blindness of the Patimkins, like Gabe, in *Letting Go*, who gives in neither to the cold *touch* of his mother, nor the anarchic embraces of his father, like Portnoy, in *Portnoy's Complaint*, who creates a new dialogic voice in his divided *mouth*, a voice balanced between "undecorous, un-Jamesian narrative liberties" and sophisticated, Freud-inspired verbiage, like Tarnopol, in *My Life as a Man*, who melds the discourses of his first two stories to strike the pulpit of meaning from his vocabulary, who learns to resist a search for a perfect *literary description* of himself, like Kepesh, in *The Breast*, who rejects *interpretation*, like the reader of *The Great American Novel*, who distrusts equally the *mythology* Smitty recounts and the mythology of American history, like Nathan Zuckerman, who, in *The Ghost Writer*, allows the *oxymorons* of life their due, who, in *The Prague Orgy*, accepts the indistinct zone between *fact* and *fiction*, story and narration, and who, in *The Counterlife*, finds *dreams* to be both achievable and fantastic, both graspable and forever out of reach, and like "Roth," in *Operation Shylock*, whose *integration* restores *mimesis* to Roth's world, a mimesis of impressions, where facts exist but where they offer no solutions, no closure: There are real events and they are funneled through the subjective consciousness; to be alive to both is to employ the vocabulary of Roth's post-Holocaust impressionism (TF 157).

The tropes - underlined above for each novel - of Roth's works point to a middle-ground within the Holocaust-thematic, a ground tempered by the fervent interplay of ideology and nihilism. Roth's works straddle that middle ground, as they straddle the ground between the past and the present. Roth's characters are the children of the ideologues of Heinrich Von Kleist's *Michael Kohlass* and Dostoevsky's *The Devils*, Kohlass (Lucy) and Pyotor Verkhovensky (Pipik, Demjanjuk), the children of the dreamers of Fitzgerald's *The Great Gatsby* and James's *The Portrait of a Lady*, Gatsby (Neil) and Isabel Archer (Gabe), the children of the divided innocent of Sherwood Anderson's "The Man Who Became a Woman," Herman Dudley (Kepesh, in

The Breast), who sees himself transformed into a girl, the children, finally, of Kafka's imprisoned men, who know that the fantasy of escape is only a less abrupt path to a new imprisonment.

But more than the children of these literary fathers and mothers, Roth's characters are the children of the real, of the Holocaust, and of Anne Frank. Roth evokes his literary predecessors to investigate a vastly altered world. Like Gatsby, Roth's Jews "beat on, boats against the current, borne back ceaselessly into the past," but now the past is not a harbor but a remembered storm (182).

"It's a comedy in the classic sense," Smilesburger says of *Operation Shylock* (394). Roth's confessional novel is, indeed, a comedy. It ends with an integrated self walking the streets of Manhattan. But comedy has not been Roth's genre, though his work lifts up with humor. Resolution remains beyond most character's reach. It is, in fact, the lack of resolution that leaves them with room to breath.

As with Kafka's "A Little Fable," Roth makes us laugh even as we sense tragedy. "You only need to change your direction," the cat tells the cloistered mouse, "and ate it up" (157). Change is not always the road to freedom; the walls, in Roth's world, are always closing in, pushed from outside and pulled from within. The air gets denser by the second. History and time suck life and freedom from the lungs of man. He is left only with himself, to see what must be seen, doubt what must be doubted, and turn and try again, changing his direction, always cognizant of the cat who might or might not be there.

As Roth moves deeper into the tides of the Holocaust he risks being submerged. But Roth is driven to turn again and again to that which most endangers him, that which most risks pain, misunderstanding, and reproof. And in that brazen drive, and in the moments when his prose sparkles with life, Roth finds a brief respite, a momentary answer. In writing his bittersweet poetry to the twentieth-century's great sadness Roth does not conquer that sadness, but he does not allow it to conquer him: In the concentrationary universe that is as much as one can attempt.

Michel Foucault, another writer interested in power and history, wrote, in *The Order of Things*, a sentence that has stood, for many, as a quintessential distillation of mans' weakness in the century of horror. He argued that man and his expressions must now disappear "like a face drawn in sand at the edge of the sea" (398). Roth's work forces an addendum: Powerless to stop the sea from erasing the words he writes, man is at least able to retrace and retrace a continually vanishing image; what is left may not be all he intended to leave behind but it is something, a mark that speaks of an "I" who was there, who saw some things, and who wrote some words against oblivion.

Obligingly Yours

Dear Milowitz,

Surprised as I am to find myself appropriated by you, I can't say I'm entirely disappointed. Roth seems to have relegated me to the past, a Tarnopol, a Portnoy, a Kepesh, used up and pushed aside. But, as his books make clear, and as you note, we are all under someone's wing; our fate is only what some seen or unseen other allows for us. Roth is my other.

Be that as it may, you ask me to comment briefly on your manuscript, to express my opinion of my maker. Obviously, anything I say must be measured against the fact that I owe him everything, good and bad, and that even now he can set me up for god-knows-what travails if this gets back to him. That said, it seems to me you've tried too hard to bring everything together, to make Roth some kind of purveyor of moderation, always right there in the center, balancing edges, consistently riding the middle lane. My Roth is much more unpredictable than that, much more exuberant, wild. My Roth thrives on the edges, pushing his imagination further and further towards various extremes; that's what gives his work its life. Straddling the median is fine for one book, or two, or even three, but once you assert "balancing" as the unifying stylistic and thematic feature of all his works you make it its own pattern, its own structure. It's a mistake to take what might be Roth's overall point and make it fit into each autonomous narrative. To me, "Portnoy," let's say, isn't about finding a middle ground but about the final exhilaration of the extremes of life, of voice. That book has power precisely because it gains momentum towards not reconciliation but towards explosion. The middle ground is often derided by Roth's very tone - his imaginative reaching ever forward - as the ground for the more satisfied writer, the more content fiction-maker. Roth is nothing if not discontented, ever striving.

That the Holocaust-makers used extremes does not make those extremes off-limits to the writer. Literature can find strength in what in life is often deadly. There's a separation between the two: One can create something moral, difficult, bloody, lively, and iconoclastic using a side of oneself that would be despicable in day to day living, anathema, even, to the social self which chats with interviewers and opines over dinners. It is these kinds of works - take Carnovsky as an example - that most challenge their readers, forcing them to question their own attraction to the angry, merciless, unhallowed voice they would uniformly and easily dismiss in any other setting. The power of fiction is the power of empathy. To make someone see inside a man they could never see inside of, to feel his thoughts, his rage, to understand his motives and his actions, is fiction's unique sorcery. Roth makes us take stock of ourselves, what we hide.

As for the Holocaust: I must resist your attempt to make the Holocaust Roth's central concern, the raison d' etre of his writing. There is no doubt it's there, but perhaps not as the central locus as it is for, let's say, Elie Wiesel, but as a marker of the ultimate degradation of man, a reminder of where of where all ideology and demagoguery can lead us, as it is for a writer like Pynchon. Remember, the epigraph to this chapter is taken not from Roth but from me. I'm the Holocaust-obsessive, and it seems you are too. Perhaps, then, it's your impressionistic perceptions leading you to read Roth as you would like to read him, as a consciousness tied to your own obsessions. That's fine; it makes for interesting reading, but you must doubt yourself at some point, wonder if your reading finally supplants Roth's texts, spins them too much your own way.

Listen: We all read from some prejudice, with some unspoken purpose. Just as Roth's characters (myself included) are often clouded by their own narrations, their own impressionistic stances, as you would have it, so, too, the reader is often blind to his own motivations. Roth's fiction asks us to jump out of our skins, fearlessly letting someone lead us, just for awhile. In that way fiction can make us free, and, contrarily, by hobbling this ability criticism can entrap. That is the difference between Roth and me, making something that lives on its own, and you, writing *about* something, indebted to us, to our originality. By using the Holocaust as the critical Rosetta stone you risk making Roth's meandering something into a stagnant artifact; it becomes too simple.

Well, as for me, anyway, I'm happy to have someone release me from the silence, if only for the few hours it took me to read your essay and compose my response. And silence and darkness have become my life, the silence of the deaf, the darkness of the blind, the emptiness of the dead. Roth has made me into an impotent old man living through others, telling their stories. Talk about closure! And thinking about my situation it occurs to me that that might just be what Roth has been writing about for all these years, not the Holocaust but death itself, loss itself, for which the Holocaust is the most spectacular trope. The loss of parents, of siblings, of girlfriends, of talent, of wives, of the pastoral, of our first love, our families, our happiness, our gifts, our curiosity, our health, our bodies, our beliefs, our dreams, and of our very lives is the persistent threat that allows no rest, no peace, no contentment, for me or for my compatriots, or, so it seems, for Roth himself. Time is the enemy, not just history, not just malice and ignorance, but time itself, that simple thing.

What amazes me now, even as I think of it, is how Roth has taken such a sad subject and used it with such versatility, how he has made loss into humor and into pleasure, into thoughtfulness and drama. What amazes is that Roth has taken the sadness of life and has often made it so beautiful - there is no other word!

Obligingly yours,

Zuckerman

Works Cited

PRIMARY SOURCES

Books

American Pastoral. New York: Houghton Mifflin, 1997.

A Philip Roth Reader. Ed. Martin Green. New York: Farrar, Straus and Giroux, 1980.

Conversations with Philip Roth. Ed. George J. Searles. Jackson and London: University Press of Mississippi, 1992.

Deception. New York: Simon and Schuster, 1990.

Goodbye, Columbus. Boston: Houghton Mifflin Company, 1959.

Letting Go. New York: Random House, 1962.

My Life as a Man. New York: Penguin Books, 1985.

Operation Shylock. New York: Simon and Schuster, 1993.

Our Gang. New York: Random House, 1971.

Patrimony. New York: Simon and Schuster, 1991.

Portnoy's Complaint. New York: Random House, 1969.

Reading Myself and Others. New York: Penguin Books, 1985.

Sabbath's Theater. New York: Houghton Mifflin, 1995

The Anatomy Lesson. New York: Farrar, Straus and Giroux, 1981.

The Breast. New York: Penguin Books, 1985.

The Facts: A Novelist's Autobiography. New York: Farrar, Straus and Giroux, 1988.

The Ghost Writer. New York: Penguin Books, 1985.

When She Was Good. New York: Random House, 1967.

Zuckerman Bound. New York: Fawcett Crest, 1985.

Zuckerman Unbound. New York: Farrar, Staus and Giroux, 1981.

Essays, Interviews, Short-Stories, and Unpublished Manuscripts

"A Coffin in Egypt." Third draft ms. *The Philip Roth Collection* 28 Oct. 1959.

"A Conversation in Prague." *New York Review of Books* 12 April 1990: 14–22.

"Armando and the Fraud." *Et Cetera* Oct. 1953: 21–28.

"Author Meets the Critics." Newsday 28 March 1993: Fan Fare 40.

"Commentary Symposium." Commentary April 1961: 11–12.

"Defender of the Faith." Goodbye, Columbus 159–200.

"Eli, the Fanatic." Goodbye, Columbus 247–298.

"Epstein." Goodbye, Columbus 201–230.

"Goodbye, Columbus." Goodbye, Columbus 1–136.

"His Mistress's Voice." Partisan Review 53.2 (1986): 155–176.

"'I Always Wanted You to Admire My Fasting'; or, Looking at Kafka." Reading Myself and
     Others 303–326.

"I Couldn't Restrain Myself." New York Times Book Review 21 June 1992: 3.

"Imagining Jews." Reading Myself and Others 271–302.

"Introduction: Goodbye, Columbus, German Edition." The Philip Roth Collection.

"Juice or Gravy? How I Met My Fate in a Cafeteria." New York Times Book Review 18 Sept.
     1994: 3.

"Novotny's Pain." A Philip Roth Reader 261–280.

"Oh, Ma, Let Me Join the National Guard." New York Times 24 Aug. 1988: A25.

"On the Air." New American Review 10 (1970): 7–49.

"Philip Roth Sees Double. And Maybe Triple, Too." New York Times 9 March 1993: C13.

"Positive Thinking on Pennsylvania Avenue." New Republic 3 June 1957: 10–11.

"Pro-Life Pro." New York Review of Books 17 Aug. 1989: 5.

"Second Dialogue in Israel." Congress Bi-Weekly 16 Sept. 1963: 4–85.

"Some New Jewish Stereotypes." Reading Myself and Others 193–203.

"The Box of Truths." Et Cetera Oct. 1952: 10–11.

"The Contest for Aaron Gold." The Best American Short Stories: 1956. Boston: Houghton
     Mifflin Company, 1956. 285–299.

"The Conversion of the Jews." Goodbye, Columbus 137–158.

"The Day it Snowed." Chicago Review 8 (1954): 34–45.

"The Fence." Et Cetera June 1953: 18.

"The Final Delivery of Mr. Thorn." Et Cetera Spring 1954: 20–28.

"The Last Jew." Draft ms. The Philip Roth Collection.

"The Mistaken." Ms. The Philip Roth Collection.

The Philip Roth Collection. The Manuscript Division of the Library of Congress, Washington D.C.

"The Prague Orgy." Zuckerman Bound 423–472.

"The Sex Fiend." Ms. The Philip Roth Collection.

"Writing About Jews." Reading Myself and Others 205–225.

"Writing About Jews - Draft." The Philip Roth Collection.

"Writing American Fiction." Reading Myself and Others 173–191.

"You Can't Tell a Man by the Songs He Sings." Goodbye, Columbus 231–246.

SECONDARY SOURCES

Appelfeld, Aharon. Beyond Despair: Three Lectures and a Conversation with Philip Roth. Trans.
     Jeffrey M. Green. New York: Fromm International Publishing Corporation,
     1994.

Arendt, Hannah. *Eichmann in Jerusalem: A Report on the Banality of Evil*. New York: Penguin Books, 1964.

Babel, Isaac. *The Collected Stories*. Ed. and Trans. Walter Morison. New York: Penguin Books USA, 1955.

Barthes, Roland. *The Pleasure of the Text*. Trans. Richard Miller. New York: Hill and Wang, 1975.

Baumgarten, Murray, and Barbara Gottfried. *Understanding Philip Roth*. Columbia: University of South Carolina Press, 1990.

Beatty, Jack. "The Ghost Writer." *New Republic* 6 Oct. 1979: 36–40.

Bell. Pearl K. "Roth and Baldwin: Coming Home." *Commentary* Dec. 1979: 72–74.

Bellow, Saul. "The Swamp of Prosperity." *Commentary* July 1959: 77–79.

Berger, Alan L. *Crisis and Covenant: The Holocaust in American Jewish Fiction*. Albany: State University of New York Press, 1985.

Bettelheim, Bruno. *Surviving and Other Essays*. New York: Vintage Books, 1980.

Bilik, Dorothy Seidman. *Immigrant-Survivors*. Middletown, Connecticut: Wesleyan University Press, 1981.

Bloom, Harold. "Introduction." Modern Critical Interpretations: Franz Kafka's The Metamorphosis. Ed. Bloom. New York: Chelsea House Publishers, 1988. 1–19.

Brent, Jonathan. "The Unspeakable Self: Philip Roth and the Imagination." Milbauer and Watson 180–200.

Chekhov, Anton. *Plays*. Trans. Elisaveta Fen. New York: Penguin Books, 1959.

——*The Darling and Other Stories*. Trans. Constance Garnett. London: Chatto and Windus, 1925.

Crane, Stephen. *Great Short Works of Stephen Crane*. New York: Harper and Row, 1968.

Deer, Irving, and Harriet Deer. "Philip Roth and the Crisis in American Fiction." *Minnesota Review* 6 (1966): 353–360.

Descartes, Rene'. *The Cambridge Companion to Descartes*. ed. John Cottingham. Cambridge: Cambridge University Press, 1992.

Des Pres, Terrence. The Survivor: An Anatomy of Life in the Death Camps. New York: Pocket Books, 1976.

Edwards, Beverly. *Zuckerman Bound: The Artist in the Labyrinth*. Diss. Lehigh University, 1987. Ann Arbor, 1987. 8714665.

Ehre, Milton. *Isaac Babel*. Boston: G.K. Hall and Company, 1986.

Epstein, Joseph. "Too Much Even of Kreplach." *Hudson Review* 33 (1980): 97–110.

Ezrahi, Sidra Dekoven. *By Words Alone: The Holocaust in Literature*. Chicago and London: The University of Chicago Press, 1980.

——"Philip Roth's Diasporism: A Symposium." *Tikkun* 8.3 (1993): 41–42.

Fowler, Marilyn Stachenfe. *The Prism of Self: The Fiction of Philip Roth*. Diss. University of California, San Diego, 1984. Ann Arbor: UMI, 1984. 8428917.

Fiedler, Leslie. *Fiedler on the Roof: Essays on Literature and Jewish Identity*. Boston: David R. godine, 1991.

Fitzgerald, F. Scott. *The Great Gatsby*. New York: Charles Scribner's Sons, 1925.

Foucalt, Michel. The Order of Things: An Archaeology of the Human Sciences. New York: Vintage Books, 1970.

Freud, Sigmund. "Contributions to the Psychology of Love." *Sexuality and the Psychology of Love.* Ed. Philip Rieff. New York: Collier Books, 1963. 39–76.

— "The Infantile Genital Organization of the Libido." *Sexuality and the Psychology of Love* 161–165.

Girgus, Sam R. "Portnoy's Prayer: Philip Roth and the American Unconscious." Milbauer and Watson 126–143.

Ginsburg, Allen. *Kaddish and Other Poems 1958–1960.* San Francisco: City Lights Books, 1961.

Green, Martin. "Half a Lemon, Half an Egg." Milbauer and Watson 82–104.

— "Introduction." *A Philip Roth Reader* ix–xxiii.

Havel, Vaclav. *Living in Truth.* Ed. Jan Vladislav. London: Faber and faber, 1986.

Hirsch, David H. *The Deconstruction of Literature: Criticism after Auschwitz.* London: University Press of New England, 1991.

Howe, Irving. *A Critic's Notebook.* Ed. Nicholas Howe. New York San Diego London: Harcourt Brace and Company, 1994.

— "Philip Roth Reconsidered." *Critical Essays on Philip Roth* 229–244.

— *Selected Writings 1950–1990.* San Diego New York London: Harcourt Brace Jovanovich, Publishers, 1990.

— "The Lost Young Intellectual." *Commentary* Oct. 1946: 361–367.

— "The Suburbs of Babylon." *New Republic* 15 June 1958: 17–18.

— *World of Our Fathers.* New York: Simon and Schuster, 1976.

Isaac, Dan. "Philip Roth: His Art and Its Origins." *Midstream* March 1981: 47–48.

James, Henry. "The Author of Beltraffio." *The Figure in the Carpet and Other Stories* 57–112.

— "The Death of the Lion." *The Figure in the Carpet and Other Stories* 259–304.

— *The Figure in the Carpet and Other Stories.* Ed. Frank Kermode. New York: Penguin Books, 1986.

— "The Figure in the Carpet." *The Figure in the Carpet and Other Stories* 355–400.

— "The Lesson of the Master." *The Figure in the Carpet and Other Stories* 113–188.

— "The Middle Years." *The Figure in the Carpet and Other Stories* 233–258.

— "The Private Life." *The Figure in the Carpet and Other Stories* 189–232.

Joyce, James. *A Portrait of the Artist as a Young Man.* New York: Penguin Books, 1944.

Kafka, Franz. "A Little Fable." *The Basic Kafka.* New York: Pocket Books, 1979. 157.

— "Selections from Diaries, 1911–1923." *The Basic Kafka* 255–268.

— "The Judgment." *Selected Stories of Franz Kafka.* Trans. Willa and Edwin Muir. New York: The Modern Library, 1952. 3–18.

Kakutani, Michiko. "With Reality Reeling, Pity the Poor Realist." *New York Times* 22 June 1994: C13.

Karl, Frederick R. *American Fictions 1940–1980.* New York: Harper and Row, 1983.

— *Franz Kafka: Representative Man.* New York: Ticknor and Fields, 1991.

Kazin, Alfred. "Introduction." *By Words Alone* ix–xiii.

Kundera, Milan. "Some Notes on Roth's My Life as a Man and The Professor of Desire." Milbauer and Watson 160–167.

— *The Art of the Novel.* Trans. Linda Asher. New York: Grove Press, 1986.

Langer, Lawrence L. *Holocaust Testimonies: the ruins of memory.* New Haven: Yale University Press, 1991.

— *The Holocaust and the Literary Imagination*. New Haven: Yale University Press, 1975.

— *Versions of Survival: The Holocaust and the Human Spirit*. Albany: State University of New York Press, 1982.

Landis, Joseph L. "The Sadness of Philip Roth: An Interim Report." *Critical Essays on Philip Roth* 164–171.

Lee, Hermione. "Kiss and Tell." *New Republic* 30 April 1990: 39–42.

— *Philip Roth*. London: Methuen, 1982.

Leonard, John. "Fathers and Ghosts." *Critical Essays on Philip Roth* 89–94.

Manea, Norman. *On Clowns: The Dictator and the Artist*. New York: Grove Weidenfeld, 1992.

Maloff, Saul. "Philip Roth and the Master's Voice: The Uses of Adversity." *Commonweal* 9 Nov. 1979: 628–631.

Marx, Leo. *The Machine in the Garden: Technology and the Pastoral Ideal in America*. London: Oxford University Press, 1964.

McDaniel, John Nobel. *Heroes in the Fiction of Philip Roth*. Diss. The Florida State University, 1972. Ann Arbor: UMI, 1972. 72–31,410.

Meeter, Glenn. *Philip Roth and Bernard Malamud: A Critical Essay*. Columbia: University of Missouri, 1973.

Milbauer, Asher Z., and Donald G. Watson, eds. *Reading Philip Roth*. New York: St. Martin's Press, 1988.

Nagel, James. *Stephen Crane and Literary Impressionism*. University Park and London: The Pennsylvania State University Press, 1980.

Nance, Guinevera A., and Judith Paterson Jones. *Philip Roth*. New York: Frederick Ungar Publishing Company, 1981.

Neel, Jasper. *Plato, Derrida, and Writing*. Carbondale and Edwardsville: Southern Illinois University Press, 1988.

O'Donnell, Patrick. "The Disappearing Text: Philip Roth's The Ghost Writer." *Contemporary Literature* xxiv.3 (1983): 365–378.

Pinsker, Sanford, ed. *Critical Essays on Philip Roth*. Boston: G.K. Hall, 1982.

— *The Comedy that Hoits: An Essay on the Fiction of Philip Roth*. Columbia: University of Missouri, 1975.

Plath, Sylvia. *Ariel*. New York: Harper and Row, 1965.

Quart, Barbara. "The Treatment of Women in the Work of Three Contemporary Jewish-American Writers: Mailer, Bellow, and Roth." Diss. New York University, 1979. *Dissertation Abstracts International* 40 (1979): 1472A.

Quart, Barbara Koenig. "The Rapacity of One Nearly Buried Alive." *Massachusetts Review* 24 (Autum 1984): 590–608.

Rodgers, Bernard F. *Philip Roth*. Boston: Twayne Publishers, 1978.

Rubin-Dorsky, Jeffrey. "Philip Roth's The Ghost Writer: Literary Heritage and Jewish Irreverence." *Studies in American Jewish Literature* 8.2 (Fall 1989): 168–185.

Said, Edward W. *Culture and Imperialism*. New York: Alfred A. Knopf, 1993.

Segev, Tom. *The Seventh Million: The Israelis and the Holocaust*. Trans. Haim Watzman. New York: Hill and Wang, 1993.

Schechner, Mark. "Philip Roth." *Critical Essays on Philip Roth* 117–132.

Steiner, George. *Language and Silence*. New York: Atheneum, 1966.

Tintner, Adeline. "Henry James as Roth's Ghost Writer." *Midstream* March 1981: 48–51.
— "Hiding Behind James." *Midstream* April 1982: 49–53.
Tolstoy, Leo. "Tolstoy's Criticism on The Darling." *The Darling and Other Stories* 23–31.
Towers, Robert. "The Lesson of the Master." *New York Times Book Review* 2 Sept. 1979: 1.
Troyat, Henri. *Chekhov.* Trans. Michael Henry Heim. New York: Fawcett Columbine, 1986.
Tucker, Martin. "The Shape of Exile in Philip Roth, pr The Part is Always Apart." Milbauer and Watson 33–49.
Updike, John. "Recruiting Raw Nerves." *New Yorker* 15 March 1993: 109–112.
— *Odd Jobs.* New York: Alfred A. Knopf, 1991.
Voelker, Joseph C. "Dedalian Sahdes: Philip Roth's The Ghost Writer." *Critical Essays on Philip Roth* 89–94.
Young, James. *Writing and Rewriting the Holocaust: Narrative and the Consequences of Interpretation.* Bloomington: Indiana University Press, 1988.

ADDITIONAL BIBLIOGRAPHY

Rodgers, Bernard F. *Philip Roth: A Bibliography.* New Jersey: Scarecrow Press, 1984.

Index

www.ingramcontent.com/pod-product-compliance
Ingram Content Group UK Ltd.
Pitfield, Milton Keynes, MK11 3LW, UK
UKHW020431010325
455677UK00029B/1105

9 781138 978393